SEX CRIMES

Sex Crimes

TRANSNATIONAL PROBLEMS
AND GLOBAL PERSPECTIVES

Alissa R. Ackerman
and Rich Furman

EDITORS

 COLUMBIA UNIVERSITY PRESS   NEW YORK

COLUMBIA UNIVERSITY PRESS
Publishers Since 1893
New York   Chichester, West Sussex

cup.columbia.edu
Copyright © 2015 Columbia University Press
All rights reserved

Library of Congress Cataloging-in-Publication Data

Sex crimes : transnational problems and global perspectives /
    [edited by] Alissa R. Ackerman and Rich Furman.
        pages   cm
    Includes index.
    ISBN 978-0-231-16948-6 (cloth : alk. paper) — ISBN 978-0-231-16949-3 (pbk.) —
ISBN 978-0-231-53948-7 (electronic)
    1. Sex crimes. 2. Human trafficking. 3. Transnational crime.
I. Ackerman, Alissa. II. Furman, Rich.
    HV6556.S423   2015
    364.15'3—dc23
                                                          2014035100

Columbia University Press books are printed on permanent and durable acid-free paper.
This book is printed on paper with recycled content.
Printed in the United States of America

c 10 9 8 7 6 5 4 3 2 1

p 10 9 8 7 6 5 4 3 2 1

Cover design: Noah Arlow

References to websites (URLs) were accurate at the time of writing.
Neither the author nor Columbia University Press is responsible for URLs
that may have expired or changed since the manuscript was prepared.

SEX CRIMES

PART 1

Foundational Chapters

Introduction

▸ *ALISSA R. ACKERMAN AND RICH FURMAN*

SEXUAL VIOLENCE, PERHAPS MORE THAN any other type of crime, elicits visceral responses from the public. Armed almost exclusively with media accounts of specific sexually violent acts or vague narratives about highly charged topics (e.g., sex trafficking), the public and politicians respond in ways that are somewhat limited or bounded by a lack of understanding about the contexts and experiences of sex crimes that occur every day around the world. While goodwill exists toward finding solutions to combat the various forms of sexual violence, the fact remains that harsh and often ineffective policies are designed and implemented because of a limited understanding about the real nature of sex crimes. This book seeks to fill this gap in knowledge by providing a global and transnational lens through which to view the subject.

Sexual violence is endemic to all parts of the world and frequently transcends national borders. The policies that are enacted to combat crimes of this nature often do not or cannot transcend these same borders. Even within a country's borders, formal criminal justice policies may not be effective at preventing or decreasing sexual crimes. For example, within national borders, as in the case of poor and developing countries such as Cambodia, criminal justice systems are ill-equipped to handle sex crimes, and outsiders see as illegal the informal tools that are often used. Sexual crimes are significant social problems in all countries, and we can learn a great deal from understanding sex crimes and sex crimes policies across the world.

A recent report found that globally one in fourteen girls and women over the age of 15, or 7.2 percent, will be sexually assaulted in their lifetime

(Abrahams et al. 2014). Such statistics quantify what can only be viewed as serious human rights violations; prevention of sexual violence is an essential human rights issue. In addition to these most intense and severe sexual crimes, various types of sexual violence represent a diverse group of sexual offenses.

Sadly, it is the few, most extreme and sensational cases that make the headlines. Far too often victims of every variety—children, adults, minorities, even animals—are ignored or forgotten while the focus remains on examples picked up, and usually distorted, by the media. Such media representations globally not only lead to erroneous conceptions of the nature of sexual crimes but also prevent a focus on the real lived experiences of many victims. This focus devalues the impacts on and experiences of countless individuals. To truly understand the depth and breadth of sexual violence worldwide and to create lasting and effective prevention measures, we must adopt a global and transnational view of the subject. We must appreciate and understand differences in approaches to combating sexual violence. When programs are effective at inducing positive change, we must learn from them. When programs fail to help survivors achieve justice and balance in their lives, we must know how to make adjustments to those programs. This book seeks to fundamentally expand the way we view sexual violence and the policies and practices aimed at reducing it.

Readers might ask, what is the importance of understanding sex crimes from a transnational and global perspective? Is it not enough to understand the nature of sexual crimes in one's own cultural context? Are the policies and practices of other countries not so different that they are irrelevant to, for example, the context of the United States? The answers to these questions help frame the rationale for this book and will help the reader place the diversity of perspectives and vantage points in context. In the following paragraphs, we explore how and why sexual crimes must be understood from a global and transnational perspective.

First, in the new millennium, no social problem exists outside of the context of globalization. Sex crimes, in spite of stereotypes about the nature of defective, sociopathic perpetrators, are not merely crimes committed by the sick and deranged; they occur within the context of social and economic upheavals that affect whole communities. Poverty, alienation, and lack of community integration and support services, for example, all influence rates of recidivism for sexual crimes. As the forces of globalization affect the economic viability of communities and have a disproportionate impact on marginalized communities in the United States and throughout the world, various social stressors serve as a context within which sexual offenses occur. Sex offender policies, as with other social policies, are bound to fail if they do not account for the full scope of social forces that contribute to the creation of the problem. Ameliorating the conditions that exacerbate sexual crimes in communities demands that policy practitioners of the future view the interconnectedness of social problems on macro, even global scales. In this sense, globalization represents an important conceptual lens for those interested in sex crime amelioration and policy.

Second, globalization has increasingly led to an acceleration of transnational migration. Transmigration, or the movement of people back and forth across nation-state boundaries, presents challenges to those concerned with a myriad of social problems in terms of creating policies that are similarly able to contend with the transitional movement of people. As several chapters explore, the movement of victims and perpetrators across nation-state boundaries is relatively easy and fluid; the movement of social institutions and organizations across the same spaces, however, is not. What we now face, then, is a world in which individuals and groups of people exist within transnational spaces, yet the organizations and institutions designed to manage and resolve their problems do not.

Third, human creativity toward solving problems is bounded by our frameworks and assumptions. When discussions and debates occur regarding "thinking outside the box," what we are really referring to is the need to find ways of challenging our assumptions and perceptions and seeing problems from different vantage points so we can find new solutions. This is a difficult challenge, as our thinking is so bound by what we know that it is often nearly impossible to break free of our context-bound possibilities. One way of pushing ourselves to think and consider problems and solutions in novel ways is to adopt new theoretical and empirical lenses that help us view our world with new eyes. We believe that a transnational and global perspective is just such a lens. By observing the ways in which scholars and practitioners from other countries and cultural contexts view various sexual crimes and their management and treatment, readers will be forced to examine their own assumptions and explore their own limitations. By comparing and contrasting both their knowledge and biases with new "data," readers will be helped to think creatively, reflectively, and, we hope, progressively.

In this book we have assembled chapters by some of the most innovative and influential scholars and practitioners from around the world. We hope that their ideas and experiences will be challenging, evocative, and educational. We know we have learned a great deal from working with these authors; we trust that readers will as well.

STRUCTURE OF THE BOOK

The first section consists of chapters foundational to an understanding of sexual crimes from a transnational/global perspective. They help provide context about the nature of globalization and transnationalism, the relationships between sexual crimes and gender, and the most common forms of sexual violence.

In chapter 1 Jay Albanese discusses the dynamics that catapulted many local sex crimes and sexual content from the local to the transnational. With the increased technology available to so many, the stigma associated with walking into an adult store or movie house no longer exists. People interested in various forms of sexually explicit materials, from sexual acts involving children and violent depictions of sexual encounters with women to sexual acts involving animals, can simply use a computer to find what they are looking for. Demand for this type of content is no longer local— it has expanded exponentially over the past twenty-five years and defines the dark side of what technology is capable of. That said, most studies on exposure to pornographic and/or obscene content indicate that it is actually quite high. Demand for pornography fuels this newfound and easily accessible supply. The nature of technology now allows a small group of individuals to quickly become a large global distribution network. We are still learning about what fuels these networks and best practices to stop them. Similarly, the introduction of Internet technology has brought into question other forms of exploitation, including the sexual exploitation and trafficking of children. Questions remain as to what it means to be trafficked or even sexually exploited. Albanese points out that while laws in some countries are certainly changing with the times, a great deal about these specific types of crimes remains unknown.

Lisa Sample and Rita Augustyn show in chapter 2 that the definition of sex crimes and more specifically rape varies across national boundaries. The authors warn that we must be cautious when we attempt to extrapolate

data on the nature and extent of sex crimes globally because the definition of what such a crime entails varies over time. For example, sexual acts
that were legal in the United States only a hundred years ago are now seen
as criminal. We have very little knowledge of what constitutes sex crimes
worldwide, and as such, actual data on the extent of rape around the world
are lacking. Sample and Augustyn analyzed the criminal codes of ninety-
three countries to determine whether the countries had statutes regarding
criminal sexual behavior and how each country defined sex crimes. The
authors stress that the lack of uniformity and consensus about what a sex
crime is makes the global policing of sex crimes impractical.

Gender is one of the essential organizing principles of human behavior.
When gender is explored vis-à-vis sexual crimes, it is typically related to
how power and patriarchy are implicated in the subordination of women
and male entitlement to sexual gratification. This is lamentable, as gender
plays a far more complex role in sexual crimes. In chapter 3 Alissa R. Ackerman, Rich Furman, Jeffrey W. Cohen, Eric Madfis, and Michelle Sanchez
explore the full implications of considering masculinities and sexual offending. They guide the reader through a discussion of the nature of masculine
scripts and roles and demonstrate the risks that various forms of masculinities entail in the perpetuation of sexual crimes. Additionally, the authors
explore the potential prosocial and positive aspects of masculinities, which
can be used in service of preventing and treating sexual crimes. The chapter
will help readers begin to see the importance of adopting a gendered lens to
understanding sexual crimes across cultures and national boundaries.

In chapter 4 Elicka Peterson-Sparks discusses intimate partner violence
in its many forms and adopts a transnational lens through which to understand risk factors of this type of violence. Intimate partner violence takes
on many forms and can be physical, psychological, and sexual in nature.
Very little research has been conducted through a transnational lens, but
the work that has been done sheds light on important risk factors that are
found in most, if not all, regions of the world. While historically most governments have been reluctant to tackle intimate partner violence as a social
issue, more recently this has begun to change. Sexual violence is now seen
as an international human rights issue, and there is a greater demand for
accountability from nations to protect women. Peterson-Sparks notes that
best efforts to prevent intimate partner violence include men and make
them more central to the process.

Sex trafficking is perhaps the sexual crime that is the most naturally trans-national and global of the topics in this book. It is also perhaps the most controversial, emotional, and contested. Sex trafficking has been frequently reported in the media, with powerful claims made by those who view it is a form of modern-day slavery, yet the debates about sex trafficking are con-tested. It most certainly is one of the most egregious of sexual crimes, and separating the various levels of fact from fiction is essential if effective social policy and treatments are to be found, promulgated, funded, and institu-tionalized. As such, the three chapters in part 2 present somewhat different perspectives on this complex transnational problem.

In chapter 5 Mary Hiquan Zhou provides a history of sex trafficking as a social problem, including the background of the current sex trafficking debate and facts about sex trafficking to date. In doing so, Zhou dispels many of the myths surrounding the topic. She argues that given the facts, sex trafficking today almost mimics the century-old moral panic about White Slavery. She notes that sex trafficking is an important social problem in need of remedy but cautions that it is not the pandemic problem that some promulgate as true. Research shows that many individuals are aware of and often consent to entering into sex work, while some may be unsure of the conditions of the work. Although some people believe the exagger-ated claim that sex trafficking rings are operated by organized crime groups, research actually shows that traffickers are more likely to be loosely con-nected individuals or small groups.

Myth is often promulgated over fact because it serves the interests of those individuals and organizations who are working to end sex traffick-ing and protect victims. Charles Anthony Smith and Cynthia Florentino conducted an analysis of international nongovernmental organizations (INGOs) and the United Nations Trafficking Protocol. The latter was entered into in December 2003 and signed by 117 countries. INGOs played a prominent role in creating and negotiating the tenets of the protocol. Most notably the very definition of "trafficking in persons" was hotly debated and ultimately driven by differing ideologies of INGOs. Two main INGO coalitions led the debate. The Human Rights Caucus, a group of INGOs involved in antitrafficking and sex workers' rights, took a regula-tionist approach, arguing for a broad definition of trafficking that includes forced labor and coercion but excludes voluntary sex work. In contrast, the International Human Rights Network adopted an abolitionist approach, defining trafficking through a victim's perspective and even arguing that prostitution is a violation of human rights. This group went as far as to say that nobody can give genuine consent to engage in prostitution. Smith and Florentino were interested in what this international UN effort amounted to at the local level. Their findings, presented in chapter 6, show that INGO engagement ultimately leads to local action, and the broad definition of trafficking finally adopted by the United Nations allows for flexibility at the local level in terms of how to deal with trafficking.

Chapter 7 takes a progressive stance on definitions of sex trafficking and sex work in general. Cathy Nguyen, Rich Furman, and Alissa R. Ackerman argue the importance of ensuring that sex trafficking and sex work are not conflated. They note that sex trafficking is an egregious wrong committed against women, girls, and boys but that prostitution and sex work are fundamentally different from sex trafficking. There must be a separation of sex work from human trafficking for a variety of reasons. For one, women should be able to control their bodies, and conflating the two robs consenting sex workers of agency and autonomy. Additionally, it draws consensual sex work into the darkness and away from well-regulated places of business. Sex workers come from a variety of backgrounds and enter into sex work for various reasons. Decriminalizing prostitution and consensual sex work values women's agency, decreases some of the stigma associated with the profession, provides economic stability, and offers the ability to creating a lasting and successful public health approach to regulate prostitution and decrease sex trafficking. The authors note that confusing sex work with trafficking draws valuable resources away from where they should actually be focused.

Part 3 explores various other sexual crimes that increasingly occur within transnational and global contexts. They represent forms of sexual violence that often are less typically considered, such as that against animals and state-supported sexual violence used for political aims. What they have in common, as with the sexual crimes explored in preceding chapters, is that each must increasingly be understood through the global, transnational lens that we have been considering. We hope that readers will have honed their ability to situate sexual crimes in this framework and will be able to apply this new, critical skill to their own areas of interest and expertise.

In chapter 8 Michele Leiby analyzes the use of sexual violence as a weapon of war in El Salvador and Peru. Too often, she notes, scholars utilize the term "weapon of war" in an uncritical way. She argues that sexual violence varies across and within armed conflicts and as such requires significant research and better understanding. Indeed, sexual violence during war has several purposes and potential benefits. For example, Leiby notes that it might be used to induce fear in the public or as a form of punishment for people in the opposition. It could also be used to acquire intelligence during interrogations of political prisoners. In the first analysis of its kind, Leiby examines accounts of sexual violence in El Salvador and Peru to determine whether it was indeed a weapon of war.

A world away, on the African continent, Helen Liebling conducted interviews with survivors of conflict and postconflict sexualized violence in Liberia, Uganda, and the Eastern Democratic Republic of Congo (DRC). In chapter 9 she relates that both men and women experienced sexual violence, but women and girls were much more likely to have survived sexual torture and sexual violence. Sexual violence perpetrated in conflict and postconflict chaos resulted in long-term and devastating effects on survivors, their children, families, and communities. Liebling argues for a holistic, gendered approach that sees women's responses to trauma as normal and not pathological. Additionally, her research highlights a strong desire for justice.

In Cambodia another problem exists. Here, over 80 percent of people live in rural areas with little access to criminal justice. In chapter 10 Catherine Burns and Kathleen Daly illustrate the dysfunction within the Cambodian criminal justice system and suggest that even if formal justice were available to citizens, they could still not afford such access. Nonetheless, local and international NGOs advocate for formal criminal justice sanctions, despite the fact that most Cambodian rape survivors, many of whom were raped by someone they know, prefer the informal and local justice practice of *somroh somruel*. In this practice, discussed at length in chapter 10, guilt and blame are less important than restoration. To this end, victim and offender often agree to some form of monetary payment. NGOs and others argue that *somroh somruel* is inequitable and substandard. These entities continue to push for formal justice mechanisms. In addition, NGOs are facing increased difficulties accruing a donor base because "everyday rape" is not seen as exciting in the way that commercial sex trafficking might be seen. In a transnational and ever-increasing global world, Burns and Daly ask us to think about some important questions: What if responses framed by universal human rights are not the best way to address rape at the local level? What if victims, families, and local communities prefer informal justice? What are the negative consequences of encouraging something that is against the will of the victim?

In chapter 11 Anne-Marie McAlinden discusses the global phenomenon of institutional child sexual abuse. Though a few high-profile institutions have been highlighted in the media in the past two decades, including the sexual abuse of children by Catholic priests, institutional child sexual abuse occurs in both religious and secular institutions. Various countries and their respective institutions have dealt with institutional child sexual abuse in a variety of ways. Importantly, one common way to address such abuse is through public accountability and blame for specific acts. This tactic, as McAlinden points out, makes examinations of broader, systemic institutional problems almost impossible. These problems stem not only from individual offenders but from institutions themselves. McAlinden argues that institutional environments facilitate institutional child sexual abuse and make it extremely difficult to discover abuse when it occurs. She offers that most institutional policies designed to combat child sexual abuse are reactive in nature and can only address the known cases of abuse. Her chapter poses a similar question to what Burns and Daly offer: What if responses to institutional child sexual abuse are not necessarily in the best interest of victims or potential victims? How can we create policy approaches that actually prevent abuse from occurring? McAlinden concludes with suggested approaches that may be effective in decreasing and preventing institutional child sexual abuse in global and transnational contexts.

In chapter 12 Karen J. Terry provides a case example concerning child sexual abuse in the Catholic Church. In 2004 John Jay College of Criminal Justice in New York was commissioned to study the nature and scope of child sexual abuse within the Church. After completion of the first study, a second study on the causes and contexts of the abuse was commissioned. Terry was the principal investigator of these studies. She highlights several important findings that echo many of the points made in chapter 11, namely, that while sex offenders are a heterogeneous group, several key similarities can be found among institutional child sexual abusers. For example, most abuse in the Church was committed by diocesan priests who had high levels of discretion, limited supervision of their daily activities, and high levels of trust. These factors support offending behavior across institutions, but Terry highlights their existence within the Catholic Church specifically as well as the importance of understanding the sexual abuse of children in the Church through a global lens.

In chapter 13 Phoenix J. Freeman articulates the importance of understanding sexual violence perpetrated against and by trans individuals in the Western world. He cautions about the limitations of available data concerning this important but often overlooked segment of the population. Data about trans populations have various shortcomings despite the fact that trans people are at increased risk of sexual violence. After a discussion of these limitations, Freeman turns to an analysis of risk factors associated with the sexual victimization of trans people. Trans people face a host of risk factors stemming from stigmatization, marginalization, and poverty, but Freeman cautions that despite risk factors for being victimized, they can and do commit sexualized violence, too. Freeman concludes by arguing that governments, NGOs, and other crisis centers can provide valuable data regarding the trans population in the absence of better research. He notes that some governments, including the United States, now document and address some forms of sexual violence against trans people, but changes are still necessary. To fully understand sexual violence by and against trans people, better-informed research is necessary.

Finally, in chapter 14 Jenny Maher adopts a comparative look at sexual assault against animals, a subject that receives little attention in the academic literature. Rarely are animals seen as victims. In fact, in many instances animal sexual assault is seen as a victimless crime. Though not viewed as common practice, animal sexual assault is probably underestimated because the victims in such cases cannot report the violence against them. Nations have taken varied stances on how to deal with animal sexual assault, with some not even viewing sexual experiences with animals as crimes. However, like intimate partner violence, there seems to be a shift in how some countries are tackling the issue. Maher points out that while many governments have previously considered animal sexual assault in anthropocentric ways, there seems to be a move toward more animal-centered legislation. The chapter asks readers to think critically about what defines animal sexual assault and what legislation should resemble.

National and international legislation are certainly factors that can help decrease sexually based offenses. However, one theme that remains central to this book is that legislation alone is not the panacea that many believe it to be. Indeed, several chapters call for multifaceted public health approaches to combat sexualized violence. Others argue that a legislative or criminal justice response stands in contrast to the desires of individuals who have been sexually victimized.

The chapters in this book represent a new way of exploring sexual violence and sexual crimes. The authors adopted complex, globally situated ways to explore different sexual crimes. We hope that they will lead readers to a new way of understanding sexual crimes and will enable students, scholars, and practitioners alike to utilize what they have learned to create new policies and practices for the management, treatment, and prevention of sexual crimes.

REFERENCES

Abrahams, N., K. Devries, C. Watts, C. Pallitto, M. Petzold, S. Shamu, and C. García-Moreno. 2014. Worldwide prevalence of non-partner sexual violence: A systematic review. *Lancet* 383:1648–54.

CHAPTER 1

The Movement of Sexual Content and Sex Crimes from the Local to the Transnational

▸ *JAY S. ALBANESE*

YOU MIGHT RECALL THE EMBARRASSING episode involving entertainer Pee Wee Herman in 1991, when an undercover vice officer caught him masturbating in an adult movie theater in Sarasota, Florida (Thomas 1991). I was in Florida not long afterward and decided to take a photo of the theater to add to my classroom presentations, but it had been torn down, following the wider trend of the decline and fall of movie houses that showed pornographic films (Slade 2001; Wells 2013).

The disappearance of the adult movie theater was a symptom of a larger social phenomenon that saw a dramatic rise in the ownership and use of personal computers and associated software (the so-called digital revolution), and the corresponding rise in access to the Internet by the masses. As Internet access became faster (via cable and Wi-Fi), allowing for easy viewing of video files beyond mere photos, and computer storage simultaneously became larger and cheaper, permitting the storage of videos on one's own equipment, the need to go to an adult movie theater to watch pornographic films vanished. There are more than 5,000 movie theaters in the United States, but as of 1990 there were only 250 left that showed adult films, a number that has declined further to under 100, as video stores, hotel rooms, cable systems, and the Internet have come to dominate the distribution of pornographic films (*Adult Theaters* 2013; Slade 2001; Wells 2013).

Of course, the same can be said of the mainstream (nonpornographic) movie industry, which now struggles to keep traditional movie theaters attractive for moviegoers in the face of competition from high-definition, flat-screen televisions, computers, and video streaming on demand at home. The past twenty-five years have witnessed a dramatic technological change in how we view photos, videos, and longer movies, and it is not surprising that the nature of the supply and demand for sexually oriented content has shifted to exploit this change.

The widespread ownership of computers and access to the Internet eliminate the social stigma that existed when a person physically had to go into a store or adult movie theater to purchase sexually oriented print or video material. But the trend did not stop there. Those persons interested in specific kinds of sex acts, or very young girls or boys, can now shop online in more anonymous fashion to fulfill their desires.

This shift of demand from the local adult bookstore or movie theater to the Internet and home computer made the location of supplier less important. Indeed, a host of existing court cases involve the legality of using the mail to send pornographic materials, the zoning of adult businesses (like theaters and strip clubs), and crossing state lines to pursue these activities (where it is illegal in some places but not in others) (Albanese 2009; Jasper 2009). But all these concerns are much less important now, in the Internet age. If there is a problem with legality in one's own jurisdiction, the Internet crosses international boundaries imperceptibly and without affecting download speeds. The past twenty-five years have seen a proliferation of sexually oriented websites designed to attract viewers of video and those interested in "live" sexual encounters with strangers, all for a fee. These sites are located in different countries around the world, because it is no longer necessary to fulfill this demand locally. The movement of sexual content and sex crimes from the local community to the transnational scene has been a significant development in the dark side of the globalization of computer ownership and Internet availability.

WHAT IS OBSCENITY AND PORNOGRAPHY?

It is important to be clear about the conduct in question. Pornography is a colloquial term that has no legal meaning, and it is generally not found in the criminal law. It refers to explicit depictions of sexually suggestive or explicit activity with the intention to arouse the viewer. This is an inadequate term because it is not specific. As U.S. Supreme Court Justice Potter Stewart infamously stated, he was not able to define what constitutes pornography, but he knows it when he sees it (*Jacobellis v. Ohio* 1964). Do suggestive photos of naked people suffice? What about simulated, versus explicit, depictions of sex? These are issues about which the U.S. Supreme Court has rendered conflicting decisions over the years (Hixson 1996; Jasper 2009).

Obscenity is the legal term used to described objectionable depictions of sex, and the U.S. Supreme Court promulgated a three-part test to determine obscenity in 1973, which still stands today: obscene material must, "taken as a whole, appeal to the prurient interest in sex," portray sexual conduct in a "patently offensive way," and lack "serious literary, artistic, political or scientific value" (*Miller v. California* 1973). This definition has not been helpful because it has been challenged in many subsequent cases owing to disagreement over what these three elements mean in practice. For example, obscenity prosecutions have been reviewed that involved R-rated movies with sexual themes but without depictions of sex, bar-room wrestling in mashed potatoes involving women and exposed breasts, sex acts with animals, magazines on display in stores that include photos of naked women and men, among many others where the line between the offensive and the obscene was unclear (Albanese 2009; Strub 2013).

Most countries do not devote much time to regulating depictions of explicit sexual activity between consenting adults. Government attention is limited primarily to concern over the age at which citizens can legally view sexually oriented material, paying special attention to depictions involving children and abusive depictions involving adults. This has been a stark change over the past twenty-five years, because previously many obscenity laws and prosecutions were concerned with the printing, distribution, and ownership of depictions of sex acts rather than with the victims being exploited in the process.

Before the technological and global changes of the past twenty-five years, the last U.S government effort to address pornography was the Attorney General's Commission on Pornography, appointed by President Ronald Reagan in 1986. The commission concluded that many video retailers sell or rent pornographic films: "Based on the evidence provided to us, it appears as if perhaps as many as half of all the general retailers in the country include within their offerings at least some material that, by itself, would commonly be conceded to be pornographic" (Commission on Pornography 1986:288), but no data or sources were provided. With regard to sexually violent material, the commission recognized that there was no consensus in the research literature about its effects on behavior. This led the commission to speculate that "finding a link between aggressive behavior towards women and sexual violence, whether lawful or unlawful, requires assumptions not found exclusively in the experimental evidence. We see no reason, however, not to make these assumptions" (325). The commission remarkably concluded, "The absence of evidence should by no means be taken to deny the existence of a causal link" (332). These conclusions were challenged by several of the researchers relied on by the commission, who claimed that the commissioners made "serious errors" of omission in their characterization of the research findings regarding the pornography-harm link (Donnerstein et al. 1987). The commission's impact on subsequent law and policy was negligible, but the rapid spread of personal computers and access to the Internet soon dominated the creation and dissemination and pornography, shifting concern from retail availability to home computer–based generation and trafficking.

HOW MUCH PORNOGRAPHY EXISTS?

A U.S. government investigation in 1970 found the pornography industry to be "primarily a localized business with no national distribution" that was "extremely disorganized" (U.S. Commission on Obscenity and Pornography 1970:22). This effort found the industry to be small: "There are no great fortunes to be made in stag film production. It is estimated that there are fewer than half a dozen individuals who net more than $10,000 per year in the business." With the subsequent broad dissemination of computer usage and Internet connectivity, there is reason to believe the situation has changed, although there are no good counts, only estimates (Albanese 2007; Carr 2004; Jenkins 2001; Wortley & Smallbone 2012). A review by the National Academy of Sciences (2013) of the commercial sexual exploitation of children concluded that "there is no reliable estimate of the incidence or prevalence of these crimes." Suffice it to say, however, that there are hundreds of thousands, if not millions, of sexually explicit videos and websites available around the world.

Perhaps more important is that, regardless of the number of sources, their usage is very high. An empirical study of males attending Evangelical colleges found that 79.3 percent of male undergraduate students at the participating colleges reported accessing Internet pornography at some point in the previous year, and 61.1 percent reported accessing Internet pornography at least some average amount of time each week (Chelsen 2011). A survey of 500 college students found that 73 percent (93 percent of male students and 62 percent of female students) reported that they had viewed online pornography before age 18 (Sabina, Wolak, & Finkelhor 2008). A study in Norway found that 82 percent of respondents reported having read pornographic magazines, 84 percent had seen pornographic films, and 34 percent had examined pornography on the Internet (Træen et al. 2006). Another review estimated that 30 percent of all data transferred across the Internet is porn, due to the large video files involved (Porn sites 2013). Therefore, regardless of the number of available sources, exposure rates appear to be quite high.

TWO KEY ISSUES: CHILDREN AND VIOLENCE

Given the wide availability of sexual material online and the general lack of concern about depictions of consensual sex between adults, it is important to note that major concerns endure. Two of these concerns will be discussed here: the commercial sexual exploitation of children in generating pornography and victims for prostitution, and pornography that depicts violence against a victim.

Commercial Sexual Exploitation of Children

A growing number of cases have been discovered in which child pornography is generated and distributed, depicting sexual acts by underage children. There is broad consensus around the world against pornography that depicts children, including a protocol to the UN Convention on the Rights of the Child that prohibits the sale of children, child prostitution, and child pornography (Dillon 2008; Gover 2007; Gozdziak & Bump 2008; Pais 2010; UNODC 2013; U.S. Department of Justice 2013a). The commercial sexual exploitation of children (CSEC) is sexual abuse of a minor for economic gain. It can involve physical abuse, pornography, prostitution, or the smuggling of children or their images for unlawful purposes. Therefore these two separate aspects (abuse of children *and* trafficking in the images of sexual exploitation) form the focus of attention for CSEC.

In a typical case, a man in Virginia was sentenced to fourteen years in prison, followed by lifetime supervised release, for running an online forum from his home that was dedicated to posting sexually explicit pictures and chatting about young girls. He was responsible for one-fourth of the images available on the forum, which was infiltrated by undercover FBI agents who logged onto a peer-to-peer file-sharing network and downloaded numerous images of child pornography from him. A forensic examination of the suspect's computer equipment revealed thousands of image files, including images of young children engaged in sexual acts with adults (U.S. Department of Justice 2013d). In this case a man in rural Virginia was able to gather and disseminate child pornography to users globally. The combination of computer equipment with large storage capacity along with a private Internet network designed to make detection difficult was all that was needed to sexually exploit children and distribute their images.

The scope of such a criminal enterprise easily expands, as was illustrated in another case in which twelve suspects were convicted and sentenced to prison terms ranging from twenty years to life. They participated in an illegal organization that used Internet news groups that shared large files of text, pictures, and videos in order to traffic images of young children engaging in sexual and sadistic acts. The group was infiltrated by police in Australia and was found to be trafficking images electronically to the United States, the United Kingdom, Germany, and Australia. The group traded more than 400,000 images and 1,000 videos before it was dismantled (U.S. Department of Justice 2009a, 2009b). Therefore comparatively small numbers of offenders can form a large global distribution network connected electronically.

A review of federal cases in the United States found that 3,661 suspects were referred to U.S. attorneys for child sexual exploitation offenses in a single year, consisting of child pornography offenses (69 percent), sexual abuse (16 percent), and transportation for illegal sexual activity (14 percent). Ninety percent of those charged were convicted and sentenced to prison, with a median sentence of more than five years imprisonment. These numbers all represented substantial increases over the previous decade (Motivans & Kyckelhahn 2007). Wolak et al. (2008) found that most Internet child molesters are not pedophiles, and that online solicitation generally involves adult men who use technology to meet underage adolescents and seduce them into sexual encounters.

Clarity is required across jurisdictions in defining what is a child and what is a child victim (i.e., dealing with age differences across jurisdictional borders and "self-exploited" young people, often runaways, who engage in consensual conduct). The number of known cases of various kinds is growing, but we do not know whether the base rate is increasing or these new cases are the result of increased law enforcement attention, better training, or improved public awareness.

The manifestations of CSEC appear varied, from family-based exploitation to "self-exploitation" of runaway and missing children, to organized crime networks of exploiters. There are no systematic data to determine which types of networks are typical in different locations. Similarly, patterns of child pornography also appear to be varied. Organized crime networks, child sex rings, pedophiles, and parents and other family members have all been identified (U.S. Department of Justice 2010; Wortley & Smallbone 2012). Systematic data have not been collected to determine which types of distribution are most common or what the trends are in the manufacture and distribution of child pornography. To date there has been no major effort to gather reliable data on the extent or trends in CSEC across locations, although there exist data to show that juvenile prostitution requires greater priority from law enforcement agencies, as more than half of large urban police departments surveyed reported no known cases (Mitchell, Finkelhor, & Wolak 2010).

Greater attention is also needed to address child sex tourism, which involves adults (usually from developed countries) traveling abroad for the purpose of sexual contact with foreign children (usually in developing countries). In many cases these trips are organized via Internet contact with third parties who arrange the exploitation. In one case of this kind, a U.S. citizen was sentenced to 165 years in prison for traveling to Haiti on multiple occasions for the purpose of engaging in illicit sexual conduct with children (U.S. Department of Justice 2013c). International enforcement efforts have increased with INTERPOL's management of the International Child Exploitation Image database (launched in 2009), which permits investigators to share data among police globally, using software to connect victim images and locations (O'Neill 2013). INTERPOL also issues "Green" notices to alert the international policing community to serious child offenders who are at large.

What is still needed is systematic, periodic research to document trends in four distinct areas:

- Risk factor trends for commercial sexual exploitation of children (i.e., social/family status, economic correlates, ease of movement, level of demand)
- Protective factor trends (i.e., laws and technology, enforcement efforts and their impact, treatment of recovered victims, and public education)
- Offender trends (i.e., typology of offenders and networks, methods of exploitation, numbers of youth exploited in known cases)
- Trends in victim patterns (i.e., from abuse to exploitation, revictimization patterns, reporting/nonreporting patterns)

Compensation and restitution to child victims of commercial sexual exploitation are now being granted in some jurisdictions (Hamblett 2013; Richey 2013b). The impact of this emerging trend needs to be studied. In sum, a great deal remains unknown about the nature and extent of commercial sexual exploitation of children, but the number of known cases is increasing, and the research needs to help guide future policy, enforcement, and practice are clear.

Pornography That Depicts Violence

Justice Antonin Scalia, writing for the majority of the U.S. Supreme Court, concluded that "speech about violence is not obscene" and upheld the right of minors to purchase violent video games (*Brown v. Entertainment Merchants Association* 2011). This continued the Court's tortured history in trying to draw an appropriate line between offensive conduct and obscenity. This case reviewed video games depicting violence where

victims by the dozens are killed with every imaginable implement, including machine guns, shotguns, clubs, hammers, axes, swords, and chainsaws. Victims are dismembered, decapitated, disemboweled, set on fire, and chopped into little pieces. They cry out in agony and beg for mercy. Blood gushes, splatters, and pools. Severed body parts and gobs of human remains are graphically shown. In some games, points are awarded based, not only on the number of victims killed, but on the killing technique employed.

It also appears that there is no antisocial theme too base for some in the video-game industry to exploit. There are games in which a player can take on the identity and reenact the killings carried out by the perpetrators of the murders at Columbine High School and Virginia Tech. The objective of one game is to rape a mother and her daughters; in another, the goal is to rape Native American women. There is a game in which players engage in "ethnic cleansing" and can choose to gun down African-Americans, Latinos, or Jews. (2738)

Legal definitions and prosecutions for obscene materials in the United States always have been directed at depictions of sexual conduct. Violence has never been part of that definition, and the U.S. Supreme Court continues in its holdings that depictions of sex are harmful, but depictions of violence are not.

The terms "patently offensive" and "prurient interest" in prior Court decisions invariably resulted in subjective line-drawing in attempting to distinguish gratuitous depictions of sex from those that have "literary, artistic, political, or scientific value" (*Miller v. California* 1973). This had led to confusion regarding what specific conduct should be criminalized. Objectively more harmful than gratuitous sex are depictions of gratuitous *violence*. A significant social concern arises when sex is depicted in a way that involves force against an unwilling victim, against children, or even when unjustified violence without sex is depicted. A similar argument can be made for depictions of violence resulting from hate, due to race, ethnicity, or sexual orientation. This concern is spilling over into the area of adult prostitution, focusing on its exploitative aspects. New York State, for example, is creating a statewide system of specialized criminal courts to handle prostitution cases and provide services to assist human trafficking victims from a cycle of exploitation and arrest (Rashbaum 2013).

The U.S. Supreme Court did not use the *Brown* case to shift the focus of obscenity from sex to unjustified violence, rejecting an opening to examine the issue of violent or degrading portrayals. Should obscenity law prohibit the depiction of gratuitous violence rather than sex alone? Depictions of violent assaultive behavior exhibited without legal justification could be deemed objectionable and punishable under law. The legal justifications for the use of force (e.g., self-defense, defense of others) are well-defined in existing law, as are the definitions of assault, so justifiable violence has clear legal meaning. An expanded definition of obscenity could include photo-graphs, videos, or broadcasts depicting assaultive behavior committed by persons without legal justification. The inclusion of sex in these depictions of violence could be a sufficient, but not necessary, element of obscenity. The only exception might be factual accounts of real events that have infor-mational or educational value.

Unlike the inconclusive link between depictions of sex and sex offenses, there is a body of research that reports on the impact of depictions of wan-ton violence on promoting aggressive behavior for its viewers (despite the Supreme Court's dismissal of these research findings) (see Anderson & Bushman 2001; Anderson et al. 2003; Diamond 2009; Donnerstein et al. 1987; Krahé et al. 2011). Therefore, descriptions of wanton violence could be declared obscene based on their effects on behavior. In addition, violence without justification could be declared as conduct more objectionable than sex without social "value" (as the *Miller* definition now holds).

The singular focus on depictions of sex as obscene led the Supreme Court to argue in regard to violent video games that the respondents "would fare better if there were a longstanding tradition in this country of specially restricting children's access to depictions of violence, but there is none" (*Brown v. Entertainment Merchants Association* 2011). The Court goes on to compare violence in the *Odyssey*, *Grimm's Fairy Tales*, and cartoons with the "astounding" violence in the video games at issue in this case, failing to make a connection between violent portrayals and their impacts on the viewer (Fisher 2013).

Therefore the U.S. Supreme Court's conclusion that gratuitously vio-lent video games are "protected speech" while depictions of sex are obscene missed an opportunity to observe that gratuitous violence has been shown to be more harmful and objectionable. Other countries, such as Iceland, have proposed a ban on online pornography, specifically that which is vio-lent or degrading, mostly toward women (Iceland 2013). Britain changed its law in 2008 to focus on a narrow band of "violent and abusive" or "extreme" pornographic material in order to distinguish portrayals of consensual sex between adults from portrayals involving violence, abuse, or children (Gold-berg 2010). And in the United States, sex-related crimes involving online harassment and extortion are increasingly being criminalized and pros-ecuted owing to their threatened violence and abusive nature (Bella 2013; Goode 2013; Jouvenal 2013; Richey 2013; U.S. Department of Justice 2013b).

These global trends reflect the view that portrayals involving violence or degradation are more harmful than portrayals of only sex.

In sum, there are two important trends as pornography has become globalized during the past twenty-five years. First, there exist data to show that violent portrayals of sex have a deleterious impact on aggression, and there are growing efforts around the world to account for degrading, abusive, and violent depictions of sex in crafting obscenity law, defining sex crimes, and enforcing them. Second, any use of children in sexually oriented images is now considered exploitative in virtually every country worldwide. As Huppin and Malamuth (2012:99) have concluded, "a limitation of obscenity's scope to only extremely violent and/or virtual child pornography, should ease constitutional concerns related to the application of community standards in the Internet Age." A focus on violence and children would permit an objective global perspective in targeting precise illegal behaviors regardless of where they occur. These are two significant steps forward in the emerging global consensus on what constitutes illegal sexual content and conduct in a world of trafficking people and images across borders.

DISCUSSION QUESTIONS

1. Argue what you believe is a more important element in a definition of obscenity: sex or violence. Defend your view, given what is known about their impact on human behavior.

2. Why do you believe that men make up the overwhelming majority of consumers of pornography? Explain why you believe that biological, psychological, or social factors may best explain this phenomenon.

3. Most people agree that sex education should occur at home, although it never happens in many homes. What do you believe should be the proper content of sex education, and where should it occur?

4. Should there be any restriction on the sale or rental of pornographic material to consenting adults, or on Internet access to such material for adults? Defend your position.

5. Explain what you believe to be the best way to inculcate healthy (i.e., nonprurient) attitudes about sex to young people.

REFERENCES

Adult Theaters Locations Locator Map and Directory. 2013. http://mapmuse.com /interest/adult-theaters.

Albanese, Jay S. 2007. *Commercial Sexual Exploitation of Children: What Do We Know and What Do We Do About It?* Washington, D.C.: National Institute of Justice Special Report.

——. 2009. Looking for a new approach to an old problem: The future of obscenity and pornography. In *Visions for Change: Crime and Justice in the Twenty-First Century,* ed. R. Muraskin and A. Roberts. 5th ed. Upper Saddle River, N.J.: Prentice Hall.

Anderson, Craig A., and Brad J. Bushman. 2001. Effects of violent video games on aggressive behavior, aggressive cognition, aggressive affect, physiological arousal, and prosocial behavior: A meta-analytic review of the scientific literature. *Psychological Science* 12:353–60.

Anderson, Craig A., Leonard Berkowitz, Edward Donnerstein, L. Rowell Huesmann, James D. Johnson, Daniel Linz, Neil M. Malamuth, and Ellen Wartella. 2003. The influence of media violence on youth. *Psychological Science in the Public Interest* 4:81–110.

Bella, Rick. 2013. Perpetrators' own families can become forgotten victims of child pornography. *Oregonian,* June 29.

Brown v. Entertainment Merchants Association. 2011. 131 S. Ct. 2729.

Carr, J. 2004. *Child Abuse, Child Pornography and the Internet.* London: NCH.

Chelsen, Paul Olaf. 2011. An examination of Internet pornography usage among male students at Evangelical Christian colleges. Ph.D. dissertation, Loyola University Chicago. http://ecommons.luc.edu/cgi/viewcontent.cgi?article =1149&context=luc_diss.

Diamond, Milton. 2009. Pornography, public acceptance and sex related crime: A review. *International Journal of Law & Psychiatry* 32 (September): 304–14.

Dillon, Sarah. 2008. What human rights law obscures: Global sex trafficking and the demand for children. *UCLA Women's Law Journal* 17 (Winter): 121–86.

Donnerstein, E., D. Linz, and S. Penrod. 1987. *The Question of Pornography.* New York: Free Press.

Fisher, Marc. 2013. Game creators are in the eye of the video-game storm. *Washington Post,* April 8.

Goldberg, William T. 2010. Two nations, one web: Comparative legal approaches to pornographic obscenity by the United States and the United Kingdom. *Boston University Law Review* 90:2121–48.

Goode, Erica. 2013. Victims push laws to end online revenge posts. *New York Times*, September 23.

Gover, Sonja. 2007. Children as chattel of the state: Deconstructing the concept of sex trafficking. *International Journal of Human Rights* 11 (Autumn): 293–306.

Gozdziak, Elzbieta, and Micah N. Bump. 2008. *Victims No Longer: Research on Child Survivors of Trafficking for Sexual and Labor Exploitation in the United States, Final Report*. Report NCJ 221891. Washington, D.C.: National Institute of Justice.

Hamblett, Mark. 2013. Joint and several liability rejected in porn case. *New York Law Journal*, September 9.

Hixson, R. 1996. *Pornography and the Justices*. Carbondale: Southern Illinois University Press.

Huppin, Mark, and Neil Malamuth. 2012. The obscenity conundrum, contingent harms, and constitutional consistency. *Stanford Law & Policy Review* 23:31–100.

Iceland: Why does liberal Iceland want to ban online pornography? 2013. *Economist*, April 23.

Jacobellis v. Ohio. 1964. 378 U.S. 184.

Jasper, Margaret. 2009. *The Law of Obscenity and Pornography*. New York: Oceana Publications.

Jenkins, Philip. 2001. *Beyond Tolerance: Child Pornography on the Internet*. New York: New York University Press.

Jouvenal, Justin. 2013. Stalkers use online sex ads as weapon. *Washington Post*, July 14.

Krahé, Barbara, Ingrid Möller, L. Rowell Huesmann, Lucyna Kirwil, Juliane Felber, and Anja Berger. 2011. Desensitization to media violence: Links with habitual media violence exposure, aggressive cognitions, and aggressive behavior. *Journal of Personality & Social Psychology* 100:630–46.

Miller v. California. 1973. 413 U.S. 15.

Mitchell, Kimberly J., David Finkelhor, and Janis Wolak. 2010. Conceptualizing juvenile prostitution as child maltreatment: Findings from the National Juvenile Prostitution Study. *Child Maltreatment* 15:18–36.

Motivans, Mark, and Tracey Kyckelhahn. 2007. *Federal Prosecution of Child Sex Exploitation Offenders*. Washington, D.C.: Bureau of Justice Statistics.

National Academy of Sciences. Institute of Medicine. 2013. *Confronting Commercial Sexual Exploitation and Sex Trafficking of Minors in the United States.* Washington, D.C.: National Academy of Sciences, September.

O'Neill, Sean. 2013. Police are "failing to halt spread of online child abuse"; Interpol issues warning on eve of web summit. *Times* (London), June 17, 11.

Pais, Marta Santos. 2010. The Protection of Children from Sexual Exploitation Optional Protocol to the Convention on the Rights of the Child on the Sale of Children, Child Prostitution and Child Pornography. *International Journal of Children's Rights* 18:551–66.

Porn sites get more visitors each month than Netflix, Amazon and Twitter combined. 2013. *Huffington Post*, May 4.

Rashbaum, William. 2013. With special courts, state aims to steer women away from sex trade. *New York Times*, September 25.

Richey, Warren. 2013a. Man in "sextortion" case might have coerced 350 women. *Christian Science Monitor*, January 29.

——. 2013b. Should child porn "consumers" pay victim millions? Supreme Court to decide. *Christian Science Monitor*, June 27.

Sabina, Chiara, Janis Wolak, and David Finkelhor. 2008. The nature and dynamics of Internet pornography exposure for youth. *CyberPsychology & Behavior* 11 (December): 691–93.

Slade, Joseph W. 2001. *Pornography and Sexual Representation: A Reference Guide.* New York: Greenwood.

Strub, Whitney. 2013. *Obscenity Rules: Roth v. United States and the Long Struggle over Sexual Expression.* Lawrence: University Press of Kansas.

Thomas, Karen. 1991. Pee-wee Herman's Florida misadventure. *USA Today*, July 29, 2D.

Træen, Bente, Toril Nilsen Sørheim, and Hein Stigum. 2006. Use of pornography in traditional media and on the Internet in Norway. *Journal of Sex Research* 43:245–54.

United Nations Office on Drugs and Crime (UNODC). 2013. *UN Crime Body to Combat Online Child Abuse.* http://www.unodc.org/unodc/en/frontpage/2013/September/un-crime-body-to-combat-online-child-abuse.html.

U.S. Commission on Obscenity and Pornography. 1970. *Report.* Washington, D.C.: U.S. Government Printing Office.

U.S. Department of Justice. 2009a. *Five Defendants Sentenced for Participation in International Child Exploitation Enterprise.* Washington, D.C.: Office of Public Affairs, March 10.

———. 2009b. *Six Defendants Sentenced for Participation in International Child Exploitation Enterprise*. Washington, D.C.: FBI Jacksonville Field Division, April 14.

———. 2010. *The National Strategy for Child Exploitation Prevention and Interdiction: A Report to Congress*. http://www.justice.gov/psc/docs/natstrategyreport.pdf.

———. 2013a. *California Man Sentenced to 980 Months for Producing Child Pornography Involving Two Young Virginia Girls*. Washington, D.C.: Office of Public Affairs. July 19.

———. 2013b. *Maine Resident Pleads Guilty to Engaging in Cyber "Sextortion" of New Hampshire Victim*. Washington, D.C.: Office of Public Affairs, September 18.

———. 2013c. *Michigan Man Sentenced to 165 Years for Child Sex Tourism Offenses*. Washington, D.C.: Office of Public Affairs, July 31.

———. 2013d. *Virginia Man Sentenced to Serve 168 Months in Prison on Child Pornography Charges*. Washington, D.C.: Office of Public Affairs, January 28.

Wells, Carrie. 2013. Last adult movie theater in Baltimore up for auction. *Baltimore Sun*. October 2.

Wolak, Janis, David Finkelhor, Kimberly J. Mitchell, and Michele L. Ybarra 2008. Online "predators" and their victims: Myths, realities, and implications for prevention treatment. *American Psychologist* 62 (February/March): 111–28.

Wortley, Richard, and Stephen Smallbone. 2012. *Child Pornography on the Internet*. Washington, D.C.: U.S. Community Oriented Policing Services.

CHAPTER 2

What Is a "Sex Crime"?

AN EXAMINATION OF THE VARIOUS DEFINITIONS OF RAPE ACROSS COUNTRIES

▸ *LISA L. SAMPLE AND RITA AUGUSTYN*

SCHOLARS HAVE LONG USED THE enactment of laws as a reflection of publicly perceived, growing social problems (Becker 1963; Best 1989; Conrad & Schneider 1980; Edleman 1988; Fonda, Eni, & Guimond 2013; Surrette 1998). The enactment of laws specific to sex offenders, such as sex-offender registration, chemical castration, or civil commitment of sex offenders to mental health institutions, has been used to infer an acceptance of sex offending as a growing problem (Evans, Lytle, & Sample 2013; Levenson, Brannon, Fortney, & Baker 2007; Sutherland 1950; Terry & Ackerman 2009), and the fact that these laws have been enacted in several countries (the United States, England, Ireland, Australia, Canada) implies that the growing sex-offender problem is occurring globally. Scant empirical or official data exist to determine the degree to which sex offending is on the rise across the globe, and this observation serves as the impetus for this chapter. Why is it that we cannot compare reports of arrests for sex crimes across countries? The answer to this question likely lies in the ways in which we come to define behaviors as problematic. In this chapter we use the existence and content of sex offender–specific and rape laws across countries to infer how people of different regions define sex crimes. First, however, a brief discussion of the constructed nature of crime is warranted.

SOCIAL CONSTRUCTIONISM AND CRIME

Constructionism holds that deviance and crime arise from someone's initiative to define a situation as problematic (Becker 1963). Deviance and crime, as social problems, are not then innate to a social environment, nor are they problems simply because of the harm they produce. Rather, deviance and crime are constructed through a process involving various actors who make subjective interpretations of events and behaviors that eventually find their way into public policy and law (Becker 1963; Ben-Yehuda 1990; Cohen 1972).

As behaviors become defined as deviant or criminal, they are also defined as social problems in need of attention. Scholars have uncovered a pathway by which deviance or crime becomes a social problem in need of solution. Problem construction usually begins after public fear is aroused by initial isolated incidents of deviance or crime (Ben-Yehuda 1990; Cohen 1972; Sutherland 1950). Many people, with varying degrees of power, prestige, and credibility, then offer their interpretations and definitions of the behavior (Becker 1963; Ben-Yehuda 1990; Cohen 1972). These "moral entrepreneurs" often use the media to manipulate political and moral symbols to mobilize support for their specific definitions and gain control over public opinion (Ben-Yehuda 1990:70). Once public support for specific definitions has been generated, solutions for the problem are offered that are congruent with popular definitions (Conrad & Schneider 1980). Solutions are typically expressed through the creation or revision of criminal law.

The consequences of the construction process result in variations in the definitions of specific crime types across time and space. For instance, what may be considered a deviant behavior in one city, state, or country may not be considered deviant in others, or the status of a behavior may not have been seen as deviant yesterday but will be next month (Ben-Yehuda 1990; Cohen 1972). While it is likely that definitions for behaviors such as theft or murder remain somewhat static and are similar across regions and countries, we have little knowledge of the degree to which definitions of "sex crimes" vary across national boundaries. For those of us living in Western democratic nations, we may assume that definitions of sex crimes and laws to prevent them are somewhat invariant across similarly situated nations, but this may not be the case. It is then important to investigate the ways in which various nations and territories within those nations define "rape" or "sex crime."

HISTORICAL DEFINITIONS OF RAPE

Despite somewhat universal condemnation of forcing children under the age of 7 to have sexual intercourse (Sample 2001), there seems to be no globally accepted definition of a sex crime or rape (John Jay College of Criminal Justice 2004; LaFree 1989). In the United States, as defined in the Federal Bureau of Investigation's Uniform Crime Reporting (UCR) Program, for eighty years prior to 2012, rape was defined as the carnal knowledge of a female forcibly and against her will. In keeping with a constructionist tradition, however, the FBI recently changed the definition to "penetration, no matter how slight, of the vagina or anus with any body part or object, or oral penetration by a sex organ of another person, without the consent of the victim" (FBI 2012). This change demonstrates the ways in which the definition of a sex crime can vary over time within the same country, but how do FBI's definitions compare with those in other countries?

Historically all sovereign nations have created their own definition of a "sex crime or assault." In a report written for the UN. Commission for Europe and the UN Office on Drugs and Crime (2004), scholars from John Jay College of Criminal Justice note the lack of a universally accepted definition of rape. For instance, despite the FBI definition of rape, which is used to determine the frequency and prevalence of sexual assault nationwide, there is no federal statute defining sexual assault. Rather, all fifty states have their own statutes to define sex crimes. Canada does not offer a definition of rape in the Canadian criminal code, thereby leaving territorial courts to define what a rape or sex crime may be. In contrast, unlike the United States or Canada, Pakistan has a national definition of sexual assault written in its criminal code. For those countries that do codify a definition of a sex crime or a sex offender, we are left to wonder how those definitions may differ across borders. One way to explore this difference is to review the solutions, or laws, countries have enacted to address sex offending as a social problem.

Laws that are meant to address whatever definition countries use for sex crimes generally come in one of two forms. Laws in individual nations' criminal codes/statutes can specifically prohibit and punish certain sexual acts (such as rape or sexual assault), and/or laws can delineate specific legal requirements for only those people criminally convicted of a sex crime.

To determine how individual nations have constructed sexual offenses, one should review both forms of legislation.

METHODS FOR DETERMINING VARIATION IN THE CONSTRUCTION OF SEX CRIMES

The data for this chapter were collected using three search engines—Google, Google Scholar, and EBSCO—focusing on two main topics: sex offender laws by country and rape laws by country. Countries were identified based on crime reporting to Interpol, which resulted in 192 possible countries to review. The following key phrases were used to search for national rape and sex-offender statutes in these countries: sex offender registry laws, public notification laws, civil commitment, chemical castration, rape laws, penal code, criminal code, and age of consent. Each phrase was used in combination with the specific country of interest. A dataset on the Woman Stats Project website (womanstats.org) was also used to collect data on rape laws. The dataset comprises existing literature and expert interviews about the status of women in 174 countries around the world. One variable (called "LRW Law 1") from the dataset was used in this study: a measure of whether these countries had laws against rape, statutory rape, and sexual assault, and an age of consent. Reference lists and other essential information (e.g., laws, coalitions, names) were used to gather additional information. The three search engines were used to locate this additional information.

After the data were collected, two tables were created: one for countries with sex offender–specific laws (table 2.1), and one for countries without laws applicable to only sex offenders (table 2.2). Both tables list four indicators of how sex crimes are defined across countries, including whether countries had a rape law, if those laws had the words "threat" and/or "violence" in their definition of rape, if formal sanctions were provided for marital rape, and the age of sexual consent within statutes. Also, we coded whether the rape law was national or differed by state or territory. After data coding concluded, we found eighty-seven countries that did not have sex offender–specific laws and had information on all our definitional measures (see table 2.1), and nine countries that did have sex offender–specific legislation (see table 2.2), for a total of ninety-six countries included in our investigation.

TABLE 2.1   Countries with Rape Laws but Not Sex Offender–Specific Laws

COUNTRY	RAPE LAW	VIOLENCE	MARITAL	AGE OF CONSENT
Afghanistan	Yes	Yes	No	18
Albania	Yes	No	No	14
Argentina	Yes	Yes	Yes	16
Armenia	Yes	M	Yes	16
Austria	Yes	M	Yes	16
Bahamas	Yes	M	No	16
Bahrain	Yes	No	No	16
Barbados	Yes	Yes	Yes	16
Belarus	Yes	M	No	16
Belize	Yes	No	Yes	16
Bhutan	Yes	M	Yes	18
Bosnia and Herzegovina	Yes	Yes	Yes	16
Botswana	Yes	M	No	16
Brunei	Yes	M	No	14
Cambodia	Yes	Yes	No	15
Cape Verde	Yes	M	Yes	16
China	Yes	Yes	No	18
Cyprus	Yes	M	Yes	16
Czech Republic	Yes	M	Yes	15
Ecuador	Yes	M	Yes	14
Egypt	Yes	Yes	No	18
El Salvador	Yes	Yes	No	16
Ethiopia	Yes	M	No	18
Finland	Yes	M	Yes	18
Gambia	Yes	M	Yes	16
Georgia	Yes	M	Yes	14
Ghana	Yes	No	No	16
Guatemala	Yes	Yes	Yes	14
Guinea Bissau	Yes	M	Yes	16
Guyana	Yes	M	Yes	13
Hungary	Yes	M	Yes	14

(continued)

TABLE 2.1 Countries with Rape Laws but Not Sex Offender–Specific Laws

COUNTRY	RAPE LAW	VIOLENCE	MARITAL	AGE OF CONSENT
India	Yes	M	Yes	16
Indonesia	Yes	Yes	No	15
Iran	Yes	Yes	No	None outside marriage
Iraq	Yes	M	No	18
Israel	Yes	M	Yes	14
Jordan	Yes	Yes	No	18
Kazakhstan	Yes	M	Yes	16
Kenya	Yes	No	No	18
Kyrgyzstan	Yes	M	Yes	16
Laos	Yes	M	No	18
Lesotho	Yes	Yes	Yes	18
Libya	Yes	M	No	14
Lithuania	Yes	M	Yes	18
Luxembourg	Yes	M	Yes	16
Malawi	Yes	M	No	16
Malaysia	Yes	M	Yes	16
Mali	Yes	Yes	No	18
Malta	Yes	Yes	Yes	18
Mauritania	No	N/A	No	None outside marriage
Mexico	Yes	Yes	Yes	Varies 12–18
Moldova	Yes	M	No	16
Mongolia	Yes	M	Yes	14
Montenegro	Yes	Yes	Yes	18
Myanmar	Yes	M	No	14
Namibia	Yes	M	No	14
New Zealand	Yes	M	Yes	16
Nigeria	Yes	M	Yes	16
Pakistan	Yes	M	No	16
Papua New Guinea	Yes	M	Yes	16
Philippines	Yes	M	Yes	18

TABLE 2.1   *(continued)*

COUNTRY	RAPE LAW	VIOLENCE	MARITAL	AGE OF CONSENT
Poland	Yes	M	Yes	15
Romania	Yes	M	Yes	15
Russia	Yes	Yes	No	14
St. Lucia	Yes	M	Yes	16
Singapore	Yes	M	No	14
Slovenia	Yes	Yes	Yes	15
Somalia	Yes	M	No	14
South Africa	Yes	M	Yes	16
South Sudan (Rep. of)	Yes	No	No	18
Spain	Yes	Yes	Yes	13
Sri Lanka	Yes	M	Yes	16
Sudan	Yes	No	No	18
Sweden	Yes	Yes	Yes	18
Syria	Yes	Yes	No	15
Tajikistan	Yes	M	No	14
Tanzania	Yes	M	Yes	16
Thailand	Yes	M	No	15
Turkey	Yes	No	Yes	16
Uganda	Yes	M	Yes	18
Ukraine	Yes	M	No	16
United Arab Emirates	Yes	Yes	No	15
Uzbekistan	Yes	M	No	18
Vietnam	Yes	M	Yes	18
Yemen	Yes	No	Yes	15
Zambia	Yes	M	No	14
Zimbabwe	Yes	M	Yes	16

Source: Data for this table were collected by using the search engine Google to locate penal or criminal codes for the majority of the countries listed (access date October 24, 2013). Additional data were collected from the womanstats.org database (access date September 29, 2013).

Note: M = Definition includes force or threat; however, also it includes additional categories.

TABLE 2.2   Countries with Sex Offender–Specific Laws

COUNTRY	SEX OFFENDER REGISTRY	RAPE LAWS	NATIONAL (N) OR TERRITORIES (T)	FORCE OR THREAT	MARITAL/ SPOUSAL RAPE	AGE OF CONSENT
Australia	Yes	Yes	T	M	Yes	Varies by territory (16–18)
Canada	Yes	Yes	T	M	Yes	16
France	Yes	Yes	N	M	Yes	15
Germany	Yes	Yes	N	M	Yes	16
Ireland	Yes	Yes	N	M	Yes	17
Japan	Yes	Yes	T	Yes	Yes	Varies by jurisdiction (13–18)
South Korea	Yes	Yes	N	Yes	No	13
United Kingdom	Yes	Yes	N	M	Yes	16
United States	Yes	Yes	T	M	Yes	Varies by state (16–18)

Source: Data for this table were collected by using the search engine Google to locate penal or criminal codes for the majority of the countries listed (access dates October 3 and 24, 2013), as well as articles found through the search engines EBSCO and Google Scholar (Department of Justice, Equality, and Law Reform 1998; Harrison & Rainey 2009; Levenson 2003; Levenson & Morin 2006; Mercado & Ogloff 2007; Newburn 2010; Obergfell-Fuchs 2011; Sample 2009; Schlesinger 2010; Vess et al. 2011; Viera 2011; Wilson et al. 2013). Additional data were collected from the womanstats.org database (access date September 29, 2013).

Note: M = Definition includes force or threat; however, it also includes additional categories.

Although several aspects of the content of rape laws can be used to infer what legislative bodies, and by extension the citizenry, consider to be a sex crime, we decided on the measures above for the following reasons. If countries had a criminal statute or law that was applicable to sex offenders only, we could infer the perceived extent of the sex-offending problem in those countries (Sample & Bray 2003) and the perceived level of dangerousness sex offenders pose in those countries. An assessment of the countries that define rape as a sex crime, a historically common definition

(LaFree 1989; Sample 2009), was inferred based on whether statutes could be found under a "rape law" key word search. To better understand national definitions of rape as a sex crime and whether these were considered violent crimes, we coded data to determine if nations included words inferring violence in their criminal codes, such as "threat," "physical force," and "threat of force." If criminal codes included punishments or formal sanctions for behaviors listed in their sex offender–specific or rape laws and the range of these sanctions in terms of supervision, imprisonment, and punishment, we could draw conclusions on the seriousness with which sex crimes are managed in countries. Taken together, the data we coded from criminal codes across nations provides a glance into the ways in which various countries construct sexual behavior as deviant or criminal. The tables we created (available on request) allowed us to make qualitative comparisons of definitions for sex crimes across countries.

QUALITATIVE OBSERVATIONS FROM INTERCOUNTRY COMPARISONS

Of the 96 nations we examined, all had a rape law or some statute in their criminal codes that identified criminal sexual behavior. This represents over half of the 174 countries reporting crime data to Interpol. This observation suggests that a majority of countries are in agreement that some sexual behaviors must be legally, and likely morally, wrong.

Of the countries that included rape in their criminal codes, the overwhelming majority mentioned language such as "force" or "threat of force," thus suggesting that their construction of rape includes notions of consent. The inference is that if force, or threat thereof, is not involved in sexual behavior, it is not criminal. Interestingly, several countries made no provisions that sex crimes can include the threats of force from a spouse. There was much variability across countries regarding whether rape can include sexual behaviors within domestic partnerships or marital relations. A cursory review of the countries without marital rape laws suggests that the religiosity of nations, the average age of their citizens, and the average level of education of residents may be variables to explore when understanding if and how sex crimes can occur within the context of legally or socially recognized relationships.

Another way in which sex crimes can be defined is the indication that there is a minimum age under which people are incapable of consenting to sexual relations. Of all ninety-six countries examined, all included an age at which consent to sexual behavior could be granted. This age, however, varied widely across countries, with a range of 12 to 18 years old. Some countries' criminal codes suggested there was no age at which someone could consent to sex if it was outside of marriage. These observations suggest to us that there is some agreement concerning consensual sex with children, but the definition of "children" varies across nations. Moreover, in some countries the age of consent varied by jurisdiction, state, or territory, suggesting some nations have not settled on a nationwide definition of "childhood."

Surprisingly, less than 10 percent of countries reviewed had determined that sex offending was of such a public concern that policy makers needed to enact laws specific to sex offenders as a group. These countries included Australia, Canada, France, Germany, Ireland, Japan, South Korea, United Kingdom, and the United States. They generally included marital rape in their definition of a sex crime, with the exception of South Korea, and varied in their age of consent, from 13 in South Korea to 18 in some states and territories in the United States and Australia. Also, most of these countries have embraced criminalizing noncontact offense against children, however that may be defined, such as possessing, manufacturing, and distributing child pornography. Given that most countries' sex offender–specific statues had been enacted within the past twenty years, the construction of a sex crime is clearly not static over time or across nations; nor are perceptions of sex offending as an increasing social problem that must be addressed legislatively.

Finally, our examination revealed that all countries in this investigation have constructed sex crimes or sexual behaviors that are considered criminal and require formal sanction or punishment, ranging from periods of community supervision to imprisonment for varying lengths, to death. Given the suggested pathways by which deviant or criminal behavior is constructed (Cohen 1972; Sutherland 1950), it was not surprising to find variability in the ways in which a sex crime may be sanctioned across nations. The solutions (laws and punishments) proposed to address a social problem are inherent in the process of defining a behavior as criminal.

DISCUSSION AND CONCLUSIONS

Most countries appear to construct notions of sex crimes based on whether reporting victims are single or married, the perpetrators were perceived to have rights to engage in sex with victims, victims were old enough to consent to sexual behavior, and this consent could be granted outside of marriage. To the degree to which religious beliefs, education, average age of citizenry, and other factors influence assessments of "appropriate" or "inappropriate" sexual behavior, contextual factors appear to play a role in the construction of criminal sexual behavior (Jenkins 1998). Perhaps these factors also influence perceptions of risk of sexual victimization and the need for legal remedies to address the "dangerousness" with which sex offenders are perceived.

Given that, globally, so few countries have felt the need to enact laws to address the behaviors of sex offenders only, we can infer that most countries reporting crime data to Interpol may not perceive sex offenders as more dangerous than other types of offenders, or that they pose a greater risk for reoffending than other groups. These countries' definitions of sex crimes have likely not expanded to include behaviors beyond rape or forced sex acts. Noncontact crimes, such as the production or possession of child pornography or the prohibition of sex offenders in public spaces, as found in definitions of sex crimes in countries' with sex offender–specific laws, may be included in many countries' definitions of sex crimes, but an expansion of the definitions of sex crimes did not prompt a perceived public outcry for the need to enact sex offender–specific laws. We are left to wonder under what conditions sex offender–specific laws are created and how these might vary across nations, given that most countries have not enacted the types of laws that single out sex offenders for additional surveillance and control measures.

The varying definitions of sex crimes across nations may affect their citizens' perceptions of the sex-offender problem internationally. For instance, in countries with broad and expansive constructions of sex crimes, citizens may perceive a growing sex-offender problem since more people and behaviors are eligible for arrest (Sample & Bray 2006), whereas citizens in countries with narrow definitions of sex crimes may perceive no growing sex-offender problem since the nature of a "sex crime" has remained somewhat static. Moreover, the diffusion of perceptions of a sex-offender problem across geographic borders may not occur to the degree that we assume.

The countries that have enacted sex offender–specific laws are geographically separated by oceans and exhibit little uniformity in their structures of government, yet to some degree they share values of democracy, exhibit similar consumer-based economies, and are considered at least somewhat "Westernized." These factors alone, however, cannot explain national views of the need for sex offender–specific laws, as countries that also share these traits have not enacted such laws (e.g., India, New Zealand, Sweden). To this end, just as the diffusion of perceptions of social problems is likely not dictated simply by "Western" values of democracy or economic structures, nor will definitions of rape and sex crimes be. We are again left to wonder if and how sexual victimization concerns spread across regions, and how this diffusion may influence the definitions of sex crimes and the enactment of laws.

The implications of the differences in the construction process of criminalizing behaviors, and differences in the definitions of resulting behaviors, are profound for the global prevention of sexual victimization. Varying constructions of what sex crimes are make it difficult to detect, monitor, and apprehend law violators outside of nation boundaries. Even within nations, differences in rape definitions (e.g., age of consent) make it difficult to consistently prosecute offenders. Our investigation suggests that global policing of sex offenders and offenses is impractical in light of the variation of sex crime definitions.

In the end, the perceptions of sex-offender problems appear contextual and thus specific to sovereign nations. Given that these perceptions are thought to be responsible for legal definitions of rape and sex crimes over time, a global condemnation of specific sex acts is not likely. Rather, actions defined as sex crimes, and laws and sanctions to address them, will likely depend on national and territorial moral values, religious beliefs, political cultures, and other factors that make nations unique. This should be kept in mind when attempting to extrapolate inferences from the enactment of sex offender–specific laws, when offering official statistics to demonstrate sex-offending rates and levels, and when suggesting measures by which sex offenses can be detected and sanctioned globally.

DISCUSSION QUESTIONS

1. What factors may influence how countries' lawmakers define a sex crime?
2. Why do you think the definition of a child varies across sovereign nations?
3. What factors do you think prompted some countries to define sex offending as a social problem in need of sex offender–specific legislation?
4. In light of the variability in the definition of rape across countries, how might we come to understand the extent of sex offending globally?

REFERENCES

Becker, H. S. 1963. *Outsiders: Studies in the Sociology of Deviance*. New York: Free Press.

Ben-Yehuda, N. 1990. *The Politics and Morality of Deviance*. New York: State University of New York Press.

Best, J. 1989. *Images of Issues: Typifying Contemporary Social Problems*. New York: Aldine De Gruyter.

Cohen, S. 1972. *Folk Devils and Moral Panics: The Creation of the Mods and Rockers*. New York: St. Martin's Press.

Conrad, P., and J. W. Schneider. 1980. *Deviance and Medicalization*. St. Louis: C. V. Mosby.

Department of Justice, Equality, and Law Reform. 1998. *The Law on Sexual Offenses: A Discussion Paper*. Dublin: Stationery Office.

Edleman, M. 1988. *Constructing the Political Spectacle*. New York: Cambridge University Press.

Evans, M. K., R. Lytle, and L. L. Sample. 2013. "Sex Offender Registration and Community Notification." In *Sex Offender Laws: Rhetoric and Reality*, ed. Richard G. Wright. New York Springer.

Federal Bureau of Investigation (FBI). 2012. UCR changes definition of rape. http://www.fbi.gov/about-us/cjis/cjis-link/march-2012/ucr-program -changes-definition-of-rape.

Fonda, M., R. Eni, and E. Guimond. 2013. Socially constructed teen motherhood: A review. *International Indigenous Policy Journal* 4 (1): 1–10.

Harrison, K., and B. Rainey. 2009. Suppressing human rights? A rights-based approach to the use of pharmacotherapy with sex offenders. *Legal Studies* 29 (1): 47–74. doi:10.1111/j.1748–121X.2008.00111.x.

Jenkins, P. 1998. *Moral Panic: Changing Concepts of the Child Molester in Modern America*. New Haven, Conn.: Yale University Press.

John Jay College of Criminal Justice. 2004. Cross-national comparisons of rape rates: Problems and issues. Joint UNECE-UNODC meeting on Crime Statistics, Geneva, November 3–5.

LaFree, G. D. 1989. *Rape and Criminal Justice: The Social Construction of Sexual Assault*. Belmont, Calif.: Wadsworth.

Levenson, J. S. 2003. Policy interventions designed to combat sexual violence: Community notification and civil commitment. *Journal of Child Sexual Abuse* 12 (3): 17–52. doi:10.1300/J070v12n03_02.

Levenson, J. S., Y. S. Brannon, T. Fortney, and J. Baker. 2007. Public perceptions and community protection policies. *Analyses of Social Issues and Public Policy* 7 (1): 1–25.

Levenson, J. S., and J. W. Morin. 2006. Factors predicting selection of sexually violent predators for civil commitment. *International Journal of Offender Therapy & Comparative Criminology* 50 (6): 609–29. doi:10.1177/0306624X06287644.

Mercado, C. C., and J. R. P. Ogloff. 2007. Risk and the preventive detention of sex offenders in Australia and the United States. *International Journal of Law & Psychiatry* 30 (1): 49–59. doi:10.1016/j.ijlp.2006.02.001.

Newburn, K. 2010. The prospect of an international sex offender registry: Why an international system modeled after United States sex offender laws is not an effective solution to stop child sexual abuse. *Wisconsin International Law Journal* 28 (3): 547–83. http://search.ebscohost.com.leo.lib.unomaha.edu/login.aspx?direct=true&db=aph&AN=67046283&site=ehost-live.

Obergfell-Fuchs, J. 2011. Experiences with sex offender registration in Germany. Paper presented at annual meeting of the ASC, Washington, D.C., November 15. http://citation.allacademic.com/meta/p515361_index.html.

Sample, L. L. 2001. The social construction of the sex offender. Ph.D. dissertation, University of Missouri- St. Louis.

——. 2009. Sexual violence. In *Handbook of Crime and Public Policy*, ed. Michael Tonry, 51–70. New York: Oxford University Press.

Sample L. L., and T. M. Bray. 2003. Are sex offenders dangerous? *Criminology & Public Policy* 3 (1): 59–82.

——. 2006. Are sex offenders different? An examination of re-arrest patterns. *Criminal Justice Policy Review* 17 (1): 83–102.

Schlesinger, L. B. 2010. Sex offenders, juvenile offenders, and cross-cultural crime research: New findings, all interesting. *International Journal of Offender Therapy*

& *Comparative Criminology* 54 (2): 147–49. http://search.ebscohost.com
.leo.lib.unomaha.edu/login.aspx?direct=true&db=aph&AN=48546010
&site=ehost-live.

Surette, R. 1998. *Media, Crime, and Criminal Justice: Images and Realities*. New
York: Wadsworth.

Sutherland, E. H. 1950. The diffusion of sexual psychopath laws. *American Journal
of Sociology* 50:142–48.

Terry, K. J., and A. R. Ackerman. 2009. A brief history of major sex offender laws."
In *Sex Offender Laws: Rhetoric and Reality*, ed. Richard G. Wright, 211–42.
New York: Springer.

U.N. Economic Commission for Europe. 2004. *Cross-national Comparison of
Rape Rates: Problems and Issues*. http://www.unece.org/fileadmin/DAM/stats
/documents/2004/11/crime/wp.18.e.pdf.

Vess, J., B. Langskaill, A. Day, M. Powell, and J. Graffam. 2011. A comparative analysis of Australian sex offender legislation for sex offender registries.
Australian & New Zealand Journal of Criminology 44 (3): 404–24. doi:10.1177
/0004865811419065.

Viera, D. 2011. Try as they might, just can't get it right: Shortcomings of the international Megan's Law of 2010. *Emory International Law Review* 25 (3): 1517–60.
http://search.ebscohost.com.leo.lib.unomaha.edu/login.aspx?direct=true&db
=aph&AN=77696007&site=ehost-live.

Wilson, R. J., J. Looman, J. Abracen, and D. R. Pake. 2013. Comparing sexual
offenders at the regional treatment centre (Ontario) and the Florida civil commitment center. *International Journal of Offender Therapy & Comparative
Criminology* 57 (3): 377–95. doi:10.1177/0306624X11434918.

Woman Stats Project. 2001. http://www.womanstats.org.

CHAPTER 3

The Use of Masculinities in the Understanding and Treatment of Male Sexual Offenders

▸ ALISSA R. ACKERMAN, RICH FURMAN, JEFFREY W. COHEN, ERIC MADFIS, AND MICHELLE SANCHEZ

RESEARCH HAS REPEATEDLY SHOWN THAT the vast majority of sex offenses perpetrated against women and children are committed by men (Snyder 2000). Additionally, some scholarship has explored the relationship between certain aspects of masculinities and those who commit sexual offenses (Cullen, Golden, & Cullen 1979). That is, when masculinities are discussed, they are viewed as singular variables that lead to an increased likelihood of men committing child sexual abuse and other sexual offenses (Cowburn & Dominelli 2001). Discussions of masculinities usually stop here and fail to address the aspects that can prevent men from committing sexual offenses. Rarely are masculinities explored in a manner that helps practitioners understand the lives of men in such a way that they can integrate lessons regarding masculinities into their interventions. So too are masculinities frequently conceptualized as risk factors or as the factor contributing to sexual offenses but rarely as a potential source of strength that helps men resist committing sexual offenses. Too infrequently are masculinities viewed as a strength that can be utilized in helping men resolve complex psychosocial dilemmas (Furman 2010). If key aspects of masculinities are implicated in sexual offenses, then it is essential for masculinities to be a component of prevention and treatment.

The purpose of this chapter is to explore the full implications of considering the relationship of masculinities to sex offenses and sexual offenders. Here we view masculinities not as a monolithic construct that is solely related to pathology but as a nuanced constellation of social expectations, behaviors, emotions, and means of constructing identity that have implications in causing, preventing, and treating men for sexual offenses. We begin by briefly exploring masculinities in general as a means of helping readers unfamiliar with this essential gender studies concept to understand their implications. Following a discussion of how the more problematic aspects of masculinities account for sexual assault and child sexual abuse, we examine the ways in which other aspects of masculinities can be utilized in the service of preventing and treating sexual offenders. That is, we show how the utilization of a strengths orientation, borrowed from social work (DeJong & Miller 1995; Maluccio 1981; Saleebey 1994; 2002; Weick et al. 1989), provides guidance in infusing masculinities into the process of treatment and prevention. This dual view of masculinities, as a prospective causal and curative feature, is an important aspect demonstrating the potential in using a gendered lens.

MASCULINITIES

Masculinities refers to the socially constructed ways in which men perform their manhood (Kilmartin 2010). That is, while men (and women) are certainly influenced by biological factors, the manner in which they enact the various roles and behaviors that men "should" perform is largely due to childhood socialization and the influence of current social forces (Kimmel 2006). Men may be born male, but they become men through complex social performances, expectations, and relationships. While this may sound fairly obvious, the implications of this basic concept of gender are powerful. The manner in which men experience and express their masculinity, while socially constructed, is not static: masculinities do change and evolve over time (O'Rand 1987) and with intervention (Kilmartin et al. 2008). Also, masculinity is not monolithic. This is reflected in the use of the preferred term "masculinities"—this plural signifies the multiplicity of masculinities and the diverse means by which men perform what it means to be a man (Brod 1987).

In spite of the diversity of masculinities, there does seem to exist, within each culture, one dominant form of masculinity, regardless of the powerful effects of globalization (Connell 1998). This dominant form, hegemonic masculinity, exists as a constellation of social structures. Connell conceptualizes the core of hegemonic masculinity within Western societies to be characterized by the dominance of women by men and a hierarchy of dominance among men in male groups. Hegemonic masculinity also serves to perpetuate male dominance and patriarchy, thereby creating differentials of power between men and women, and men who do not live up to the hegemonic ideal. It serves as a standard by which all men are judged and likewise judge themselves (Connell 1987) and defines the accepted feelings, traits, roles, thoughts, and behaviors that are preferred for men within each society (Thorpe 2010). Hegemonic masculinity is that form of masculinity to which all men learn they must strive in order to be "real men." However, the attributes encompassed by this ideal are not available or achievable to many men, even if they wish to attain them (Connell 1990; de Visser, Smith, & McDonnell 2009).

Brannon's (1985) typology of traditional (hegemonic) masculinity remains one of the clearest and most relevant to date. His model includes four characteristics: antifemininity, status and achievement, inexpressiveness and independence, and adventurousness and aggressiveness. Put colloquially, men are to engage in "no sissy stuff," be "the big wheel," be the "sturdy oak" or the "male machine," and "give 'em hell." As we shall see, several of these characteristics are especially implicated in sexual offenses and can be viewed as highly problematic in other domains in men's lives. There are several ways in which the hegemonic masculine ideal becomes problematic. First, even if all the attributes of this form of masculinity were desirable (which they are not), many men are not willing or able to achieve them. Further, the powerful external and internal expectations to achieve and constantly perform each of these attributes, and a man's lack of ability or willingness to achieve them, have powerful effects on the psychosocial well-being of men. The conflicts created by the discrepancy between how men actually perform their masculinity and these powerful expectations has been referred to as gender role conflict (O'Neil, Good, & Holmes 1995) or gender role strain (Pleck 1995). Research has demonstrated numerous psychosocial consequences of not fully conforming to gender roles and expectations. For example, gender role conflict/strain has been linked to psychological distress, as indicated by measures of somatization, depression, and anxiety (Liu & Iwamoto 2006; Wester et al. 2007) as well as obsessive-compulsive problems, interpersonal sensitivity, and hostility (Wester, Kuo, & Vogel 2006).

In addition to the difficulties men experience when they are unable to successfully meet hegemonic gender roles, there are problems that they may experience when they do successfully meet them. In this subtype of gender role strain, or dysfunction strain, the actual fulfillment of the roles or the intensity in which they are fulfilled is problematic (Pleck 1995). For instance, Iwamoto, Liao, & Liu (2010) found that Asian American men who conform to the use of avoidant coping strategies such as drinking and endorsing the hegemonic trait of dominance reported higher levels of depression. In addition, Liu and Iwamoto (2007) found that Asian American men's conformity to certain masculine norms predicted marijuana use and binge drinking. As we shall explore in the next section, many of these masculine norms are highly correlated not only to symptoms of psychological distress but also to the performance of violence, and often sexual violence.

A final dynamic regarding hegemonic masculinity may offer additional insight. Specifically, it is important to note that hegemonic masculinity operates at both the macro and micro levels. Not only can we identify broad cultural ideals of masculinity, but we can also "unpack the interactional processes through which the most honored way to be a man is locally constituted" (Schrock & Padavic 2007:630; see also Dekeseredy et al. 2006; Yeung, Stombler, & Wharton 2006). When taking this into account, we are able to identify instances in which broader cultural ideals associated with hegemonic masculinity may conflict with more locally constituted forms.

For instance, Yeung, Stombler, and Wharton (2006) point out that the construction of masculinity among a particular group can be used as a way to cope with and/or deconstruct the hegemonic masculinity of the larger cultural milieu within which that group operates. In this sense, masculinities may work as both a risk and, in some instances, a protective factor. Similarly, in response to their finding that conformity to the hegemonic masculine ideal of "emotional control" had an inverse relationship with alcohol use and binge drinking among a sample of college-age Asian American men, Liu and Iwamoto (2007:35) suggested that this particular aspect of conformity to masculine norms "may potentially serve as a protective factor of alcohol consumption and binge drinking behavior."

Along these lines, in his qualitative study of physically violent, sexually violent, and nonviolent boys, James Messerschmidt (2000) identified additional ways in which masculinities can be constructed to buffer the negative aspects of hegemonic masculinities. As Messerschmidt points out, hegemonic masculinities at both the macro and micro levels are constructed in relation to other forms of masculinities (i.e., subordinated, oppositional, and accommodating masculinities). By situating masculine accomplishments as structured actions within and across situational contexts, Messerschmidt illustrates that the construction of a nonviolent hegemonic masculinity in one context (e.g., the family) may mediate the need to perform a violent (physically or sexually) hegemonic masculinity in another context (e.g., at school).

THE PROBLEM OF MASCULINITIES: A HISTORICAL APPROACH TO UNDERSTANDING SEX CRIMES

The literature on masculinities has documented that male sex offenders commit sex offenses for a variety of reasons, and no one factor can account for all sexual offending; contrary to popular belief, sex offenders represent an extremely heterogeneous group. Yet the majority of sex crimes (Snyder 2000), as is the case with most other crimes, are committed by men (Truman 2011). This has led to a body of literature that explores masculinities or gender-related issues as the problem, or the factor that influences both sexual and nonsexual offending. Exploring the gendered nature of men's sexual offenses allows practitioners and policy advocates alike to develop new practices, programs, and policies from what we term a gender-competent perspective. Gender competence is analogous to cultural competence, which is recognized as an essential aspect of providing and desiring services (Rivera 2009).

Rapists

With regard to rape, common characteristics emerge, regardless of the overall impetus for offending. For example, most rapists exhibit negative views toward women, are likely to endorse rape myths, condone violence, and often identify with a hypermasculine role (Scully & Marolla 1984). Many of these men exhibit a sense of worthlessness and vulnerability, low self-esteem, and/or the mismanagement of aggression. The research shows that power and dominance are highly correlated with various types of sexual offenses (Groth 1979). Groth (1983:165) stated that rape is the "sexual expression of aggression, rather than the aggressive expression of sexuality." Groth (1983) found that only 5 percent of all rapes included primarily sexual motivations. The other 95 percent were characterized as "power rape" or "anger rape." In the first type, power rape, the rapist's primary motivations are to dominate and control the victim. In anger rapes, the primary objective is to harm women. In both classifications of rapes, sex is conceptualized more as a vehicle than as an aim. The commission of a rape provides the goal of power or dominance rather than the goal of sexual gratification. Brownmiller (1975) pointed out that this is true of violent rape as well as date rape. Specifically, the use of Rohypnol, alcohol, other date rape drugs, or any combination of these, provides the offender with control over the victim (Sturman 2000).

O'Neil (2005) contends that in Brannon's original typology, antifemininity is the most central feature of hegemonic masculinity. Misogyny is a powerful message that boys receive growing up, and one that many men continue to hold as a constellation of cognitive beliefs; this antipathy must be somehow experienced emotionally. However, men are not typically encouraged to experience feelings of loss, sadness, regret, or other "softer feelings"; therefore this antipathy must be experienced in a manner that is acceptable to hegemonic notions of masculinity. Since men are traditionally allowed and encouraged to express only two feelings—anger and lust—these become easily integrated and confused, thereby providing the affective currency for the performance of rape. Therefore sexualized anger can be conceptualized as the affective correlate to antifemininity.

Further, research on gendered experiences of emotion suggests that men (presumably through gendered socialization around hegemonic masculinity) are more likely to experience anger in isolation, as opposed to women, who tend to experience anger concomitantly with guilt, shame, fear, and other self-targeted emotions (Broidy & Agnew 1997). Gendered differences in externalization and internalization of threats may also play a role. Men (as compared to women) tend to externalize threats, protecting against feelings of shame and depression, while simultaneously increasing feelings of anger toward others (Broidy & Agnew 1997). Since men are taught that they must act on their emotions, and that they should act aggressively toward those whom they perceive as a threat, this antifemininity becomes a powerful contributor to sexual violence.

Perhaps no other factor is so clearly related to hegemonic masculinities and sexual offenses as dominance. Cheng (1999) holds the notion of dominance as the most central feature of hegemonic masculinity. This, perhaps indirectly, makes it the most powerful factor in the perpetuation of rape. Similarly, Brownmiller (1975) argues that all rape is an exercise in power and dominance. In her classic best seller, she provides a historical account of rape from ancient times through the mid-twentieth century and details how power and control have dominated rape across all cultures, through times of war and within institutions of power. Perhaps the clearest illustration of the relationship among power, dominance, hegemonic masculinity, and rape is found during wartime rape (Connell & Messerschmidt 2005, Zurbriggen 2010)

Brownmiller notes that rape entered the criminal code only as a property crime, where the rape of a woman was actually a crime against another man. Women were seen merely as property. The belief that women remained the property of their husband is still visible today in many parts of the world; it was not until the 1970s that the United States began to see a societal shift away from the *women as property* zeitgeist (Bergen 1999). It was less than twenty years ago that the last U.S. state—North Carolina—outlawed spousal rape. Several states continue to distinguish between marital and nonmarital rape, a distinction that results in lesser penalties being applied to marital rape. These facts expose the manner in which men generally maintain power and control over women and, as Brownmiller (1975) suggests, utilize the threat or commission of rape to continue to gain control or power over them. Bergen (1999) articulates that, while there is no clear picture of the husband-rapist, one point that seems to be clear is that these men feel a sense of entitlement to do what they please with their property. This remains true for men who rape women who are not their spouses or significant others. Brownmiller provides the historical evidence that rape has most often been used to gain control over *property*.

While some scholars take issue with this approach to understanding power/control and rape (LaFree 1989), they also point to research that suggests that at least part of Brownmiller's critique has merit. For example, Brownmiller contends that rape "is nothing more or less than the conscious process of intimidation by which *all* men keep *all* women in a state of fear" (1975:15). LaFree (1989:150) takes issue with this stance, questioning the extent to which "men consciously calculate the effect that rape will have on women in general." While this may be true, research suggests that women are very much aware of the threat of rape, and though men are disproportionately the victims of violent crime—with rape the exception—women remain much more fearful (Cossman & Rader 2011; Karmen 1991). As a result, many women take numerous precautions to protect themselves from rape or other violence, and many women are fearful to walk alone at night (Gallup 2010; Katz 2006). To the extent that Brownmiller was correct, rape, or the threat of rape, serves to keep women inferior to men.

Some scholars argue that the feminist literature on rape has not been fully versed in science but engages in propagandizing to further the "gender war" (Sommers 2000). Sommers argues that much of the literature on males, gender, and privilege is mysteriously missing from the peer-reviewed literature and full of errors. Though the question remains as to whether there is sufficient empirical evidence to support the claim that rape serves as a broad form of power and control over women, some evidence, at both the macro and micro levels, does indicate this. At the macro level, some scientific evidence reveals that societal gender roles and rape myths are controlled by rape. For example, LaFree (1989) found that gender-role nonconformity was a factor in the decision to arrest. Young girls who lied, ran away from home, or were perceived as being promiscuous or liking sex were more likely to have the police believe that their rape allegation was fabricated. Similarly, girls under 18 who were acquainted with the offender were less likely to have their cases charged as felonies, because date or acquaintance rapes were not considered to be sufficiently serious (LaFree 1989).

LaFree also found that, while some judges were very sympathetic to rape victims, others held several rape myths to be true. For example, one judge, who had presided over many rape cases stated:

> The typical rape case involves a tremendous amount of asking for it. The average rape is a girl . . . well-endowed . . . went to a tavern, drank all night, expected a sexual encounter and got raped—he used more force than she expected. . . . I believe biologically it is wrong to entice a man knowing the situation you're creating and then saying "no." There is a button a man has that cannot be turned off and on like a light switch. And a man can go to prison for a very long time because of it. (95–96)

As such, a girl who was raped in her home, especially when she invited the man into the home, was less likely to have the rapist found guilty. Similarly, if a girl had frequented bars or was picked up in certain places or at certain times, the case was less likely to end in a guilty verdict.

While much of the research on gender roles and rape comes out of the 1970s and 1980s, many of the findings hold true today, in that both men and women continue to hold and support rape myths. For example, though the majority of rapes against college-aged women are date rapes, Littleton and colleagues (2009) found that this demographic of women still describes the typical rape as a violent assault by a stranger. Similarly, Polaschek and Ward (2002) provide an overview of the evidence that correlates rape myths with sexually aggressive behavior. Research still shows that an increased adherence to rape myths is significantly related to sexual aggression (Lonsway & Fitzgerald 1995). Several scholars point out that adherence to rape myths provides a justification to engage in date rape. Abbey et al. (2001) and Ryan (2004) suggest that teasing or promiscuity on the part of the woman is still regarded as a justification to coerce or force sex. Women who allow some sexual activity to occur but do not allow the activity to escalate beyond a certain level are perceived as somehow blameworthy (Ryan 2004). Macrolevel societal ideologies and practices influence individual level beliefs and actions. While not all men who rape explicitly articulate their behavior as an expression of these macrolevel forces, such structural dynamics do work to construct cultural contexts in which rape becomes expected, unchallenged, and, in some ways, accepted.

Child Sexual Abusers

Child sexual abusers commit a variety of offenses for various reasons; however, they share several characteristics with men who commit rape, including low self-esteem, feelings of inadequacy, a sense of worthlessness or vulnerability, and ineptitude or awkwardness in adult relationships (Terry 2006). In addition, many child sexual abusers lack appropriate social skills and often feel a sense of loneliness and isolation (Terry 2006). For instance, Marshall (1989) found that many sex offenders had not developed the necessary social skills and self-confidence to form appropriate intimate relationships with peers. However, Seidman and colleagues (1994) found that rapists and nonfamilial child molesters exhibited more intimacy deficiency.

While the majority of these men have a sexual attraction to age-appropriate individuals, their sexual behavior toward children is generally the result of external stressors (Simon et al. 1992). These stressors may be situational or based on one's negative affective state (Terry 2006).

For example, there is a wide range of stressors that may be the impetus for the offense cycle, including unemployment or marital problems (which are situational) and isolation or loneliness (which are negative affective states). Often these stressors are seen as an affront to one's masculinity. While scholars have suggested that they may lead to low self-confidence or self-esteem (Schwartz 1995), few have examined the link between gender and these problematic feelings.

Similarly, while rapists often adhere to rape myths that stem from cultural values to condone their sexually assaultive or coercive behavior (Marshall, Laws, & Barbaree 1990), child sexual abusers develop attitudes that allow them to cope or neutralize their behavior as it conflicts with social norms (Abel, Becker, & Cunningham-Rathner 1984). While rape myths may be the cause or justification for sexual assault against adults, the attitudes and cognitive distortions developed by child sexual abusers are the result of their behavior. However, rape myths and cognitive distortions are similar in nature (Burt 1998). Some cognitive distortions include minimization and denial, justification, and lack of victim empathy (Terry 2006).

While several of these factors are similar to those seen in rapists, there remain stark contrasts as well. For instance, rapists tend to exhibit higher levels of aggression than child sexual abusers, just as rapists are more likely to identify with a hypermasculine role (Scully & Marolla 1984). Child molesters tend to show more sensitivity toward the victim's feelings than do many rapists. Finally, rapists are more likely to act on impulse than are child sexual abusers, who are likely to carefully plan and groom their victims (Groth 1979; Pryor 1996; Terry 2006). Regardless of the similarities and/ or differences between rapists and child molesters, one thing remains clear. Studies, especially those stemming from the feminist movement of the 1970s, focus on the negative role of men and masculinities in the offending cycle. Many of the factors related to offending, for both rapists and child molesters, inevitably link back to one's role as a man. While exploring the negative consequences of pathological masculinities is a valuable means of understanding how and why men perpetrate sexual offenses, it can also be beneficial to help men utilize the more functional aspects of their masculinities in order to resist perpetration and augment treatment. In the following section, we explore how knowledge of both the problematic aspects of masculinities as well as their strengths may be utilized in both the development of social policy and practice with individual sex offenders.

THE PROMISE OF MASCULINITIES: IMPLICATIONS
FOR POLICY AND PRACTICE

Lessons from psychology and social work practice with at-risk men can help inform those who provide services to male sex offenders on a day–to–day basis. The strengths perspective of social work helps practitioners focus on utilizing key strengths and resources from an individual's life in service of their treatment goals. It begins with the recognition that even the most psychologically or behaviorally disturbed individual desists from deviant and criminal behavior more often than he acts. Therefore each individual possesses the capacity to control his impulses but needs to maximize motivation, engage in contexts and systems that support healthy choices, and learn skills to maximize prosocial impulses. Saleebey (2002:3) notes that "practicing from a strengths orientation means that everything you do as a social worker (or therapist) will be predicated, in some way, on helping to discover and embellish, explore and exploit clients' strengths and resources in the service of assisting them to achieve their goals, realize their dreams, and shed the irons of their own inhibitions and misgivings."

What too infrequently has been explored is how practitioners can help men use masculinities as a source of strength (Kosberg 2005). As we have noted, key aspects of masculinities are deeply implicated in creating and perpetuating sexual offenses. How then can masculinities simultaneously be a source of strength and fodder for change?

Three key aspects of masculinities provide guidance: their performative nature, their diversity, and their contextual nature. Essentialist views of masculinity minimize the performative and contextual aspects. Masculinities change over time and vary greatly by context. For instance, men who respond in sexist and derogatory ways with peers may not behave in the same manner with their children or significant others (McMahon 2010; Quin 2002). Therefore men can be encouraged to perform their masculinities in new ways, and learn to reframe them as well.

As previously noted, men do not possess one masculinity but perform multiple masculinities. Helping men to access aspects of their masculinities that serve their well-being is an important part of the change process. For instance, the concept of "toughness" is as central to the hegemonic ideal as is stoicism and constrictive effect (Katz 2006). Typically, these two traits are linked: a tough man does not express his feelings. However, treatment providers and programs can help men reconceptualize toughness as the willingness to withstand and tolerate difficult feelings (Brooks 1998). In a similar manner, paternalistic notions can be shifted from one of objectification to protection—a real man just learns to protect women and children, and part of this is to control one's impulses against committing sexual violations.

As part of their developing the capacity to utilize the strengths of masculinities in service of helping men change, practitioners must engage in their own self-reflective process of challenging what is considered "healthy." For instance, while it is clear that one must possess the capacity to be in touch with one's softer feelings as a way of increasing empathy toward one's victims, most men know that stoicism plays an important and highly functional role in many social contexts (Scharrer 2012). For example, being able to not engage with nor react to fear is an essential aspect of responding to crisis. Practitioners ought to recognize this more nuanced view of many masculine norms in order to most effectively treat and counsel men.

Currently there are a substantial number of programs that seek to alter men's adherence to destructive forms of masculinities that lead to violence (Barker, Ricardo, & Nacimento 2007). Many of these programs engage boys and men in dialogues and psychoeducational experiences that have demonstrated a reduction in strict adherence to masculine norms. Too few of these programs are geared toward sex offenders. However, key lessons from these programs on how to transform men's overly rigid adherence to these forms of masculinities are highly relevant to sex offenders.

THE GOOD LIVES MODEL

Though originally conceived of as a general strengths-based model for offenders, the Good Lives Model (GLM) has been extensively used with sex offenders (McGrath, Cumming, & Bouchard 2009). This is not to say that it has not been used with other populations, nor that it cannot be used. In fact, recently the GLM was applied to individuals convicted of violent, nonsexual crimes (Langlands, Ward, & Gilchrist 2009; Whitehead, Ward, & Collie 2007). The core principles of the GLM suggest that offenders should be helped to acquire core competencies, such as being intimate, stress management, and other skills that are of interest to the particular offender based on his interests and abilities (Laws & Ward 2011). The theoretical assumptions of the GLM are guided by research and suggest, among other things, that "human agents' physical embodiment has a profound impact on their cognitive functioning and interface with the world" (Laws & Ward 2011:181). One's physical embodiment and one's gender(s) can and do influence goals, socialization, and experience. However, individuals can use their bodies and their gender (or other physical characteristics) to change themselves and their worlds. While the GLM does not specifically discuss masculinities, its focus on capacity building is congruent with the masculine norm of focusing on "doing." That is, men can be encouraged to take specific actions to change the social conditions that influence their sexual offending, or to learn skills for resisting. Additionally, the GLM's focus on the development of intimacy mandates that men must be helped to challenge the hegemonic trait of lack of expressiveness. By developing new capacities for feelings through improving intimate relationships, the GLM can help men develop the empathy that is needed to identify with their past or potential victims.

Another area of intervention is for advocates to continue to shine the light on media representations connecting masculinities and rape. Perhaps the most blatant example of sexual violence in film comes from the 1970s movie *Blazing Saddles* (McIntosh et al. 2003). When criminals signing up for a paid job in a gang are asked their qualifications, one man answers "rape, arson, murder, and rape." The enrolling men inform the applicant that he said rape twice, to which he responds, "I like rape." This casual, almost deadpan response is followed by an uproarious, joyous, and intense bout of laughter from the other applicants. While current media presentations are less clear, they are perhaps even more insidious owing to their lack of subtlety. The *Twilight* series offers a potent example about hegemonic masculinities via subtle messages to young girls about gendered identity and subservience to men.

CONCLUSION

In this chapter we have discussed the potential use of masculinity principles as they apply to various sex offenders. We pointed out that most often the focus has been on the negative aspects of masculinities and their relation to sexual offending. We argued, however, that masculinities can also be utilized in a positive, strengths-based approach to decreasing sexually based offenses. We do not intend to imply a causal relationship in this discussion but instead explored how key aspects of hegemonic and other forms of masculinities may be associated with the sexual abuse of children and rape. This is meant to help treatment providers, practitioners, and academics begin thinking around new potential targets for intervention.

We also hope this review will stimulate new research into the relationship between masculinities and sexual offending. Specifically, we believe that further research is needed that explores specific attributes and components of masculinities and their relationship to specific sex crimes. The development of such a typology of sex crimes through a gendered lens would help identify the dimensions of masculinities that contribute to particular sex crimes and that may be leveraged in attempts to treat sex offenders and prevent sex offenses.

Research is also needed to uncover the salience of gender and masculinities in the lives of men who commit sex crimes. As discussed in this chapter, the construction and performance of masculinities occur at both macro and micro levels. We "do" masculinities to varying degrees across time and space. While scholars and practitioners may accurately interpret a particular sex crime as an expression of a violent hegemonic masculinity, this may not resonate with or be articulated by the men who actually commit such crimes. Understanding the implications of both macrolevel masculine ideologies and microlevel masculine performances is an important aspect of research in this area.

Finally, we believe there is also a need for explorations of the specific social contexts that (re)inforce toxic aspects of masculinities, and how these environments can be modified to decrease the likelihood of offending. If, as we and others argue, masculinities are differentially structured across social settings, time periods, and environments, then we must begin to identify those contexts in which men (individually and collectively) are exposed to the more toxic constructions of masculinity and those in which they are exposed to more positive constructions. In so doing, we may be able to more fully address the complexity of sexual offending in ways that minimize the problems while maximizing the promises of masculinities and, therefore, be better situated to engage men more meaningfully as gendered beings.

DISCUSSION QUESTIONS

1. The definition of masculinities offered in this chapter is broad. Explain the importance of this definition. Why is it essential to have a broad understanding of the concept of masculinity?
2. Masculinity is the lens through which the chapter discusses sexually based offenses. Describe the similarities and differences between rapists and child molesters and their performance of masculinities.
3. Can gender-based treatment programs prevent sexual violence? Why or why not?

REFERENCES

Abbey, A., P. McAuslan, T. Zawacki, A. M. Clinton, and P. O. Buck. 2001. Attitudinal, experiential, and situational predictors of sexual assault perpetration. *Journal of Interpersonal Violence*, 16:784–807.

Abel, G. G., J. V. Becker, and J. Cunningham-Rathner. 1984. Complications, consent, and cognitions in sex between children and adults. *International Journal of Law and Psychiatry* 7:89–103.

Barker, G., C. Ricardo, and M. Nacimento. 2007. *Engaging Men and Boys in Changing Gender-Based Inequity in Health*. Geneva: World Health Organization.

Bergen, R. K. 1999. *Marital Rape. National Electronic Network on Violence Against Women.* http://www.hawaii.edu/hivandaids/Marital%20Rape.pdf.

Brannon, R. 1985. Dimensions of the male sex role in America. In *Beyond Sex Roles*, ed. A. G. Sargent, 2nd ed., 296–316. St. Paul: West.

Agnew, R., & I. Broidy. 1997. Gender and strain: A General Strain Theory perspective. *Journal of Research in Crime and Delinquency* 34:275–306.

Brod, H., ed. 1987. *The Making of Masculinities: The New Men's Studies*. Boston: Allen and Unwin.

Brooks, G. R. 1998. A new psychotherapy for traditional men. San Francisco: Jossey-Bass.

Brownmiller, S. 1975. *Against Our Will: Men, Women, and Rape*. New York: Ballantine.

Burt, M. 1998. Rape myths. In *Confronting Rape and Sexual Assault*, ed. M. Odem and J. Clay-Warner. Worlds of Women, no. 3. Wilmington, Del.: SR Books/ Scholarly Resources.

Cheng, C. 1999. Marginalized masculinities and hegemonic masculinity: An introduction. *Journal of Men's Studies* 7:295–315.

Connell, R. W. 1987. *Gender and Power: Society, the Person, and Sexual Politics.* Stanford, Calif.: Stanford University Press.

——. 1990. An iron man: The body and some contradictions of hegemonic masculinity. In *Sport, Men and the Gender Order,* ed. M. A. Messner and D. F. Sabo, 83–95. Champaign, Ill.: Human Kinetics Books.

——. 1998. Masculinities and globalization. *Men and Masculinity* 1 (1): 3–23.

Connell, R. W., and J. W. Messerchmidt. 2005. Hegemonic masculinity: Rethinking the concept. *Gender and Society* 19:829–59.

Cossman, J. S., and N. E. Rader. 2011. Fear of crime and personal vulnerability: Examining self-reported health. *Sociological Spectrum* 31:141–62.

Cowburn, M., and L. Dominelli. 2001. Masking hegemonic masculinity: Reconstructing the pedophile as the dangerous stranger. *British Journal of Social Work* 31 (3): 399–415.

Cullen, F. T., K. M. Golden, and J. B. Cullen. 1979. Sex and delinquency: A partial test of the masculinity hypothesis. *Criminology* 17 (3): 301–10.

De Jong, P., and S. D. Miller. 1995. How to interview for client strengths. *Social Work* 40 (6): 729–36.

Dekeseredy, W. S., M. D. Schwartz, D. Fagen, and M. Hall. 2006. Separation/divorce sexual assault: The contribution of male support. *Feminist Criminology* 1 (3): 228–50.

De Visser, R. O., J. A. Smith, and E. J. McDonnell. 2009. That's not masculine. *Journal of Health Psychology* 14 (7): 1047–58.

Furman, R. 2010. *Social Work Practice with Men at Risk.* New York: Columbia University Press.

Gallup. 2010. http://www.gallup.com/poll/144272/nearly-americans-fear-walking-alone-night.aspx.

Groth, A. N. 1979. *Men Who Rape: The Psychology of the Offender.* New York: Plenum.

——. 1983. Treatment of the sexual offender in a correctional institution. In *The Sexual Aggressor: Current Perspectives on Treatment,* ed. J. G. Greer and I. R. Stuart. New York: Van Nostrand Reinhold.

Iwamoto, D. K., L. Liao, and W. M. Liu. 2010. Special section: Recent research on masculine norms. *Psychology of Men & Masculinity* 11:15–24.

Kamen, A. 1991. Victims of crime. In *Criminology: A Contemporary Handbook,* ed. J. F. Sheley. Belmont, Calif.: Thomson-Wadsworth.

Katz, J. 2006. *The Macho Paradox*. London: Sourcebooks.

Kilmartin, C. 2010. *The Masculine Self*. 4th ed. Cornwall-on-Hudson, N.Y.: Sloan.

Kilmartin, C., T. Smith, A. Green, M. Kuchler, H. Heinzen, and D. Kolar. 2008. A real time social norms intervention to reduce male sexism. *Sex Roles: A Journal of Research* 59 (3): 264–73.

Kimmel, M. S. (2006). *Manhood in America: A Cultural History*. 2nd ed. New York: Oxford University Press.

Kosberg, J. I. (2005). Meeting the needs of older men: Challenges for those in the helping professions. *Journal of Sociology and Social Welfare* 32 (1): 9–31.

——. 2011. Social work outreach and practice with men. Paper presented at NASW New Mexico conference, Albuquerque, February 24–25.

LaFree, G. D. 1989. *Rape and Criminal Justice: The Social Contruction of Sexual Assault*. Belmont, Calif.: Wadsworth.

Langlands, R., T. Ward, and E. Gilchrist. 2009. Applying the Good Lives Model to male perpetrators of domestic violence. In *Strengths Based Batter Intervention: A New Paradigm in Ending Domestic Violence*, ed. P. Lehmann and C. Simmons. New York: Springer.

Laws, D. R., and T. Ward. 2011. *Desistance from Sex Offending: Alternatives to Throwing Away the Keys*. New York: Guilford.

Littleton, H., H. Tabernik, E. G. Canales, and T. Backstrom. 2009. Risky situation or harmless fun: A qualitative examination of women's bad hook-up and rape scripts. *Sex Roles* 60:793–804.

Liu, W., and D. Iwamoto. 2006. Asian American men's gender role conflict: The role of Asian values, self-esteem, and psychological distress. *Psychology of Men & Masculinity* 7 (3): 153–64.

——. 2007. Conformity to masculine norms, Asian values, coping strategies, peer group influences and substance use among Asian American men. *Psychology of Men & Masculinity* 8 (1): 25–39.

Lonsway, K. A., and L. F. Fitzgerald. 1995. Attitudinal antecedents of rape myth acceptance: A theoretical and empirical reexamination. *Journal of Personality and Social Psychology* 68:704–11.

Maluccio, A. N. (1981). *Promoting Competence in Clients*. New York: Free Press.

Marshall, W. L. 1989. Intimacy, loneliness, and sexual offenders. *Behavior Research and Therapy* 27:491–503.

Marshall, W. L., and H. E. Barbaree. 1990. Outcome of comprehensive cognitive-behavioral treatment programs. In *Handbook on Sexual Assault: Issues, Theories, and Treatment of the Offender*, ed. W. L. Marshall, D. R. Laws, and H. E. Barbaree. New York: Plenum.

Marshall, W. L., D. R. Laws, and H. E. Barbaree. 1990. Issues in sexual assault. In *Handbook on Sexual Assault: Issues, Theories, and Treatment of the Offender*, ed. W. L. Marshall, D. R. Laws, and H. E. Barbaree. New York: Plenum.

McGrath, R. J., G. F. Cumming, and B. L. Bouchard. 2009. The safer society 2009 North American survey: Current practices and emerging trends in sexual abuser management. Paper presented at the 28th Annual Research and Treatment Conference of the Association for the Treatment of Sexual Abusers, Dallas, Texas.

McIntosh, W. D., J. D. Murray, R. M. Murray, and S. Manian. 2003. What's so funny about a poke in the eye? The prevalence of violence in comedy films and its relation to social and economic threat in the United States, 1951–2000. *Mass Communication and Society* 4:345–60.

McMahon, S. 2010. Rape myths and bystander attitudes among incoming college students. *Journal of American College Health* 59 (1): 3–11.

Messerschmidt, J. W. 2000. *Nine Lives: Adolescent Masculinities, the Body, and Violence*. Boulder, Colo.: Westview.

O' Neil, J. M. 2005. Summarizing 25 years of research on men's gender role conflict using the Gender Role Conflict Scale: New research paradigm and clinical implications. *Counseling Psychologist* 36:358–445.

O'Neil, J. M., G. E. Good, and S. Holmes. 1995. Fifteen years of theory and research on men's gender role conflict. In *The New Psychology of Men*, ed. R. F Levant and W. S. Pollack, 164–206. New York: Basic Books.

O'Rand, A. M. 1987. Gender. In *The Encyclopedia of Aging*, ed. G. L. Maddox, 271–84. New York: Springer.

Pleck, J. H. 1995. The gender role strain paradigm: An update. In *A New Psychology of Men*, ed. R. Levant and W. Pollack, 11–32. New York: Basic Books.

Polaschek, D. L. L., and T. Ward. 2002. The implicit theories of potential rapists: What our questionnaires tell us. *Aggression and Violent Behavior* 7:385–406.

Pryor, D. 1996. *Unspeakable Acts: Why Men Sexually Abuse Children*. New York: New York University Press.

Quin, B. A. 2002. Sexual harassment and masculinity: The power and meaning of "girl watching." *Gender & Society* 16 (3): 386–402.

Rivera, J. A. 2009. Cultural and gender competence: An essential ingredient for behavioral healthcare. Paper presented at 16th Annual Children's Behavioral Health Conference. http://www.ok.gov/odmhsas/documents/Rivera,%20Jose'%20-%20Understanding%20Cultural%20Competence.pdf.

Ryan, K. M. 2004. Further evidence for a cognitive component of rape. *Aggression and Violent Behavior* 9:579–604.

Saleebey, D. 1994. Culture, theory, and narrative: The intersection of meanings in practice. *Social Work* 9 (4): 352–59.

——. 2002. *The Strengths Perspective in Social Work*. Boston: Allyn and Bacon.

Scharrer, E. 2012. More than "Just the facts"? Portrayals of masculinity in police and detective programs over time. *Howard Journal of Communications* 23 (1): 88–109.

Schrock, D. P., and I. Padavic. 2007. Negotiating hegemonic masculinity in a batterer intervention program. *Gender & Society* 21 (5): 625–49.

Schwartz, B. K. 1995. Characteristics and typologies of sex offenders. In *The Sex Offender: Corrections, Treatment, and Legal Practice*, ed. B. Schwartz and H. R. Cellini. Kingston, NJ: Civic Research Institute.

Scully, D., and J. Marolla. 1984. Convicted rapists' vocabulary of motive: Excuses and justifications. *Social Problems* 31 (5): 530–44.

Seidman, B. T., W. L. Marshall, S. M. Hudson, and P. J. Robertson. 1994. An examination of intimacy and loneliness in sex offenders. *Journal of Interpersonal Violence* 9:518–34.

Simon, L. M. J., B. Sales, A. Kaskniak, and M. Kahn. 1992. Characteristics of child molesters: Implications for the fixated-regressed dichotomy. *Journal of Interpersonal Violence* 7:211–25.

Snyder, H. N. 2000. *Sexual Assault of Young Children as Reported to Law Enforcement: Victim, Incident, and Offender Characteristics*. NIBRS Statistical Report. Washington, D.C.: U.S. Department of Justice, Office of Justice Programs, Bureau of Justice Statistics.

Sommers, C. H. 2000. The war against boys. *Atlantic Monthly* (May). http://www.theatlantic.com/past/issues/2000/05/sommers.htm.

Sturman, P. 2000. *Drug Assisted Sexual Assault*. London: Home Office, Police Research Award Scheme.

Terry, K. 2006. *Sexual Offenses and Offenders: Theory, Practice, and Policy*. Belmont, Calif.: Thomson-Wadsworth.

Thorpe, H. 2010. Bourdieu, gender reflexivity, and physical culture: A case of masculinities in the snowboarding field. *Journal of Sport & Social Issues* 34 (2): 176–214.

Truman, J. 2011. *Criminal Victimization in 2010*. Washington, D.C.: Bureau of Justice Statistics.

Weick, A., C. A. Rapp, W. P. Sullivan, and W. E. Kishardt. 1989. A strengths perspective for social work practice. *Social Work* 89:350–454.

Wester, S., H. Christianson, D. Vogel, and M. Wei. 2007. Gender role conflict and psychological distress: The role of social support. *Psychology of Men & Masculinity* 8 (4): 215–24.

Wester, S., B. Kuo, and D. Vogel. 2006. Multicultural coping: Chinese Canadian adolescents, male gender role conflict, and psychological distress. *Psychology of Men & Masculinity* 7 (2): 83–100.

Whitehead, J. T., T. Ward, and R. Collie. 2007. Time for a change: Applying the Good Lives Model of rehabilitation to a high-risk violent offender. *International Journal of Offender Therapy and Comparative Criminology* 51:578–98.

Yeung, K. T., M. Stombler, and R. Wharton. 2006. Making men in gay fraternities: Resisting and reproducing multiple dimensions of hegemonic masculinity. *Gender & Society* 20 (1): 5–31.

Zurbriggen, E. I. 2010. Rape, war and the socialization of masculinity: Why our refusal to give up war ensures that rape cannot be eradicated. *Psychology of Women Quarterly* 34: 538–49.

CHAPTER 4

A World of Hurt

AN INTERNATIONAL LOOK AT INTIMATE PARTNER VIOLENCE

▸ ELICKA S. PETERSON-SPARKS

Everyone has the right to life, liberty and security of person.
—UN Universal Declaration of Human Rights, Article 3

INTIMATE PARTNER VIOLENCE IS A transnational problem that consistently garners less attention than it warrants. Worldwide, a quarter of all violent crimes reported to police involve a man assaulting his intimate partner (EU Campaign against Domestic Violence 2000), and women are more likely to be assaulted, raped, injured, and killed by their current or past intimate partner than by any other person (Ellsberg & Heise 2005). Yet even in nations with progressive outlooks on this serious human rights issue, violence in the context of relationships tends to be viewed as somehow less serious than violence among strangers; the very designation of "domestic violence" connotes a tamer version of violence, which seems to require no further description based on the relationship between victims and offenders to attenuate it. This global phenomenon of downplaying intimate partner violence is at least largely responsible for its prolific nature—around the world, roughly 30 percent of women who have had an intimate relationship have experienced violence in the context of a relationship, and 38 percent of female homicide victims were killed by their intimate partners (WHO 2013a).

In this chapter global rates of intimate partner violence will be examined with respect to major variables affecting rates, including cultural, religious, and economic factors. The consequences and responses to intimate partner

violence internationally will also be reviewed, including targeted preven-
tion and measures such as the International Violence Against Women Act
(IVAWA, H.R. 4594, S. 2982), the Universal Declaration of Human Rights
(G.A. res. 217A (III)), and the application of the due diligence standard
to intimate violence in the Declaration on the Elimination of Violence
Against Women (DEVAW, article 4(c)).

Though men are victimized in intimate partner relationships, the lack
of severity in these instances relative to women has resulted in very little
research on the topic, particularly in an international context. Similarly,
research related to intimate partner violence in the context of homosexual
relationships is extremely limited in this context. As such, only heterosexual intimate partner violence with female victims can be addressed in the
context of this chapter.

AN INTERNATIONAL COMPARISON OF INTIMATE
PARTNER VIOLENCE

As with many criminal offenses, it is difficult to generate good cross-
national comparisons for rates of intimate partner violence owing to a
number of factors, including social issues affecting levels of reporting, cost,
logistical and other considerations limiting access, and cross-cultural differences in legal definitions (Ali 1986; Kishor & Johnson 2004; Veronique,
Johnson, & Fisher 2011). Where international comparisons of intimate
partner violence are concerned, the World Health Organization's study on
*Global and Regional Estimates of Violence Against Women: Prevalence and
Health Effects of Intimate Partner Violence and Non-Partner Sexual Violence*
(2013a) is by far the most comprehensive undertaking to date, with the statistics presented here derived from survey data from seventy-nine countries
in seven regions with varying economic and cultural environments.

The World Health Organization (WHO) defines intimate partner violence as "any behavior within an intimate relationship that causes physical,
psychological or sexual harm to those in the relationship" (2012:1). This
definition includes acts of physical violence, sexual violence and coercion,
psychological abuse, and controlling behaviors such as restricting a woman's
access to financial resources, education, medical care, or employment, or
isolating her and monitoring her movements. Most research indicates that
these different varieties of violence coexist in intimate relationships: where

there is physical violence, it is not uncommon to find sexual violence, and both are frequently accompanied by emotional abuse (Jewkes 2010).

Using this definition, the WHO (2013a) collected data to estimate the global and regional prevalence of intimate partner violence. The regions capture low- and middle-income countries in the Americas, Africa, the Eastern Mediterranean, Europe (a region encompassing Albania, Azerbaijan, Georgia, Lithuania, Republic of Moldova, Romania, Russian Federation, Serbia, Turkey, and Ukraine, with the rest situated in the high-income region), Southeast Asia, the Western Pacific, and a category of "high-income" countries from the various regions (including the United States). The WHO team also analyzed other, less comprehensive data, such as their own *Multi-Country Study on Women's Health and Domestic Violence Against Women Survey* (García-Moreno et al. 2005), the *International Violence Against Women Survey* (Johnson, Ollus, & Nevala 2008), the *Gender, Alcohol and Culture: An International Study* (Hettige 2012), and USAID's Demographic and Health Survey data (Hindin, Kishor, & Ansara 2008). The resulting analysis provides the clearest picture of global intimate partner violence available to date, despite its weaknesses (WHO 2010, 2013a).

By and large the areas with the highest lifetime prevalence rates of intimate partner violence (~37 percent overall) are Africa (36.6 percent), the Eastern Mediterranean (37 percent), and Southeast Asia (37.7 percent), followed by the Americas (29.8 percent). The lowest rates were found in the high-income (23.3 percent), European (25.4 percent), and Western Pacific (24.6 percent) regions (overall ~25 percent) (WHO 2013a:16–17). Despite differences in prevalence by region, intimate partner violence appears to be transnational in nature, with some demographic and behavioral factors influencing variations in lifetime prevalence rates fairly consistently both within and between countries.

Globally, WHO researchers found that the prevalence of violence in relationships is fairly high among young women between the ages of 15 and 19 (29.4 percent) but reaches its peak from ages 40 to 44 (37.8 percent) (2013a:24). Fewer data points were available for women 50 and older, as many of the surveys only included women 49 years and younger, and those data were skewed toward higher-income countries, so while lower rates were found, the confidence intervals were far wider. As such, it is not clear that older women experience less partner violence so much as that less is known about their situations, particularly in low- and middle-income countries.

RISK FACTORS ASSOCIATED WITH INTIMATE PARTNER
VIOLENCE AROUND THE WORLD

In terms of assessing risk factors for intimate partner violence, its transnational nature is again thrown into sharp relief: numerous international studies show a surprising similarity in risk factors across nations and vastly different cultures (for an overview, see Stith et al. 2004). Accurate identification of these risk factors is essential to developing effective prevention and intervention programs, and while some cultural features will surely require specialization, many common rudimentary indicators of risk—and common insulating traits—suggest that programs can be created and exported worldwide with few complications (Vashakidze 2013).

A number of factors influencing intimate partner violence are similar across most regions of the world. Secondary education for both partners shows the most significant protective effect, compared with those with primary education or less, or couples in which only one partner completed a secondary degree or certificate (in Bangladesh, Ethiopia, and Tanzania, primary education had the same positive effect due to the rarity of secondary education) (Abramsky et al. 2011). A history of abuse in partners is also significantly associated with intimate partner violence, whether through either or both partners' mothers. Further, a history of childhood sexual abuse for female partners, childhood beatings for male partners, or both was consistently associated with intimate partner violence, and at highest risk were relationships in which both partners were abused as children (Abramsky et al. 2011; see also Capaldi, Kim, & Pears 2009; Cornelius & Resseguie 2007; Fargo 2009).

Youthful victims are at increased risk for intimate partner violence regardless of country, while age gaps in either direction between partners appear to make little difference in victimization risk. Similarly, women who believe that husbands have the right to beat their wives were at significantly higher risk for intimate partner violence in every region (Abramsky et al. 2011). Not surprisingly, alcohol is a major risk factor in intimate partner violence. In all countries studied, the odds of such violence were much higher where either or both partners had problems with alcohol, with frequent inebriation of male partners significant in the majority of countries (Abramsky et al. 2011; see also Foran & O'Leary 2008). Women with children from previous relationships, with unfaithful partners, or who are cohabitating but not married to their partners were found to be at greater risk for intimate partner violence in all or most of the countries studied as well, as were women in polygamous relationships in every country where polygamy is legal. Dowry and bride price practices showed mixed effects, varying by according to country and the amount of remuneration (Abramsky et al. 2011; Krishnan 2005; Naved & Persson 2005; Parish et al. 2004; Rastogi & Therly 2006; Vickerman & Margolin 2008).

SELECTED CONSEQUENCES OF INTIMATE PARTNER VIOLENCE

The consequences of intimate partner violence are pernicious and costly for both those directly victimized and the larger societies in which this violence occurs. The impact is so far-reaching that it would be difficult to adequately summarize the research in the space of a book. Here the focus will be consequences that are less commonly addressed and particularly problematic in regions of the world where lifetime prevalence rates are high.

Aside from the obvious physical injuries (Campbell et al. 2002; García-Moreno et al. 2006; Jackson et al. 2002; Sheridan & Nash 2007; Yanqiu, Yan, & Lin 2011), the negative impact of intimate partner violence on child health and development outcomes is clearly an issue in any country and has been firmly established in the literature, as have anxiety and depressive disorders (PTSD), teen pregnancy, hypertension, cancer, and cardiovascular diseases (Black 2011; Black & Breiding 2008; Chowdhary & Patel 2008; Coker et al. 2002; Holt, Buckley, & Whelan, 2008; Jones, Hughes, & Unterstaller 2001; Quinlivan & Evans 2001; Wolfe et al. 2003). While these are serious issues, in less developed regions other consequences merit additional consideration. HIV and other sexually transmitted infections (STI) (Dunkle et al. 2004), along with unwanted pregnancies, low birth weight (Weiss Patel et al. 2008), and preterm labor (Dunkle et al. 2006), are a particular problem in terms of global health efforts in such venues.

Findings from numerous studies indicate that men who perpetrate violence against their intimate partners are more likely than their nonviolent counterparts to engage in high-risk behaviors that impact the likelihood of their female partners contracting HIV or STIs, such as having an STI themselves, having multiple sex partners and engaging sex workers, and frequent alcohol use (Abrahams et al. 2004; Dunkle et al. 2006; Maman et al. 2000;

Osinde, Kaye, & Kakaire 2011; Raj et al. 2006; Santana et al. 2006; Zablotska et al. 2009). Large studies in Africa and India have produced biologically confirmed positive associations for HIV, syphilis, and chlamydia and gonorrhea (Jewkes, Levin, & Penn-Kekana, 2003; Weiss Patel et al. 2008).

A large body of research shows significantly higher rates of problems associated with reproduction in women who experience intimate partner violence (for an overview, see Coker 2007). These threats to women's health are likely due to sexual violence and coercion common to violent relationships, and factors influencing the use of contraception, such as male partners preventing or sabotaging efforts at birth control through fear of violence (Moore, Frohwirth, & Miller 2010; Pallitto, Campbell, & O'Campo 2005; Silverman et al. 2007). Induced abortions among women with histories of intimate partner violence are higher as well and expose women to serious health risks in areas with less advanced medical care (García-Moreno & Stöckl 2013; Ko Ling 2009; Sedgh et al. 2012). Seventeen studies to date have confirmed that the stress of living in a violent relationship is a significant and important risk factor in pregnancies resulting in both low birth weight and preterm birth (for an overview, see Howard et al. 2013; Devries et al. 2010).

In addition to the consequences felt by victims, the cost to countries already struggling economically further reduces resources to address intimate partner violence. Across nations, victims of such violence are more likely to be hospitalized, seek medical mental health care, and present in emergency rooms subsequent to and as a direct result of victimization (Bonomi et al. 2009; National Center for Injury Prevention and Control 2003; Wisner et al. 1999). This effect is most pronounced during the period of victimization but continues beyond the violence.

A GLOBAL RESPONSE TO INTIMATE PARTNER VIOLENCE

Historically, governments have been reluctant to address intimate partner violence as a social problem for a variety of reasons, from not knowing what to do, to a reluctance to pry into what were believed to be private, family matters, to cultural acceptance of intimate violence. More recently, however, tolerance for such violence has declined, and multinational efforts are being undertaken both to change these attitudes and to address the problem aggressively.

One reason for this shift is found in a newer perception of domestic violence as an international human rights issue (European Institute for Gender Equality 2012; Meyersfeld 2010; United Nations General Assembly 1993; UNFPA Eastern Europe & Central Asia 2013; WHO 2010), as well as a shift toward demanding greater accountability from countries for protecting women from such violence (see Bettinger-Lopez 2008; Engle Merry 2005). Another, related legal shift toward the application of the due diligence standard in determining what actions should be required of states in protecting women from intimate partner violence has gained a strong foothold transnationally (Benninger-Budel 2008; Farrior 2004). It is too soon to say whether these shifts will result in reduced levels of intimate violence, but early assessments give cause for hope (Meyersfeld 2010). If governments are not held legally responsible for protecting their citizens—enforcing protection orders and prosecuting intimate partner violence perpetrators, for example—they become complicit in those acts of violence, which is a violation of human rights (Engle Merry 2005; Farrior 2004). Meyersfeld (2010) refers to this phenomenon as systemic intimate violence.

Globally there has also been a decided shift toward making men more central in efforts to curb intimate partner violence; instead of focusing on women as responsible for protecting themselves from victimization, men are being called on to change their behaviors (see, e.g., Kimball et al. 2013). A great example of a program focusing on men controlling the violence rather than women responding to it was founded in 1997 in Israel. The Beit Noam Residential Treatment Facility's approach to intimate violence is something of a model for holding offenders accountable for their violence against their partners, providing intensive treatment with an eye toward developing skills for greater self-control and other changes in normative behavior. A revolutionary feature of this program is its allowing battered women and their children to stay in the home, whereas victims are commonly the ones required to uproot their lives to escape the violence (seeking help at shelters or with relatives). Through requiring the men to stay in residential treatment, there is also the hope that transgenerational cycles might also be disrupted (Keynan et al. 2003).

There are now a number of programs using tenets from this model, as well as many efforts to increase men's awareness about their responsibility in intimate partner violence, and the normative pattern of cultural support for violence against women that allows it to continue (see, e.g., Bunch 2013).

International eradication efforts also focus on the economic empowerment of women, particularly in poorer regions of the world. While research findings are mixed regarding the role of women becoming financially self-sufficient in terms of risk for intimate partner homicide, most studies showing increased violence took place in countries where women were formerly very repressed and had only recently been given the opportunity for greater financial freedom (Rocca et al. 2008; Shrivastava & Shrivastava 2013). It is very likely that rates of violence against women may rise as a backlash to such emancipation and then diminish as women's rights become more accepted within cultures (for an overview, see Vyas & Watts 2009). Worldwide, programs are becoming increasingly more sensitive to the needs of women suffering intimate partner violence, and to the seriousness of this human rights issue.

DISCUSSION QUESTIONS

1. Why would viewing intimate partner violence as a human rights issue lead to increased efforts to address the issue?
2. How would criminal justice practices change if intimate partner violence were treated like violence perpetrated by a stranger?
3. What are some ways that we can increase men's involvement in reducing violence against women?

REFERENCES

Abrahams, N., R. Jewkes, M. Hoffman, and R. Laubsher. 2004. Sexual violence against intimate partners in Cape Town: Prevalence and risk factors reported by men. *Bulletin of the World Health Organization* 82 (5): 330–37.

Abramsky, T., C. H. Watts, C. Garcia-Moreno, K. Devries, L. Kiss, and M. Ellsberg. 2011. What factors are associated with recent intimate partner violence? Findings from the WHO multi-country study on women's health and domestic violence. *BMC Public Health* 11 (109).

Ali, B. 1986. Methodological problems in international criminal justice research. *International Journal of Comparative and Applied Criminal Justice* 10 (1–2): 163–76.

Benninger-Budel, C. 2008. *Due Diligence and Its Application to Protect Women from Violence.* Leiden: Koninklijke Brill.

Bettinger-Lopez, C. 2008. *Jessica Gonzales v. United States*: An emerging model for domestic violence & human rights advocacy in the United States. *Harvard Human Rights Journal* 21.

Black, M. C. 2011. Intimate partner violence and adverse health consequences. *American Journal of Lifestyle Medicine* 5 (5): 428–39.

Black, M. C., and M. J. Breiding. 2008. Adverse health conditions and health risk behaviors associated with intimate partner violence—United States, 2005. *Morbidity and Mortality Weekly Report* 57 (5): 113–17.

Bonomi, A. E., M. L. Anderson, E. P. Rivara, and R. S. Thompson. 2009. Health care utilization and costs associated with physical and nonphysical-only intimate partner violence. *Health Services Research* 44 (3): 1052–67. doi: 10.1111/j.1475-6773.2009.00955.x.

Bunch, T. 2013. Ending violence against women. *A Call to Men: Promoting Healthy Manhood*. http://www.acalltomen.org/sites/default/files/Ending%20 Violence%20Against%20Women.TB_.pdf.

Campbell, J., A. S. Jones, J. Dienemann, J. Kub, J. Schollenberger, P. O'Campp, A. C. Gielen, and C. Wynne. 2002. Intimate partner violence and physical health consequences. *Archives of Internal Medicine* 162 (10): 1157–63.

Capaldi, D., H. Kim, and K. Pears. 2009. The association of partner violence to child maltreatment: A common conceptual framework. In *Preventing Partner Violence: Research and Evidence-based Intervention Strategies*, ed. D. K. Whitaker and J. Lutzker, 93–111. Washington, D.C.: American Psychological Association.

Chowdhary, N., and V. Patel. 2008. The effect of spousal violence on women's health: Findings from the Stree Arogya Shodh in Goa, India. *Journal of Postgraduate Medicine* 54 (4): 306–12.

Coker, A. L. 2007. Does physical intimate partner violence affect sexual health? A systematic review. *Trauma Violence and Abuse* 8 (2): 149–77.

Coker, A. L., K. E. Davis, I. Arias, S. Desai, M. Sanderson, and H. M. Brandt. 2002. Physical and mental health effects of intimate partner violence for men and women. *American Journal of Preventive Medicine* 24 (4): 260–68.

Cornelius, T. L., and N. Resseguie. 2007. Primary and secondary prevention programs for dating violence: A review of the literature. *Aggression and Violent Behavior* 12 (3): 364–75.

Devries, K. M., S. Kishor, H. Johnson, H. Stöckl, L. J. Bacchus, C. Garcia-Moreno, and C. Watts. 2010. Intimate partner violence during pregnancy: Analysis of prevalence data from 19 countries. *Reproductive Health Matters* 18 (36): 158–70.

Dunkle, K. L., R. K. Jewkes, H. C. Brown, G. E. Gray, J. A. McIntryre, and S. D. Harlow. 2004 Gender-based violence, relationship power, and risk of HIV infection in women attending antenatal clinics in South Africa. *Lancet* 363 (9419): 1415–21.

Dunkle, K. L., R. K. Jewkes, M. Nduna, J. Levin, N. Jama, N. Khuzwayo, M. P. Koss, and N. Duvvury. 2006. Perpetration of partner violence and HIV risk behavior among young men in the rural Eastern Cape, South Africa. *AIDS* 20 (16): 2107–14.

Ellsberg, M., and L. Heise. 2005. *Researching Violence Against Women: A Practical Guide for Researchers and Activists*. Washington, D.C.: World Health Organization. http://www.path.org/publications/files/GBV_rvaw_front.pdf.

Ellsberg, M., L. Heise, R. Pena, S. Agurto, and A. Winkvist. 2001. Researching domestic violence against women: Methodological and ethical considerations. *Studies in Family Planning* 32 (1): 1–16.

Engle Merry, S. 2005. *Human Rights & Gender Violence: Translating International Law into Local Justice*. Chicago: University of Chicago Press.

Engle Merry, S., S. Shimmin, and J. Shimmin. 2011. The curious resistance to seeing domestic violence as a human rights violation. In *Human Rights in the United States: Beyond Exceptionalism*, ed. S. Hertel and K. Libal, 113–30. Cambridge: Cambridge University Press.

European Institute for Gender Equality. 2012. *Review of the Implementation of the Beijing Platform for Action in the EU Member States: Violence Against Women—Victim Support*. http://eigi.europa.edu/sites/default/files/Violence-against-Women-Victim-Support-Report.pdf.

Fargo, J. D. 2009. Pathways to adult sexual revictimization: Direct and indirect behavioral risk factors across the lifespan. *Journal of Interpersonal Violence* 24 (11): 1771–91.

Farrior, S. 2004. The due diligence standard and violence against women. *Interights Bulletin* 14 (4). SSRN: http://ssrn.com/abstract=1747936.

Foran, H. M., and K. D. O'Leary. 2008. Alcohol and intimate partner violence: A meta-analytic review. *Clinical Psychology Review* 28 (7): 1222–34.

García-Moreno, C., H. A. Jansen, M. Ellsberg, L. Heise, and C. Watts. 2005. *WHO Multi-Country Study on Women's Health and Domestic Violence Against Women: Initial Results on Prevalence, Health Outcomes and Women's Responses*. Geneva: World Health Organization. http://www.who.int/gender/violence/who_multicountry_study/en/.

——. 2006. Prevalence of intimate partner violence: findings from the WHO multi-country study on women's health and domestic violence. *Lancet* 368 (9543): 1260–69.

García-Moreno, C., and H. Stöckl. 2013. Violence against women: Its prevalence and health consequences. In *Violence against Women and Mental Health*, ed. C. García-Moreno and A. Riecher-Rössler, 1–11. Vol. 178. Key Issues in Mental Health. Basel: Karger. doi: 10.1159/000343777.

Hettige, S. 2012. *GENACIS: Gender, Alcohol and Culture: An International Study*. http://genacis.org/.

Hindin, M. J, S. Kishor, and D. L. Ansara. 2008. Intimate partner violence among couples in 10 DHS countries: Predictors and health outcomes. *DHS Analytical Studies* 18. Calverton, Md: Macro International.

Holt, S., H. Buckley, and S. Whelan. 2008. The impact of exposure to domestic violence on children and young people: A review of the literature. *Child Abuse & Neglect* 32 (8): 797–810.

Howard, L. M., Oram, K. Trevillion, and G. Feder. 2013. Domestic violence and perinatal mental disorders: A systematic review and meta-analysis. *PLoS Med* 10 (5). doi:10.1371/journal.pmed.1001452.

Jackson, H., E. Philp, R. L. Nuttall, and L. Diller. 2002. Traumatic brain injury: A hidden consequence for battered women. *Professional Psychology: Research and Practice* 33 (1): 39–45.

Jewkes, R. K. 2010 Emotional abuse: a neglected dimension of partner violence. *Lancet* 376 (9744): 851–52.

Jewkes, R. K., J. B. Levin, and L. A. Penn-Kekana. 2003. Gender inequalities, intimate partner violence and HIV preventive practices: Findings of a South African cross-sectional study. *Social Science & Medicine* 56 (1): 125–34.

Johnson, H., N. Ollus, and S. Nevala. 2008. *Violence Against Women: An International Perspective*. New York: Springer.

Jones, L., M. Hughes, and U. Unterstaller. 2001. Post-traumatic stress disorder (PTSD) in victims of domestic violence: A review of the research. *Trauma, Violence, and Abuse* 2 (2): 99–119.

Keynan, O., H. Rosenberg, B. Beili, M. Nir, S. Levin, A. Mor, I. Agabaria, and A. Tefelin. 2003. Beit Noam: Residential program for violent men. *Journal of Aggression, Maltreatment & Trauma* 7 (1): 207–36.

Kimball, E., J. L. Edleson, R. M. Tolman, T. B. Neugut, and J. Carlson. 2013. Global efforts to engage men in preventing violence against women: An international survey. *Violence Against Women* 19 (7): 924–39.

Kishor S., and K. Johnson. 2004. *Profiling Domestic Violence: A Multi-Country Study*. Calverton, Md.: ORC Macro International.

Ko Ling, C. 2009. Sexual violence against women and children in Chinese societies. *Trauma, Violence & Abuse* 10 (1): 69–85.

Koenig, M. A., R. Stephenson, S. Ahmed, S. J. Jejeebhoy, and J. Campbell. 2006. Individual and contextual determinants of domestic violence in North India. *American Journal of Public Health* 96 (1): 1–7.

Krishnan, S. 2005. Do structural inequalities contribute to marital violence? Ethnographic evidence from rural South India. *Violence Against Women* 11: 759–75.

Maman, S., J. Campbell, M. D. Sweat, and A. C. Gielen. 2000. The intersections of HIV and violence: Directions for future research and interventions. *Social Science & Medicine* 50 (4): 459–78.

Mayhew, S., and C. Watts. 2002. Global rhetoric and individual realities: Linking violence against women and reproductive health. In *Health Policy in a Globalising World*, ed. K. Lee and K. Buse, 159–80. Cambridge: Cambridge University Press.

Meyersfeld, B. 2010. *Domestic Violence and International Law*. Oxford: Hart.

Moore A. M., L. Frohwirth, and E. Miller. 2010. Male reproductive control of women who have experienced intimate partner violence in the United States. *Social Science and Medicine* 70 (11): 1737–44.

National Center for Injury Prevention and Control. 2003. *Costs of Intimate Partner Violence Against Women in the United States*. Atlanta: Centers for Disease Control and Prevention. http://www.cdc.gov/ncipc/pub-res/ipv_cost/ipvbook-final-feb18.pdf.

Naved, R. T., and L. A. Persson. 2005. Factors associated with spousal physical violence against women in Bangladesh. *Studies in Family Planning* 36 (4): 289–300.

Office for Official Publications of the European Communities. 2000. *Breaking the Silence: European Campaign Against Domestic Violence*. Luxembourg.

Osinde, M. O., D. K. Kaye, and O. Kakaire. 2011. Intimate partner violence among women with HIV in rural Uganda: Critical implications for policy and practice. *BMC Womens Health* 11:50. doi: 10.1186/1472-6874-11-50.

Pallitto, C. C., J. C. Campbell, and P. O'Campo. 2005. Is intimate partner violence associated with unintended pregnancy? A review of the literature. *Trauma, Violence, and Abuse* 6 (3): 217–35.

Parish, W. L., T. Wang, E. O. Laumann, S. Pan, and Y. Luo. 2004. Intimate partner violence in China: National prevalence, risk factors and associated health problems. *International Family Planning Perspectives* 30 (4): 174–81.

Quinlivan, J. A., and S. F. Evans. 2001. A prospective cohort study of the impact of domestic violence on young teen pregnancy outcomes. *Journal of Pediatric and Adolescent Gynecology* 14 (1): 17–23.

Raj, A., M. C. Santana, A. La Marche, H. Amaro, K. Cranston, and J. G. Silverman. 2006. Perpetration of intimate partner violence associated with sexual risk behaviors among young adult men. *American Journal of Public Health* 96 (10): 1873–78.

Rastogi, M., and P. Therly. 2006. Dowry and its link to violence against women in India: Feminist psychological perspectives. *Trauma, Violence & Abuse* 7 (1): 66–77.

Rocca, C. H., S. Rathod, T. Falle, R. P. Pande, and S. Krishnan. 2008. Challenging assumptions about women's empowerment: Social and economic resources and domestic violence. *International Journal of Epidemiology* 38 (2): 577–85.

Santana, M. C., A. Raj, M. R. Decker, A. La Marche, and J. G. Silverman. 2006. Masculine gender roles associated with increased sexual risk and intimate partner violence perpetration among young adult men. *Journal of Urban Health* 83 (4): 575–85.

Sedgh, G., S. Singh, I. H. Shah, E. Ahman, S. Henshaw, and A. Bankole. 2012. Induced abortion: Incidence and trends worldwide from 1995 to 2008. *Lancet* 379 (9816): 625–32. doi:10.1016/S0140-6736(11)61786-8.

Sheridan, D. J., and K. R. Nash. 2007. Acute injury patterns of intimate partner violence victims. *Trauma, Violence, and Abuse* 8 (3): 281–89.

Shrivastava, P. S., and S. R. Shrivastava. 2013. A study of spousal domestic violence in an urban slum of Mumbai. *International Journal of Preventive Medicine* 4 (1): 27–32.

Silverman, J. G., J. Gupta, M. R. Decker, N. Kapur, and A. Raj. 2007. Intimate partner violence and unwanted pregnancy, miscarriage, induced abortion, and stillbirth among a national sample of Bangladeshi women. *BJOG: An International Journal of Obstetrics and Gynecology*, 114 (10): 1246–52.

Stith, S., D. Smith, C. Penn, D. Ward, and D. Tritt. 2004. Intimate partner physical abuse perpetration and victimization risk factors: A meta-analytic review. *Aggression and Violent Behavior* 10 (1): 65–98.

United Nations General Assembly. 1993. *Declaration on the Elimination of Violence Against Women*. UN Doc. A/Res/48/104. http://www.un.org/documents/ga /res/48/a48r104.htm.

UNFPA Eastern Europe & Central Asia. 2013. *Domestic Violence in Georgia: Breaking the Silence.* http://eeca.unfpa.org/public/pid/13529;jsessionid=C D332E58191C6550755C0D5BFBB7C3FF.jahia01/cache/bypass/template /news_rss.rss.

Vashakidze, T. 2013. *UNFPA, Dimensions of Violence against Women and Girls, and How to End It.* UNFPA. http://unfpa.org/public/site/global/home /news/pid/13634.

Véronique, J., S. Johnson, and B. S. Fisher. 2011. Research methods, measures, and ethics. In *Sourcebook on Violence Against Women*, ed. C. M. Renzetti, J. L. Edleson, and R. K. Bergen, 23–45. 2nd ed. Thousand Oaks, Calif.: Sage.

Vickerman, K. A., and G. Margolin. 2008. Trajectories of physical and emotional marital aggression in midlife couples. *Violence & Victims* 23:18–34.

Vyas, S., and C. Watts. 2009. How does economic empowerment affect women's risk of intimate partner violence in low and middle income country settings? A systematic review of published evidence. *Journal of International Development* 21:577–602.

Weiss, H. A., V. Patel, R. W. Peeling, B. R. Kirkwood, and D. Mabey. 2008. Spousal sexual violence and poverty are risk factors for sexually transmitted infections in women: A longitudinal study of women in Goa, India. *Sexually Transmitted Infections* 84 (2): 133–39.

Wisner, C. L., L. E. Saltzman, and T. M. Zink. 1999. Intimate partner violence against women: Do victims cost health plans more? *Journal of Family Practice* 48 (6): 439–43.

Wolfe, D. A., C. V. Crooks, V. Lee, A. McIntyre-Smith, and P. G. Jaffe. 2003. The effects of children's exposure to domestic violence: A meta-analysis and critique. *Clinical Child and Family Psychology Review* 6 (3): 171–87.

World Health Organization (WHO). 2010. *Preventing Intimate Partner Violence and Sexual Violence Against Women: Taking Action and Generating Evidence.* Geneva: World Health Organization.

——. 2012. *Understanding and Addressing Violence Against Women: Intimate Partner Violence.* Geneva: World Health Organization. http://apps.who.int/iris /bitstream/10665/77432/1/WHO_RHR_12.36_eng.pdf.

——. 2013a. *Global and Regional Estimates of Violence Against Women: Prevalence and Health Effects of Intimate Partner Violence and Non-Partner Sexual Violence.* Geneva: World Health Organization. http://apps.who.int/iris/bitstre am/10665/85239/1/9789241564625_eng.pdf.

——. 2013b. *Responding to Intimate Partner Violence and Sexual Violence Against Women: WHO Clinical and Policy Guidelines.* Geneva, World Health Organization

Yanqiu, G., W. Yan, and A. Lin. 2011. Suicidal ideation and the prevalence of intimate partner violence against women in rural Western China. *Violence Against Women* 17:1299–1312.

Zablotska, I. B., R. H. Gray, M. A. Koenig, D. Serwadda, F. Nalugoda, N. Sewankambo, T. Lutalo, F. Wabwire Mangen, and M. Wawer. 2009. Alcohol use, intimate partner violence, sexual coercion and HIV among women aged 15–24 in Rakai, Uganda. *AIDS and Behavior* 13 (2): 225–33.

PART | 2

Sex Trafficking in a Transnational World

Global Sex Trafficking Overview

FACTS, MYTHS, AND DEBATES

▸ *MARY HIQUAN ZHOU*

OVER THE PAST TWENTY YEARS, intense international concern has been raised about a perceived rise in the number of people being trafficked across international borders for commercial sexual exploitation. Viewed as an organized crime problem, an immigration problem, a human rights violation, and an issue of economic injustice, the phenomenon has been popularly defined as sex trafficking, a modern-day slavery (United Nations Office on Drugs and Crime, 2012a).

Although all agree that victims should be helped and that such a crime against humanity should not exist in our society, people disagree on the scope and nature of the sex trafficking phenomenon and thus have different opinions regarding intervention and prevention strategies. Some believe the problem is severe and call for tighter border control, harsher punishment for traffickers, better assistance to victims, and education for potential victims. Others, however, suggest that the problem may not be as serious as described in the media, and that the various estimated numbers on the scope of the problem are just "guesstimates." Some believe that the majority of the trafficking victims are women and children, and that they have been forced, coerced, or enticed into the sex trade by traffickers. Others, however, dismiss such iconic victimization stories, arguing that they do not represent the majority of the cases and would not help the antitrafficking work. Some believe that traffickers are usually members of an organized crime group and will use physical threats, psychological control, debt bondage, or other illegal means to hold the victims against their will and make profits from selling the innocent human bodies (and souls). Others, however argue that the fear of transnational organized crime, including sex trafficking, is just a result of our fear of globalization.

Surrounded by different numbers, stories, and claims, it seems difficult to get a real picture of the global sex trafficking phenomenon. Without such a picture, we will not be able to come up with effective and efficient antitrafficking strategies. But how can we get a real picture? As will be presented later, researchers have carried out empirical studies in the field aiming to find the "truth," but their findings are also conflicting, adding more fuel to the already heated debated. Is sex trafficking an increasingly severe problem that affects millions, or is it a myth? How many people are trafficked into the sex trade? What are the victims and their traffickers like? What are the factors that contribute to sex trafficking? These questions are still unanswered.

Instead of feeling overwhelmed and frustrated, maybe we should take a step back and remind ourselves that social problems are "fundamentally products of a process of collective definition" instead of objective conditions (Blumer 1971:298). During the stages of collective problem definition, individuals and groups initiate and frame public discussion about issues of concern, which ultimately leads to some level of public agreement about the nature of and policy implications for an identified problem (Kingdon 1984). Then perhaps we will ask a different set of questions: Instead of asking "What is the fact?" maybe we should ask "Why are there so many different numbers, stories, and claims?" Instead of asking "Who is telling the truth?" maybe we should ask "Why are we having such a debate?" And, instead of asking "What are the factors contributing to the sex trafficking phenomenon?" maybe we should ask "Why are we suddenly so concerned about global sex trafficking?"

This chapter attempts to address the alternative questions by reviewing the background of the sex trafficking debate and discussing the various myths, facts, and opinions about sex trafficking. The goal is to present not only the different viewpoints and evidence but also the historical, political, economic, and ideological background of these claims, so that readers can critically evaluate our current knowledge of and discussion about sex trafficking.

HISTORICAL BACKGROUND: IS MODERN-DAY SLAVERY
REALLY MODERN?

Before diving into the discussion of modern-day slavery, it is important to point out that sex trafficking is not new. It may have had a different name in the past, or no name at all, but it has existed for longer than any of us have lived. Our last large-scale campaign against global sex trafficking ended only about a century ago. At that time sex trafficking was called "White Slavery." There were stories about white British girls and women being drugged, kidnapped, and sold abroad into the sex trade (Bristow 1977), and narratives about evil pimps (usually foreign) kidnapping (white) American farm girls and selling them into brothels in the city (Connelly 1980; Langum 1994). Horrified Victorian reformers campaigned against the White Slavery trade. A series of legislation was introduced to prohibit the importation of women (and later men, too) for the purpose of prostitution, and many progressive institutions were set up to rescue the victims (Connelly 1980).

Although there was not much debate at that time, many researchers today question the scope and nature of White Slavery. They point out that the majority of the immigrant women involved in the sex trade were lower-class migrants who lacked the skills and social networks to get a well-paid job; they had to exchange sex for money to support themselves and their children, especially if their husband died (Hobson 1990). Historical research also found that many of the incidents prosecuted as interstate trafficking cases in the United States involved consenting adults (Langum 1994). The innocent American farm girls or working-class daughters rescued by progressive reformers were mostly rebellious teenagers seeking independence (Odem 1995). White Slavery is now widely considered a myth or a moral panic.

How did such a myth become a serious social problem? Researchers believe that the progressive reformers were reacting to rapid social and economic changes at the turn of the twentieth century, namely, industrialization, urbanization, and the influx of immigrants, all of which threatened traditional values, lifestyles, and social structure (Connelly 1980; Langum 1994). When Chinese laborers in the United States brought in Chinese women to start families, the public feared the accumulation of this unwanted group who had bizarre customs and "sexual aberrations" (Abrams 2005; Chang 2003). Thus the United States introduced the Page Law to prohibit the importation of Chinese women for the purpose of prostitution, but in fact the law excluded virtually all Chinese women from entering the country and successfully prevented Chinese immigrants from creating families (Peffer 1999). Later, to prevent the influx of "unassimilable" Roman Catholics and Jews, the U.S. government issued reports claiming that the majority of prostitutes, brothel owners, and pimps were foreign born, with the French, Jews, and Italians as the leaders of the business (Langum 1994). Hence the immigration laws were amended to deport all immigrants (both men and women) found to be involved in prostitution before acquiring U.S. citizenship. Using these restrictive immigration policies, the United States successfully kept out many lower-class, non-Protestant immigrants (Cordasco & Pitkin 1981).

When rapid industrialization brought young women out of the domestic sphere and into the factory, parents feared that they would lose control of their daughters, who now had economic independence and were seeking independence in other aspects of life (Abrams 2000; Abrams & Curran 2000). The White Slavery myth, together with many other urban myths, such as the "seduction myth," were derived from these fears and served to deter the adventurous young women and to restore the patriarchal social order. The Mann Act, for example, was a direct product of the campaign against White Slavery. It prohibited the transportation of women and girls across state borders for immoral purposes. Violation of the law depended entirely on a woman's movement across state border, if the man she was with at that time intended any *immoral* purposes. Under the disguise of protection, the Mann Act barred women from taking trips with their male friends, depriving them of opportunities for vacations and preventing them from using interstate vehicles to express their own sexuality, which caused harm to nobody. At the same time, men were free to travel anywhere to meet with women. Hence American women as a group, as Langum (1994:11) argued, were "far more victimized by the Mann Act then by so-called white slavery." Angry parents and concerned social workers also brought these "wayward girls" to court. The charges being pressed often involved statutory rape or trafficking, while in reality the young women or girls were merely engaging in activities that parents would not approve of (e.g., staying out late), wanting to move in with boyfriends whom their parents did not like, not turning in wages to their parents, or running away from home to escape heavy domestic duties (Odem 1995).

By mounting the campaign on the backs of the most innocent victims, conservatives framed the social problems at the turn of the century as an immigration, organized crime, and morality issue. This diverted public attention from fundamental social injustices. For instance, some people pointed out that there might be a relationship between prostitution and low wages for women, because urban girls were paid only six dollars per week, while a minimum of eight dollars per week was needed in order to live independently (Hobson 1990). However, such voices were seldom heard in the sex trafficking/prostitution/White Slavery discussion. The reason is not hard to comprehend: had the discussion been framed in that way, it would have aided the feminists' fight for a minimum wage and the women's suffrage movement, both of which white male authorities opposed.

Now, in the early twenty-first century, the level of social and economic development in the world is significantly different from a hundred years ago. However, the social and economic challenges we face look similar: the world is becoming increasingly mobile. According to the United Nations, in 2013 international migrants constituted about 3.2 percent of the world's population (United Nations 2013). Unlike in the previous century, when migrants were mostly moving from less developed parts of the world to more developed countries, today migration within the global South is comparable to South-North migration. Hence almost everywhere in the world people will come into contact with individuals who are different from them. Also, women are becoming more and more mobile and now constitute half the international migrant population—in some countries, as much as 70 or 80 percent (United Nations Population Fund 2013). Social movements, such as the civil rights movement and the sexual liberation movement, have challenged traditional gender roles, as well as traditional codes of behavior related to sexuality and interpersonal relationships. However, moral conservatism has kept making powerful comebacks, as conservatives try to "reaffirm traditional values and disciplines, through law if necessary, and to stigmatize immoral behaviors" (Jenkins 1998:121). The Cold War is over, and the power of state-centric political and military rivalries that once dominated international relations has diminished. We are in a new era of globalization, which involves the integration of economic, social, and cultural relations across borders (Keohane & Nye 2000). These changes are not only transforming individuals' lives but also challenging the West-phalia system of governance, which is based on the principles of statehood and sovereignty (Held 1989). Will the state wither away in the face of globalization?

It is during this period of rapid and drastic transformations that we have rediscovered sex trafficking and given this old issue a new name: modern-day slavery. How have the challenges above shaped our discussion about sex trafficking? In the remaining sections of this chapter, I shall present three topics that are often debated in the sex trafficking field: the scope, the characteristics of victims, and the characteristics of traffickers. The vari-ous numbers, stories, and claims will be analyzed in the context of the con-temporary social changes and the struggles between different value systems brought about by these changes.

THE SEX TRAFFICKING DEBATE

Numbers: Estimates? Guesstimates? Does It Matter?

Over the past ten to fifteen years, many have attempted to estimate the scope of sex trafficking, or human trafficking in general. For instance, the U.S. Department of State (2002:1) claimed that "at least 700,000, and pos-sibly as many as four million men women and children worldwide were bought, sold, transported and held against their will in slave-like condi-tions," and the majority of them were trafficked into commercial sexual exploitation. The United Nations Children's Fund (2001) made a similar estimation, claiming that approximately one million children (mainly girls) enter the multibillion-dollar commercial sex trade every year.

These early claims were made without providing any information on the methodology of estimation. Increasingly, over the years, researchers have called into question these various estimations. Steinfatt (2011) for instance, responding to the claim that there were 80,000 to 100,000 sex trafficking victims in Cambodia, conducted several studies to provide more evidence-based statistics. Comparing his results with other studies conducted by different researchers, he concluded that the real number is much smaller—only around two thousand. Zhang (2011) studied the red-light district in a Mexican border city. The results showed that "there were no shortage of women willing to work in the sex industry, suggesting limited pros-pect for coerced prostitution" (509). No support was found for the claim that "approximately 135,000 Mexican children have been kidnapped and trafficked into illegal adoption, prostitution, and pornography" (Ugarte, Zarate, & Farley 2003:155).

In short, newly emerged empirical data seem to contradict the early claims made by various governmental and nongovernmental bodies. Some researchers suggested that the early claims were not derived from sound scientific methods and were thus merely guesstimates. Others went so far to accuse the different entities of fabricating figures to achieve their own agendas. Of course, researchers conducting empirical sex trafficking research acknowledge the difficulty in getting an accurate estimate of the victims, owing to the hidden nature of the population, and admit that their studies also have limitations. However, they point out that rumors and propaganda do not help the antitrafficking efforts. In fact, in recent years, fewer and fewer entities report estimated numbers. The United Nations, for example, reports confirmed cases. According to the U.N., between 2007 and 2010 a total of 34,800 victims were detected in eighty-one countries around the world, and between 57 and 62 percent of victims were trafficked for sexual exploitation (United Nations Office on Drugs and Crime 2012a).

It may be true that rumor and propaganda will not help the antitrafficking efforts, but will accurate estimations really make a difference? Are we willing to embrace people who are different from us? Many countries have singled out certain groups of "blameless," unfortunate migrants (e.g., refugees and victims of human trafficking) and made them eligible for humanitarian relief. However, attitudes toward immigrants as a whole can be hostile. The United States, for example, just before introducing the Trafficking Victim Protection Act (TVPA), passed the Personal Responsibility and Work Opportunity Reconciliation Act, and the Illegal Immigration and Immigrant Responsibility Act. These laws denied immigrants many welfare benefits, which led to further deterioration in poor immigrants' living conditions in United States (Srikantiah 2007). Of course, if an immigrant woman voluntarily chooses to make money through sex work, she will not be considered a sex trafficking victim. It is very likely that she will be deported upon identification by authorities, just as a hundred years ago. Furthermore, although the TVPA shows sympathy toward trafficking victims, many efforts have been made to investigate who deserves a T-visa to remain in America and who should be deported. As a result, only a small portion of the trafficking victims who have applied for a T-visa have received one; the majority of the applications were denied or are still pending (Chacon 2006). Such a hostile attitude toward unwanted immigrants is detrimental to antitrafficking efforts because it makes it easier for traffickers to threaten or to mislead victims.

The Victims: Lost Women? Loose Women? What Should We Do About Them?

The classic sex trafficking story today reads very similar to the White Slavery narratives of a hundred years ago. It often involves an innocent girl from a village in a third world country, kidnapped and sold into an urban brothel (as told in the documentary *The Day My God Died*), or a young woman from a former Soviet country, answering an advertisement for a nanny job but ending up a prostitute in a strip club (as told in *The Natashas: Inside the Global Sex Trade*). These stories can easily win the public's sympathy. In reality, however, sex trafficking may take many different forms, which are much more complicated than media portrayals. It may involve consenting adults, who later find themselves in exploitative situations such as debt bondage (International Labor Office 2008); partially voluntary children, who are convinced by their family that being trafficked for labor or sexual purposes will improve the economic well-being of the family (Bastia 2005; Taylor 2005); or even consenting juveniles (although the law does not recognize their voluntariness) (Estes & Weiner 2001).

It is widely agreed that children should not be involved in commercial sex acts. Thus it is not necessary to discuss the extent to which their involvement in sex trafficking is voluntary. However, when it comes to adults, social workers, politicians, and researchers alike continue to debate their "willingness" to participate in the commercial sex industry. Some have argued that all sex workers are victims because they must have been tricked or forced into the business, if not by traffickers, then by poverty (Barry 1997). Others, however, believe that there is currently an enormous demand for sexual services and there are women who do not mind this occupation or prefer it to others available to them (Agustin 2006). Empirical studies seem to find evidence supporting both claims. Mai (2013:107), for instance, studied the experience of migrant female sex workers and their male agents and partners. The results confirmed that "a minority of women are coerced into the sex industry," but most "negotiate their aspiration to cosmopolitan late modern lifestyles against the prevalence of essentialist patriarchal gender values and sexual mores at home." Likewise, Zhang (2011:523) interviewed pimps in a Mexican red-light district. Although some pimps reported using "persuasion" to recruit women, in general women "enter sex trade out of financial necessity." Many organizations working with "trafficking victims" also found that the majority of the women know that they are going to work in the sex industry but are lied to about the conditions under which they will work, such as wage levels, and how much they need to pay their traffickers (Doezema 2000).

How can the same evidence support both sides of the debate? The reason is simple: the debate has little to do with what happens to women and more to do with whether sex work is legitimate, and whether anyone willingly chooses to become a sex worker. Such disagreements have existed for decades, particularly within the feminist movements, between abolitionists, who aim to eradicate the sex industry as a gendered exploitation, and regulationists, who see sex work as a legitimate type of work, and advocate regulation as a way to improve the rights and lives of sex workers (Doezema 2010). Subscription to different types of ideology gives rise to different policies and intervention/prevention programs. Some countries have tightened up their border controls and prescribed harsher punishment for traffickers; others countries have legalized prostitution, hoping that this will improve the welfare of sex workers and sex trafficking victims (Chacon 2006; Chapkis 2003; Duarte 2012; Jakobsson & Kotsadam 2013; Outshoorn 2012; Yen 2008). Both approaches have been criticized. While all policies are about the struggle over values, some have pointed out that prostitution policy, as well as trafficking policy, is "morality policy," which is ruled by explicit ideologies, emotionally charged, resistant to facts, and subject to abrupt changes (Wagenaar & Altink 2012). Morality policy will not help solve problems. Maybe, instead of making value judgments, as argued by some, it is more important to "learn to locate and talk with those who are oppressed, listen to what they want and will accept" (Steinfatt 2011:460).

But who are the oppressed? In the midst of the prostitution discussion, just like a hundred years ago, women's welfare in a general sense has been left out. For instance, the sex trafficking discussion seldom mentions the discrimination women face in general. Almost a century has passed since women won their right to vote, but women are still earning less than their male counterparts (Anderson, Binder, & Krause 2003; Budig & England 2001). Immigrant women will suffer a double-negative effect because of their gender and their immigrant status (Beach & Worswick 1993; Husted et al. 2000). Such discrimination affects not only lower-class women (e.g., the poor and uneducated women portrayed in sex trafficking stories) but also well-educated ones. For example, studies show that female managers tend to concentrate in lower-paid niches, and there is a significant wage penalty for female-dominated occupations (Cohen, Huffman, & Knauer 2009). The reason, as proposed by some, is that while employers may view single women as honorary males, they see married women with working husbands as making only a secondary contribution to the family income (Ferree 1990). Women are paid less because they are seen as dependents of men.

Such a patriarchal view has also shaped our discussion of female migration. As mentioned earlier, women around the world are becoming more mobile. However, women are often depicted as being "forced" to migrate, while male migration is often described as brave, adventurous, and admirable (Dannecker & Sieveking 2009). Such a discourse reflects a desire to control the "loose women," to reinforce female dependence and purity (Doezema 2000). It denies women their autonomy, agency, and history. If policy is developed based on the assumption of female passiveness, women will be forced to either accept such an assigned image (i.e., to become a victim) or forgo the potential benefits of the policy, or even be punished (i.e., become an immigration or prostitution law offender).

The Traffickers: Mafia? Loosely Connected Criminals? Whom Do We Fear?

Human trafficking is often linked to organized crime. The United Nations has claimed that human trafficking is a lucrative business for organized crime groups, and that traffickers are making an estimated thirty-two billion dollars annually (United Nations Office on Drugs and Crime 2012b). The U.S. government also believes that human trafficking is the third largest source of profits for international organized crime, behind only drugs and guns (Miko & Park 2002).

However, such an alleged connection between human trafficking and organized crime groups is not based on empirical research but on the notions that (1) people of different nationalities can be part of the same group of trafficking victims or illegal migrants; (2) trips over long distance and traveling in a group both seem to require a well-oiled organization; (3) substantial amounts of money are involved; (4) ability to change itineraries quickly is needed; (5) there must be fast and readily available legal services; and (6) there is a strong reaction to counteroffensives by law enforcement (Salt & Hogarth 2000). Despite the lack of empirical support, many people still believe that human trafficking is conducted by organized crime groups (Juhasz 2000; Taibly 2001). Some researchers further suggest that three types of criminal networks are involved in international sex trafficking: large-scale networks with political and financial contacts in both countries of origin and destination countries; medium-sized networks that traffic women from a specific country; and small networks that traffic one or two women at a time when a club or brothel places an order (Bertone 2000:7)

Some other researchers, however, have pointed out that we need to distinguish between criminal activities that involve a group of people and organized crime groups (Finckenauer, cited by Salt & Hogarth 2000). According to the U.N. Convention Against Transnational Organized Crime, an organized criminal group is "a structured group of three or more persons, existing for a period of time and acting in concert with the aim of committing one or more serious crimes or offenses . . . in order to obtain, directly or indirectly, a financial or other material benefit" (United Nations 2011: Article 2.a). Such a definition excludes loosely connected criminals or episodic offenders from organized crime groups. What proportion of sex trafficking, then, is done by organized crime groups, and what proportion is done by other loosely connected criminals?

This question is of course very hard, if not impossible, to answer. To date we have only limited empirical studies that look at the offender side of the story. Shannon (1999), for example, used newspaper and magazine articles to explore the geographic overview of organized crime's involvement in sex trafficking and concluded that organized crime is involved at various levels, but the nature and the scale of the involvement is hard to determine. Caldwell and colleagues (1999) investigated the role of Russian Mafia in sex trafficking. Based on their interviews with pimps, law enforcement officials, traffickers, and others, they concluded that organized crime groups either directly control sex trafficking operations or provide protection for such activities; the international operations are usually controlled by small criminal groups that are less visible to law enforcement and competitors. Richard (2000), who studied sex trafficking in the United States, echoed the conclusion that sex trafficking is not in the hands of major criminal organizations but rather run by "smaller crime groups, smuggling rings, gangs, loosely linked criminal networks, and corrupt individuals" (vii).

Zhang's (2011:509) study on the Mexican border city red-light district, however, found "no evidence of any systematic collaborations with either local criminal organizations or foreign traffickers." Pimps and other sex trade facilitators in this study behaved like entrepreneurs in an illicit niche business. They treated sex workers as commodities and tried hard to ensure that their business ran smoothly, including avoiding reluctant women who were not willing to work in the sex industry. As a result, sex trade facilitators do not need force to control a large number of unwilling sex workers. Furthermore, because sex work is legal in the area, facilitators do not even need organized crime groups to protect their business, since police are offering protection.

In short, the limited empirical studies do not deny the involvement of organized crime groups in sex trafficking, but evidence seems to suggest that the role of large major crime syndicates, such as the Russian Mafia, has been exaggerated. Traffickers, according to empirical data, are more likely to be loosely connected individuals and small crime groups.

Thus the question is, why are we so obsessed with the Mafia, even though the evidence suggest otherwise? Scholars have pointed out that the idea of organized crime itself, whether linked with sex trafficking or not, is a product of moral panics. From the White Slavery panic until now, whenever we feel that something is threatening our existing value system, be it drinking, vice, gambling, drug, or street gangs, we will try to tighten up social control by "absolving the mainstream society of responsibility for a perceived decline in moral values and exaggerating the threat from an alien and nebulous enemy" (Woodiwiss & Hobbs 2009:106). Such a strategy is often quite effective in pushing for new legislation and setting up new institutions of control, because the public, out of fear, may be willing to accept things they would not usually accept. Organized crime, especially the American type, was socially constructed by lumping different social issues, such as gangs and violence, together to maximize the fear effect.

Other scholars point out that our specific fear of transnational organized crime activities, such as sex trafficking, stems from our fear of globalization, a fear of "a world without borders," where there is not only free movement of goods but free movement of terrorists, criminals, drugs, diseases, and illegal migrants (van der Pijl, Breuil, & Siegel 2011:573). Such accounts of transnational organized crime, including sex trafficking, as pointed out by Andreas (2013:22), "in many ways echo the old familiar arguments in the globalization literature about the withering away of the state in the face of increasingly globalized markets—but in this case, the market actors and forces are considered particularly threatening and sinister." Out of fear, we may prescribe costly and counterproductive solutions and forget that history has already taught us many lessons (Andreas & Greenhill 2010).

CONCLUSION AND LOOKING FORWARD

To end this chapter, it is important to point out that although the current facts, myths, and debates around sex trafficking are similar to those about White Slavery, I am not suggesting that we denounce the existence of such a complicated phenomenon. Rather, the purpose of this chapter is to provide a review of the different opinions so that readers can adopt a critical view of the facts and discussions they read and see elsewhere. Progressive reformers, in their response to the White Slavery panic, might have had some class and cultural biases, but they had a genuine concern for the young women and a commitment to social justice and human progress. Their work became the foundation of modern social work. Now, facing various challenges brought by globalization, rather than panicking and repeating past mistakes, we may take a better look at empirical evidence and investigate the real needs of those who are involved so as to respond with effectiveness and efficiency.

DISCUSSION QUESTIONS

1. Do you think we have a fear of globalization? Why?
2. Can you think of a way to get the regulationists and the abolitionists to work together?
3. Most of the discussion has centered on women and children. How do you think this is going to influence men and transgender people?

REFERENCES

Abrams, K. 2005. Polygamy, prostitution, and the federalization of immigration law. *Columbia Law Review* 105 (3): 641–716.

Abrams, L. S. 2000. Guardians of virtue: The social reformers and the "girl problem," 1890–1920. *Social Service Review* 74 (3): 436–52.

Abrams, L. S., and L. Curran. 2000. Wayward girls and virtuous women: Social workers and female juvenile delinquency in the progressive era. *Affilia—Journal of Women and Social Work* 15 (1): 49–64.

Agustin, L. 2006. The disappearing of a migration category: Migrants who sell sex. *Journal of Ethnic and Migration Studies* 32 (1): 29–47.

Anderson, D. J., M. Binder, and K. Krause. 2003. The motherhood wage penalty revisited: Experience, heterogeneity, work effort, and work-schedule flexibility. *Industrial & Labor Relations Review* 56 (2): 273–94.

Andreas, P. 2013. Illicit globalization: Myths, misconceptions, and historical lessons. *Political Science Quarterly* 126 (3): 403–25.

Andreas, P., and K. M. Greenhill. 2010. *Sex, Drugs, and Body Counts: The Politics of Numbers in Global Crime and Conflict.* Ithaca, N.Y.: Cornell University Press.

Barry, K. 1997. Prostitution of sexuality: A cause for new international human rights. *Journal of Personal & Interpersonal Loss* 2 (1): 27–48.

Bastia, T. 2005. Child trafficking or teenage migration? Bolivian migrants in Argentina. *International Migration* 43 (4): 57–89.

Beach, C. M., and C. Worswick. 1993. Is there a double-negative effect on the earnings of immigrant women? *Canadian Public Policy* 19 (1): 36–53.

Bertone, A. M. 2000. Sexual trafficking in women: International political economy and the politics of sex. *Gender Issues* 18 (1): 4–22.

Blumer, H. 1971. Social problems as collective behavior. *Social Problems* 18:298–306.

Bristow, E. J. 1977. *Vice and Vigilance: Purity Movements in Britain Since 1700.* Totowa, N.J.: Rowman and Littlefield.

Budig, M. J., and P. England. 2001. The wage penalty for motherhood. *American Sociological Review* 66 (2): 204–25.

Caldwell, G., S. Galster, J. Kanics, and N. Steinzor. 1999. Capitalizing on transition economies: The role of the Russian Mafia in trafficking women for forced prostitution. In *Illegal Immigration and Commercial Sex: The New Slave Trade,* ed. P. Williams. London: Frank Cass.

Chacon, J. M. 2006. Misery and myopia: Understanding the failures of US efforts to stop human trafficking. *Fordham Law Review* 74:2977–3040.

Chang, I. 2003. *The Chinese in America: A Narrative History*. New York: Penguin.

Chapkis, W. 2003. Trafficking, migration, and the law—protecting innocents, punishing immigrants. *Gender & Society* 17:923–37.

Cohen, P. N., M. L. Huffman, and S. Knauer. 2009. Stalled progress? Gender segregation and wage inequality among managers, 1980–2000. *Work and Occupations* 34 (4): 318–42.

Connelly, M. T. (1980). *The Response to Prostitution in the Progressive Era*. Chapel Hill: University of North Carolina Press.

Cordasco, F., and T. M. Pitkin. 1981. *The White Slave Trade and the Immigrants: A Chapter in American Social History*. Detroit: Blaine Ethridge Books.

Dannecker, P., and N. Sieveking. 2009. *Gender, Migration and Development: An Analysis of the Current Discussion on Female Migrants as Development Agents*. Bielefeld, Germany: Centre on Migration, Citizenship and Development.

Doezema, J. 2000. Loose women or lost women? The re-emergence of the myth of white slavery in contemporary discourses of trafficking in women. *Gender Issues* 18 (1): 23–50.

——. 2010. *Sex Slaves and Discourse Masters: The Construction of Trafficking*. London: Zed.

Duarte, M. 2012. Prostitution and trafficking in Portugal: Legislation, policy, and claims. *Sexuality Research and Social Policy* 9 (3): 258–68.

Estes, R. J., and N. Weiner. 2001. *The Commercial Sexual Exploitation of Children in the U.S., Canada and Mexico*. Philadelphia: University of Pennsylvania, School of Social Work, Center for the Study of Youth Policy.

Ferree, M. M. 1990. Beyond separate spheres: Feminism and family research. *Journal of Marriage and Family* 52:866–84.

Held, D. 1989. *Political Theory and the Modern State*. Stanford, Calif.: Stanford University Press.

Hobson, B. M. 1990. *Uneasy Virtue: The Politics of Prostitution and the American Reform Tradition*. Chicago: University of Chicago Press.

Husted, L., H. S. Nielsen, M. Rosholm, and N. Smith. 2000. Hit twice? Danish evidence on the double-negative effect on the wages of immigrant women. Working paper. Centre for Labour Market and Social, Universitetsparken, Building. Aarhus, Denmark.

International Labor Office. 2008. *ILO Action Against Trafficking in Human Beings*. Geneva: International Labour Organization.

Jakobsson, N., and A. Kotsadam. 2013. The law and economics of international sex slavery: Prostitution laws and trafficking for sexual exploitation. *European Journal of Law and Economics* 35 (1): 87–107.

Jenkins, P. 1998. *Moral Panic: Changing Concepts of the Child Molester in Modern America*. New Haven, Conn.: Yale University Press.

Juhasz, J. 2000. Migrant trafficking and human smuggling in Hungary. In *Migrant Trafficking and Human Smuggling in Europe: A Review of Evidence with Case Studies from Hungary, Poland and Ukraine*, ed. F. Laczko and D. Thompson, 167–232. Geneva: International Organization for Migration.

Keohane, R., and J. S. Nye. 2000. Globalisation: What's new? What's not? (And so what?). *Foreign Policy* 118:104–9.

Kingdon, J. W. 1984. *Agendas, Alternatives and Public Policy*. Boston: Little Brown.

Langum, D. J. 1994. *Crossing over the Line: Legislating Morality and the Mann Act*. Chicago: University of Chicago Press.

Mai, N. 2013. Embodied cosmopolitanisms: The subjective mobility of migrants working in the global sex industry. *Gender, Place & Culture* 20 (1): 107–24.

Miko, F. T., and G. Park. 2002. *Trafficking in Women and Children: The U.S. and International Response*. Washington, D.C.: Library of Congress, Congressional Research Service.

Odem, M. E. 1995. *Delinquent Daughters: Protecting and Policing Adolescent Female Sexuality in the United States, 1885–1920*. Chapel Hill: University of North Carolina Press.

Outshoorn, J. 2012. Policy change in prostitution in the Netherlands: From legalization to strict control. *Sexuality Research and Social Policy* 9 (3): 233–43.

Peffer, G. 1999. *If They Don't Bring Their Women Here: Chinese Female Immigration Before Exclusion*. Urbana: University of Illinois Press.

Richard, O. N. A. 2000. *International Trafficking in Women to the United States: A Contemporary Manifestation of Slavery and Organized Crime*. Washington, D.C.: Center for the Study of Intelligence, CIA.

Salt, J., and J. Hogarth. 2000. Migrant trafficking and human smuggling in Europe: A review of the evidence. In *Migrant Trafficking and Human Smuggling in Europe: A Review of Evidence with Case Studies from Hungary, Poland and Ukraine*, ed. F. Laczko and D. Thompson, 11–164. Geneva: International Organization for Migration.

Shannon, S. 1999. Prostitution and the Mafia: The involvement of organized crime in the global economy. In *Illegal Immigration and Commercial Sex: The New Slave Trade*, ed. P. Williams, 119–44. London: Frank Cass.

Srikantiah, J. 2007. Perfect victims and real survivors: The iconic victim in domestic human trafficking law. *Boston University Law Review* 87 (1): 157–211.

Steinfatt, T. M. 2011. Sex trafficking in Cambodia: fabricated numbers versus empirical evidence. *Crime, Law and Social Change* 56 (5): 443–62.

Taibly, R. 2001. Organised crime and people smuggling/trafficking to Australia. *Australian Institute of Criminology* 208:1–6.

Taylor, L. R. 2005. Dangerous trade-offs—The behavioral ecology of child labor and prostitution in rural northern Thailand. *Current Anthropology* 46 (3): 411–31.

Ugarte, M. B., L. Zarate, and M. Farley. 2003. Prostitution and trafficking of women and children from Mexico to the United States. In *Prostitution, Trafficking and Traumatic Stress*, ed. M. Farley, 147–65. Binghampton, N.Y.: Haworth Maltreatment & Trauma Press.

United Nations. 2011. *United Nations Convention Against Transnational Organized Crime*. (G.A. Res. 25, annex I, U.N. GAOR, 55th Sess., Supp. No. 49, at 44, U.N. Doc. A/45/49 C.F.R.).

——. 2013. *World Migration in Figures*. http://www.un.org/en/development/desa/population/publications/pdf/migration/migration/World_Migration_Figures_UNDESA_OECD.pdf.

United Nations Children's Fund. 2001. *Profiting from Abuse: An Investigation into the Sexual Exploitation of Our Children*. New York: Author.

United Nations Office on Drugs and Crime. 2012a. *Global Report on Trafficking in Persons*. Vienna: Author.

——. 2012b. *Human Trafficking: Organized Crime and the Multibillion Dollar Sale of People*. http://www.unodc.org/unodc/en/frontpage/2012/July/human-trafficking_-organized-crime-and-the-multibillion-dollar-sale-of-people.html.

United Nations Population Fund. 2013. *Migration: A World on the Move*. http://www.unfpa.org/pds/migration.html.

U.S. Department of State. 2002. *Trafficking in Persons Report 2002*. Washington, D.C.: U.S. Department of State, Office to Monitor and Combat Trafficking in Persons.

van der Pijl, Y., B. C. O. Breuil, and D. Siegel. 2011. Is there such thing as "global sex trafficking"? A patchwork tale on useful (mis)understandings. *Crime Law and Social Change* 56 (5): 567–82.

Wagenaar, H., & S. Altink. 2012. Prostitution as morality politics or why it is exceedingly difficult to design and sustain effective prostitution policy. *Sexuality Research and Social Policy* 9 (3): 279–92.

Yen, I. 2008. Of vice and men: A new approach to eradicating sex trafficking by reducing male demand through educational programs and abolitionist legislation. *Journal of Criminal Law & Criminology* 98 (2): 653–86.

Zhang, S. X. 2011. Woman pullers: Pimping and sex trafficking in a Mexican border city. *Crime Law and Social Change* 56 (5): 509–28.

CHAPTER 6

INGOs and the UN Trafficking Protocol

▶ *CHARLES ANTHONY SMITH AND CYNTHIA FLORENTINO*

HUMAN TRAFFICKING, OFTEN CATEGORIZED AS one form of modern-day slavery, is a transnational crime that affects marginalized populations across the globe (Brysk & Choi-Fitzpatrick 2011). The clandestine nature of the crime coupled with the fact that the most vulnerable people in society are targeted makes it difficult to create and implement legislation that adequately addresses the problem (Smith & Smith 2011b; Smith & Smith-Cannoy 2013). Still, legislation constructed as an antitrafficking measure rather than as an antiprostitution measure is a more effective way to combat the global problem of human trafficking. A crucial step forward in combating human trafficking was the *United Nations Convention Against Organized Crime*. The convention is a thorough and binding instrument in international law designed to combat transnational organized crime. It was also an attempt by the international community to inject international law into combating human trafficking domestically (Gallagher 2001; Smith & Smith-Cannoy 2013).

The convention was signed in Palermo, Italy, in December 2000. The international community came together to provide a political solution to a human security problem. The convention also provided three other protocols for related aspects of organized crime: the *Protocol Against the Smuggling of Migrants by Land, Sea and Air*; the *Protocol Against the Illicit Manufacturing of and Trafficking in Firearms, Their Parts and Components and Ammunition*; and the *Protocol to Prevent, Suppress and Punish Trafficking in Persons, Especially Women and Children*. We focus exclusively on the third protocol and refer to it hereafter as the UN Trafficking Protocol. It not only deals exclusively with a specific type of organized crime, human trafficking, but also addresses issues like prosecution of the people accused of engaging in trafficking and emphasizes the need for support and protection for human trafficking victims.

One of the focal points of the convention is the emphasis on the protection of human trafficking victims and their families. Article 24 requires states to protect victims, their families, and witnesses who provide testimonies during criminal proceedings. The article discourages states from using intimidation or retaliation (or threats of retaliation) during criminal proceedings. It encourages states not only to offer physical protection of victims and witnesses but also to conceal their identities and offer relocation for safety purposes (*UN Convention Against Transnational Organized Crime* 2000).

The Trafficking Protocol entered into force in December 2003 and was signed by 117 countries. United Nations Secretary General Kofi A. Annan urged the member states to sign and ratify the protocol in order to bring a global approach to the struggle with human trafficking. He argued that since the crime crosses borders, so must any effective law enforcement protocol. Annan observed that because human trafficking is a global issue, he strongly believed that the ratification of the protocol was critical so that the international community would be better equipped to combat such trafficking (*UN Convention Against Organized Crime* 2000).

Domestic governmental law enforcement and local policy makers were assisted in structuring the fight against human trafficking by international nongovernmental organizations (INGOs) dedicated to amelioration of this problem. The INGOs played a critical role in both the UN Trafficking Protocol negotiations and its implementation. Numerous INGOs, as well as some domestic NGOs, worked closely with state delegates to draft the protocol in a relatively short period of time. Although INGOs engage in a wide range of activities, including cooperation with local governments to strengthen laws, collaboration on prosecutions, public awareness campaigns, and the provision of direct victim assistance programs, here we specifically examine the lobbying and negotiations efforts that occurred during the drafting of the UN Trafficking Protocol. The hard work put in by the INGO's, including the Office of the United Nations High Commissioner for Human Rights and the United Nations High Commissioner for

Refugees, was critical in shaping the protocol (Fitzpatrick 2003). We then consider the differing INGO concerns that had an impact in the negotiations, as well as the role of INGOs in implementation after the protocol was signed.

NGOS AND THE NEGOTIATION OF THE PROTOCOL

The definition of human trafficking adopted by the UN Trafficking Protocol was the result of negotiations among countries and the INGOs. The protocol defines trafficking in persons as "the recruitment, transportation, transfer, harboring or receipt of persons, by means of the threat or use of force or other forms of coercion, of abduction, of fraud, of deception, of the abuse of power or of a position of vulnerability or of the giving or receiving of payments or benefits to achieve the consent of a person having control over another person, for the purpose of exploitation" (UN Office of Drugs and Crime 2004). The exploitation mentioned in this protocol refers not only to sexual exploitation or exploitation for the purposes of prostitution but also to forced labor or services, slavery or practices similar to slavery, servitude, or removal of organs.

The negotiations regarding the final definition of "trafficking in persons" were driven by the differing ideologies of the engaged INGOs. The controversy over the definition represented the INGO lobbying blocs' different approaches on how best to combat human trafficking. A clear definition of "trafficking in persons" and an understanding of what constituted trafficking were crucial if the protocol was going to be effective as a human trafficking amelioration tool. The final definition was arrived at after an intensive lobbying effort led by two INGO coalitions, the Human Rights Caucus and the International Human Rights Network. The Human Rights Caucus involved a number of antitrafficking and sex workers rights organizations and activists and was predominantly led by the International Human Rights Law Group (IHRLG) and the Global Alliance Against Traffic in Women (GAATW). The American-based Coalition Against Trafficking in Women (CATW), the European Women's Lobby (EWL), and the International Abolitionist Federation (IAF) led the International Human Rights Network (Ditmore & Marjan 2003).

The Human Rights Caucus advocated for the inclusion of a very broad definition of trafficking, one that included forced labor and coercion

TABLE 6.1   Major NGO Lobbying Blocs in UN Trafficking Protocol
            Negotiations

LOBBYING AGENDA	MAIN AFFILIATED NGOS
Human Rights Caucus	
(sex workers' stance)	Definition of trafficking excludes voluntary sex work, coercion, debt, and bondage.
Advocated for human rights of trafficked persons.	
Sought to "empower" rather than "protect" through laws.	Global Alliance Against Traffic in Women
International Human Rights Law Group	
Asian Women's Human Rights Council	
International Human Rights Network	
(victims' stance)	Definition of trafficking should be tied to both consensual and nonconsensual prostitution.
Prostitution per se is a violation of women's human rights.	
Maintained an abolitionist perspective.	Coalition Against Trafficking in Women
European Women's Lobby	
International Abolitionist Federation	

(Ditmore & Marjan 2003). The main goal of this coalition was to grant
trafficked persons rights through the definition rather than merely creating a victimhood status. Since the Human Rights Caucus consisted of
both antitrafficking groups and groups in favor of sex workers rights, it
emphasized that forced labor and slavery are also considered trafficking,
and it excluded voluntary, noncoercive prostitution or any other forms of
voluntary sex work. Fearing that the protocol might turn into an antiprostitution document, the Human Rights Caucus emphasized the belief that
prostitution is no different from other types of labor (Doezema 2002). In
contrast, the International Human Rights Network approached the problem of human trafficking through the victims' perspective and with a focus
on prostitution. It emphasized that prostitution is an egregious violation

of human rights and that the victims should not be punished or blamed because "any distinction which refers to the will or consent of the women concerned is meaningless, as no person, not even an adult, is believed to be able to give genuine consent to engage in prostitution" (Ditmore & Marjan 2003).As a result, the CATW-led network wanted the definition to consider prostitution as the primary focus of the trafficking protocol and not allow for the acceptability of sex work even in the absence of coercion.

Despite the differences between the two lobbying groups, they shared some approaches when it came to battling human trafficking. The lobbying bloc led by the International Human Rights Network took the position that victims of human trafficking should be treated fairly and given a host of rights under international human rights law. The GAATW also urged countries to treat human trafficking victims with respect and local governments to constantly analyze and review existing legislation to ensure that human trafficking victims would not face discriminatory practices during trials based on their race, color, language, political opinion, or country of origin. The *Human Rights Standards for the Treatment of Trafficked Persons*, a report jointly developed by the GAATW, IHRLG, and Coalition Against Trafficking in Women, focused on the importance of protecting the rights of trafficked persons. The report is also used in lobbying efforts both nationally and internationally. It identifies the state responsibilities toward human trafficking victims and explains that "States are obligated to respect and protect the human rights of the persons within its territorial boundaries, as well as to enable such persons to realize those rights, which includes the concept that human rights encompass not only states' obligations to respect and protect but also their obligation to provide or make available the means (including information, capacity and structures) to ensure the realization of rights possible by each person" (GAATW 1999).

The UN Trafficking Protocol negotiations were shaped by the INGOs, in particular with respect to the basic parameters of the protocol and the language used in it. The two major INGO lobbying blocs advocated for their respective positions and urged their incorporation into the language of the protocol. The Human Rights Caucus sought to empower rather than merely protect through laws, and the International Human Rights Network considered prostitution to be a violation of human rights per se and held an abolitionist perspective.

Leaders of the CATW and the GAATW played a significant role as these are nongovernmental organizations that hold consultative status in the United Nations. To analyze the level of influence exercised by both INGO blocs, we consider the importance of the leading INGOs in the series of negotiations that took place during the drafting of the UN Trafficking Protocol, the impact they had on the final definition of human trafficking, and the language used in the final draft of the protocol.

Article 3 of the UN Trafficking Protocol defines "trafficking in persons" and is divided into four parts. We analyzed parts A, B, and C as they contain the bulk of the germane information. Part A establishes the following:

> Trafficking in persons shall mean the recruitment, transportation, transfer, harboring or receipt of persons, by means of the threat or use of force or other forms of coercion, of abduction, of fraud, of deception, of the abuse of power or of a position of vulnerability or of the giving or receiving of payments or benefits to achieve the consent of a person having control over another person, for the purpose of exploitation. Exploitation shall include, at a minimum, the exploitation of the prostitution of others or other forms of sexual exploitation, forced labor or services, slavery or practices similar to slavery, servitude or the removal of organs. (UNODC 2004)

In its *Victory in Vienna* document (2000), the CATW celebrates the accomplishments of the International Human Rights Network, which lobbied to maintain the integrity of the *Convention for the Suppression of the Trafficking in Persons* (1949). The CATW's interest was in preserving the historical framework and ensuring that the new protocol did not stray far from its 1949 model. Specifically, the new definition uses the phrase "exploitation of the prostitution." The CATW argued that since trafficking is often intertwined with prostitution, it was critical to maintain a reference to prostitution in the new definition. The Human Rights Caucus, however, explained this inclusion differently. In its annotated guide to the UN Trafficking Protocol, the IHRLG states that "exploitation of the prostitution" is left undefined in the protocol because different countries view prostitution differently, and therefore the agreement leaves this particular phrase open to interpretation for each country.

Part B of the definition establishes that "the consent of a victim of trafficking in persons to the intended exploitation set forth in subparagraph

(a) of this article shall be irrelevant where any of the means set forth in subparagraph (a) have been used." The CATW embraced the language in this case because of the organization's stance on prostitution; the protocol legitimizes the irrelevance of victim consent. The IHRLG argued that consent is not possible under the already established coercion, abduction, force, and so on, but when the law is not fully defined, consent can mean different things. Accordingly, it should not prevent prosecutions of traffickers in the individual countries. The main goal is to prevent the revictimization of the trafficked person through the protocol.

Part C of the protocol states: "The recruitment, transportation, transfer, harboring or receipt of a child for the purpose of exploitation shall be considered 'trafficking in persons' even if this does not involve any of the means set forth in subparagraph (a) of this article." The CATW did not take a specific position for or against this section, but the Human Rights Caucus stated that the language is not clear and that children and their needs have to be considered on a greater, more defined scale when it comes to trafficking.

Ultimately the language of the protocol suggests that one lobbying bloc, the International Human Rights Network, had more influence than the other. The lobbying bloc led by the International Human Rights Network clearly exerted a significant amount of influence during the UN Trafficking Protocol negotiations. As set forth in *Victory in Vienna* (2000), while the definition of trafficking in persons is the result of a compromise among INGOs and country delegations, it consists in its majority of aspects advocated for by the CATW and the network. The Human Rights Caucus acknowledged this and stated that there is weakness evident in the language used in the protocol. The caucus argued that law enforcement, not human rights, is the focus of this protocol. This led to the creation by the Human Rights Caucus of recommendations for countries to fill the gap between the protocol and their aspirations.

DOMESTIC IMPLEMENTATION OF THE PROTOCOL

We now turn to a consideration of the influence that INGOs had on the ratification of the UN Trafficking Protocol in six different countries. The complexity of human trafficking and the nature of the crime hinder the ability to collect comprehensive measurements and data. For this reason we rely on the U.S. Department of State's *Trafficking in Persons Report* (2013). Although the data used in the report may not be perfect or error free, they are the best available data to use for comparing and contrasting the role of INGOs in combating human trafficking. We also take into account that each country has a different political environment, and INGOS are welcomed at different levels.

The *Trafficking in Persons Report* is an annual report issued to monitor and combat human trafficking on a global level. The report ranks countries based on their progress in the fight against human trafficking. It also provides information regarding the numerous antitrafficking measures and how prevention, protection, and prosecution programs are used to battle human trafficking. It is used not only as a crucial tool to combat the global problem of modern slavery but also by various nongovernmental organizations and governments to examine how resources can be allocated effectively to combat trafficking. The report classifies countries and regions into three tiers based on the government's efforts to comply with the "minimum standards for the elimination of trafficking found in Section 108 of the Trafficking Victims Protection Act" (U.S. Department of State 2013).

The United Nations *List of Signatories to the Protocol to Prevent, Suppress and Punish Trafficking in Persons, Especially Women and Children*, supplementing the United Nations *Convention Against Transnational Organized Crime*, was used to gather the dependent variable. However, it should be noted that not all countries listed as signatories have ratified the protocol, and therefore they were not considered here. Moreover, the level of INGO participation in the six countries was determined by the information about initiatives and programs in the selected countries that were self-reported on the INGOs' respective websites. We use four different INGOs.

The countries have been chosen based on geographic diversity, and the regions chosen for this study align with the regions described in the U.S. Department of State's *Trafficking in Persons Report* released in 2013. These regions and select countries are Nigeria for the African region, Philippines for East Asia and Pacific, Bosnia and Herzegovina for Europe, Egypt for the Near East, India for South and Central Asia, and Brazil for the Western Hemisphere.

The six countries are all classified tier 2 status by the U.S. Department of State, which means that they are countries whose governments do not fully comply with the Trafficking Victims Protection Act's minimum standards but are making significant efforts to bring themselves into compliance with those standards. By selecting countries of the same tier, we can do a better job of measuring and comparing countries as their responsiveness to human trafficking and the implementation of antitrafficking legislation are very similar. The Trafficking Victims Protection Act (TVPA) was passed in 2000 and contains guidelines and regulations that help deal with the issue of human trafficking in the United States and also on a global scale. The U.S. Department of State designates countries' tiers based on their level of compliance with the TVPA, so that countries will tend to acknowledge the problem of human trafficking and continue to implement antitrafficking measures. With the passing of this act, the president of the United States gained increased authority to deny humanitarian and trade-related aid to countries that do not attempt to comply with the TVPA and to provide more aid to those who try to meet the minimum standards.

The independent variable in the study is the level of influence exercised by the INGOs in the countries. The amount of significance that the INGOs had during the drafting of the UN Trafficking Protocol is based on the amount of INGO participation (initiatives/conferences/ advocacy) in the specific countries. The information collected on the participation of the various INGOs in different countries has been taken from the INGOs' websites, which described in detail the different initiatives taken during the drafting of the protocol.

The countries selected were then measured on scale of 0 to 4 based on the level of INGO involvement in their respective countries during the drafting negotiations of the protocol. A classification of 0 means that none of the INGOs listed was active in the country, and a classification of 4 means that the INGOs used in our study have shown a considerable amount activity in these countries. The INGOs used in these case studies are categorized in conjunction with the first part of the analysis of INGO lobbying blocs: the Human Rights Caucus and the International Human Rights Network. The GAATW and the IHRLG represented the Human Rights Caucus; the CATW and the EWL represented the International Human Rights Network. After looking at the list of signatories to the UN Trafficking Protocol, we removed the countries that had not yet ratified the protocol. After this we gathered a list of the countries that had both signed and ratified the protocol. Again, only the countries that were classified as tier 2 status were used in this study.

TABLE 6.2   Countries, Times, Participation

COUNTRY AND REGION	TIME RANGE	NGO PARTICIPATION
Nigeria (Africa)	0.53	4
Philippines (East Asia and Pacific)	1.45	4
Bosnia and Herzegovina (Europe)	1.36	4
Egypt (Near East)	1.85	2
India (South and Central Asia)	8.41	3
Brazil (Western Hemisphere)	3.13	3

From the list of signatories to the protocol we calculated the difference in time between the date the country signed and when it officially ratified it. The difference in time was then converted from months to years. The relationship between time range and level of INGO participation developed is described below. The independent variable is the level of INGO participation, while the dependent variable is the amount of time between the date a country signed the protocol and the date it ratified the protocol. The results are shown in table 6.2.

What do the time ranges tell us about INGOs and human trafficking? As detailed above, the debate among the INGOs combating the problem of human trafficking remains an issue because of the ideological extremes on both sides. The Human Rights Caucus holds progressive views, while the International Human Rights Network embraces more conservative approaches. The Human Rights Caucus argues for prostitution to be considered like any other form of labor, while the International Human Rights Network looks at this issue from a sex workers' perspective. This position counters that of the Coalition Against Trafficking in Women, which advocates for women's rights and holds a neo-abolitionist perspective.

The manner in which INGOs exercise power and activity in the countries depends on the level of government commitment. Some governments may be in denial and not as accepting of the influence of INGOs in their countries. If local governments do not share the same passion as the INGOs for the battle against human trafficking, it will be less effective because, although the problem is global, implementation of the protocol is local (Smith & Hunt 2012). Indeed, when enacting antitrafficking

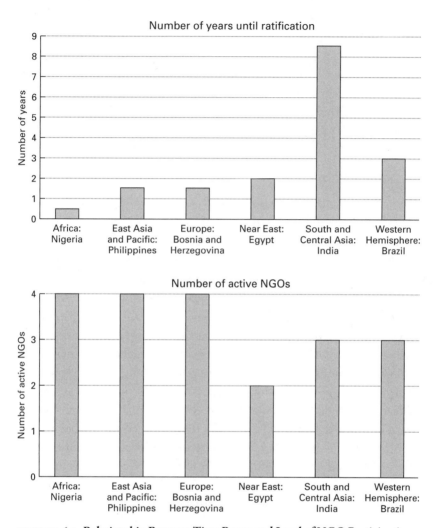

FIGURE 6.1 **Relationship Between Time Range and Level of NGO Participation**

legislation, "governments must be involved, both to steer the process and to strengthen their capacity to fight human trafficking" (United Nations Office of Drugs and Crime 2004).

The comparison between the amount of time a country took to sign and ratify the protocol and the level of the INGO participation shows a negative relationship between the date of ratification and the level of INGO participation. This relationship, presented in figure 6.1, shows that INGOs are using different initiatives to push countries to embrace the issue of human trafficking and take action and the necessary steps in fighting this transnational issue. This means that the higher the level of INGO participation in a certain country, the less time it took for that country to ratify the UN Trafficking Protocol after it signed it and vice versa. INGO engagement leads to local action.

CONCLUSION

The findings of this study suggest the role INGOs played in global governance within the framework of the UN Trafficking Protocol. The INGO lobbying agenda and efforts at the negotiations showcased their agendas, which were then translated into local action to the extent that the INGOs followed through domestically. Thus the INGOs filled in gaps left between government, citizens, and intergovernmental organizations in relation to human trafficking. The reasons for the increase in INGO participation may vary based on region and/or country, but the presence and impact of these organizations are clearly evident. The underlying question is whether the INGOs will continue to take center stage in crafting and implementing human trafficking amelioration policies.

In terms of global governance, INGOs exert influence over international and domestic law and have effectively utilized their lobbying and negotiation skills to combat human trafficking through implementation of the policies they prefer (Smith & Miller-de la Cuesta 2011; Smith & Smith-Cannoy 2013). The differing ideologies of the two INGO lobbying blocks—the International Human Rights Network and the Human Rights Caucus—led to the adoption of a broad definition of human trafficking. This discord between the groups leads to local flexibility. INGOs are often welcomed in the international realm because of their neutrality and their nonaffiliation with governments. This leads some countries to welcome extensive INGO participation and financial help, which in return causes the INGOs to have a significant amount of power over the structure and implementation of policies regarding human trafficking in various countries. As INGOs participate in global governance, collaboration and coordination where possible will continue to be tied to the ultimate efficacy of the efforts. Similarly, it is also critical that the INGOs remain in constant engagement domestically. Policy implementation by domestic governments can be shaped by the actors in global governance, especially the INGOs, only to the extent those actors also engage the local. The commitment of the INGOs to the fight against human trafficking continues. Both lobbying factions of the movement demonstrated effective strategies during the negotiations to institutionalize their principles.

DISCUSSION QUESTIONS

1. How have international nongovernmental organizations that are concerned with human trafficking influenced global governance approaches to the issue?
2. Can you make an argument that sex workers should always be thought of as victims of human trafficking? Can you also make an argument that sex workers should *not* always be thought of as victims of human trafficking?
3. Discuss the role of consent in human trafficking.
4. Explain how international organizations can alter the local, domestic approach to combatting human trafficking.

REFERENCES

Abramson, K. 2003. Beyond consent, toward safeguarding human rights: Implementing the United Nations trafficking protocol. *Harvard International Law Journal* 44 (2): 473–502.

Annotated Guide to Complete UN Trafficking Protocol. http://www.hrlawgroup. org/resources/content/Traff_AnnoProtocol.pdf.

Brysk, Alison, and Austin Choi-Fitzpatrick, eds. 2011. *From Human Trafficking to Human Rights: Reframing Contemporary Slavery.* Philadelphia: University of Pennsylvania Press.

Center for International Crime Prevention. 2002. United Nations Convention Against Transnational Organized Crime. New York: United Nations.

Coalition Against Traffic in Women. 2000. *Victory in Vienna.* http://www.utopia. pcn.net/puta3-i.html.

Ditmore, M., & W. Marjan. 2003. The negotiations on the UN protocol on trafficking in persons. *Nemesis* 4:73–88.

Doezema, Jo. 2002. Who Gets to Choose? Coercion, Consent, and the UN Trafficking Protocol. *Gender & Development* 10 (1): 20–27.

———. 2005. Now you see her, now you don't: Sex workers at the UN trafficking protocol negotiation. *Social & Legal Studies* 14 (1): 61–89.

Fitzpatrick, J. 2003. Trafficking as a human rights violation: The complex intersection of legal frameworks for conceptualizing and combating trafficking. *Michigan Journal of International Law* 24:1150.

Gallagher, Anne. 2001. Human rights and the new UN protocols on trafficking and migrant smuggling: A preliminary analysis. *Human Rights Quarterly* 23 (4): 975–1004.

Global Alliance Against Traffic in Women. 1999.. *Human Rights Standards for the Treatment of Trafficked Persons*. Bangkok.

Smith, Charles A., and Tyler H. Hunt. 2012. Best practices in domestic human trafficking policy. *Law Enforcement Executive Forum* 12 (1): 22–35.

Smith, Charles A., and Brandon Miller-de la Cuesta. 2011. Human trafficking in conflict zones: The role of peacekeepers in the formation of networks. *Human Rights Review* 12 (3): 287–99.

Smith, Charles A., and Heather Smith. 2011a. Human trafficking: The unintended effects of United Nations intervention. *International Political Science Review* 32 (2): 139–60.

———. 2011b. Peacekeepers and human trafficking: The new security dilemma. In *From Human Trafficking to Human Rights: Reframing Contemporary Slavery*, ed. Alison Brysk and Austin Choi-Fitzpatrick. Philadelphia: University of Pennsylvania Press.

Smith, Charles A., and Heather Smith-Cannoy. 2013. Human trafficking and international cheap talk: The Dutch government and the island territories. *Journal of Human Rights* 11 (1): 51–65.

United Nations Office of Drugs and Crime. 2004. *United Nations Convention Against Transnational Organized Crime And the Protocols Thereto*. http://www.unodc.org/documents/treaties/UNTOC/Publications/TOC%20Convention/TOCebook-e.pdf.

———. 2007. *The Global Initiative to Fight Human Trafficking*. http://www.unodc.org/pdf/gift%20brochure.pdf.

U.S. Department of State. 2013. *Trafficking in Persons Report*. http://www.state.gov/g/tip/rls/tiprpt/2013.

CHAPTER 7

Sex Work and Agency

DECRIMINALIZATION OF PROSTITUTION

▸ CATHY NGUYEN, RICH FURMAN, AND ALISSA R. ACKERMAN

HUMAN SEX TRAFFICKING AND THE sexual abuse of minors constitute horrible crimes against two vulnerable and at-risk populations (Schatz & Furman 2003). Each year thousands of women and children are trafficked for the purpose of sexual abuse and sex tourism. In this book, other chapters deal with the dehumanizing effects of these two often interrelated problems, neither of which should ever be minimized. Too frequently, however, discourses, programs, and policies designed to respond to human sexual trafficking and transnational sexual offenses against minors inadvertently, and sometimes intentionally, criminalize sex work performed by adult women. Such practices are a concern for in a paternalistic attempt to protect adult women they harm their sense of agency, reduce their employment options, and represent a form of social control over women's bodies (Bouhours et al. 2012; Crago 2008; Hayes-Smith & Shekarkhar 2010; Shields 2012). Many feminist scholars advocate for the right of women to engage in sex work (Bouhours et al. 2012; Crago 2008; Hayes-Smith & Shekarkhar 2010; Shields 2012), though this idea is certainly contested. They argue that women who choose to engage in sex work are exercising self-determination and agency, using their bodies not only for their survival but also for their advancement. For instance, Hoang (2011), in her study of sex workers and sex work clients in Vietnam, explores how sex workers may utilize more advanced psychosocial skills in discourses and actions that transcend pure sexual encounters to ones that are more complicated, nuanced relationships. Diverging from the contention that sex work is solely an exploitative act, she argues that it must be analyzed using a relationship lens, and that "sex work is an *intimate relationship* best illustrated by the complex inter-mingling of money and intimacy" (367).

Further, there are significant consequences for criminalizing sex work and confusing sex work with trafficking. Conflating the two may lead to several harmful consequences, such as preventing women from seeking health care (Crago 2008; Hayes-Smith & Shekarkhar 2010) and discourag-ing women from reporting sexual abuse (Shields 2012). The purpose of this chapter is to explore the distinctions between sex trafficking and sex work. This becomes essential in a transnational world, as without this distinction, advocates, policy makers, and criminal justice systems run the risk of two deleterious problems: (1) the disempowerment of adult women who choose to engage in sex work, and (2) the dilution of social resources away from women and minors who have been trafficked. Understanding the distinc-tions between the two can help those concerned with the most exploited and vulnerable women and children to focus on these populations. It is of the utmost importance that we focus on the vulnerable and not on women who are engaging in sex work of their own free will and volition, who may often utilize this as a conscious strategy for economic advancement.

SEX WORK, PROSTITUTION, AND TRAFFICKING: DYNAMICS AND DIFFERENCES

Not carefully separating consensual sex work from instances of human traf-ficking can have severe negative implications. In this section, we explore key differences between trafficking and consensual sex work and discuss the importance of delineating between them.

There are several reasons why distinctions between consensual sex work and human trafficking and the abuse of minors should be made. First, adult women should have the right to control their bodies and how they use them. Second, confusing sex work with sex trafficking draws valuable social resources away from where they should be focused: on the sexual exploitation of women and children. For instance, recent laws and their subsequent enforcement, under the guise of reducing trafficking, have sought to reduce the number of venues where sex workers can work. These laws have had the effect of drawing sex workers away from controlled and regulated institutions, such as bars, and into uncontrolled contexts, such as the street or unregulated discos (Hayes-Smith & Shekarkhar 2010). The increase in unregulated contexts creates the likelihood that sex tourists will inadvertently be drawn to minors or women who may have been trafficked. Also, by focusing on noncoerced sex workers, the authorities are giving the impression that they are focusing on sex trafficking, yet little to no evidence exists that trafficking has been reduced.

Contrary to popular belief, sex workers come from a number of different backgrounds. While many sex workers tend to be of lower socioeconomic status, this does not define them all. Many sex workers alternate between formal employment and engagement in sex work to earn their income (Rosen & Venkatesh 2008). Moreover, individuals who are involved in sex work are varied in age (Bouhours et al. 2012; Rosen & Venkatesh 2008). As the sex work industry exists in varying forms across the globe, sex workers identify with a large range of ethnic and cultural groups and come from different educational backgrounds (Bouhours et al. 2012; Rosen & Venkatesh 2008; Shields 2012). With sex workers occupying varied and unique social locations, it is no coincidence that each woman's reasons for and circumstances surrounding entering and staying in sex work are different, as are their experiences of agency and oppression in the work that they do.

In an examination of the literature and a study of the commercial sex industry in Cambodia, it was found that a majority of sex workers are inaccurately labeled as "trafficked" and are actually aware of their recruitment into the industry and willing to engage in the work. A handful of these "trafficked" individuals regard their work as honorable because it allows them to provide a means to sustain and support their family's socioeconomic welfare. For some, entrance into this informal economy is initiated by their own family members. Few of these individuals report having experienced abuse, and whereas dominant political institutions regard sex work as a grave moral issue, most do not consider it to be so (Bouhours et al. 2012).

WOMEN'S AGENCY AND SEX WORK

Agency is a concept that derives from feminist scholarship and explores notions of empowerment, will, and self-determination. It connotes the capacity to adapt to difficult and oppressive contexts (Lindsey 2010), such as extreme poverty and deprivation.

Because each sex worker occupies a unique social location, there are many layers of power and oppression in each worker's experience. Just as the lifestyles, needs, and external circumstances of any individual are not fixed, the experience of agency by the sex worker is not fixed, either. Over time and across varying contexts, the sex workers' sense of agency shifts within their place of work and larger social institutions, causing them to shift along the spectrum of power or perceived agency. It is crucial, then, that the exploration of sex workers' experience with agency is undertaken with the recognition that this experience is not "either-or"; rather this experience fluctuates because the sex worker's perception of agency is situationally experienced.

Many sex workers are drawn to sex work because, as coined by Rosen and Venkatesh (2008), it "satisfices." This term implies that sex work is often opted for because it is a job that allows for both personal autonomy and a sufficient means for fulfilling constraining financial demands. This multitiered function of sex work "satisfices," in that it both satisfies the individual's relative sense of agency (e.g., scheduling flexibility, selection of one's own clientele, determination of services one provides) and suffices, given the individual's constrained circumstances and options (e.g., unstable living conditions, lack of required educational background or professional skills, inaccessibility of affordable childcare, etc.). The concept of "satisfices" is especially relevant because it invites social workers to move beyond dichotomous "empowering vs. exploiting" debates to analyze the underlying roots of the sex worker's "constrained circumstance and options," and to recognize the ways in which agency is exercised in nontrafficked prostitution.

In their ethnographic study conducted with sex workers in Chicago, Rosen and Venkatesh (2008) found that the sex workers entered the work because it adequately met their economic needs and allowed a substantial amount of personal autonomy and satisfaction. After assessing other accessible and available options to earn a living in their immediate environment, individuals often found that sex work offers them the most flexibility, control, and income in relation to jobs that require the same level of education or skills. While their living circumstances make a significant impact on their choice of occupation, sex workers can and do engage in an intentional process of decision making in order to determine the option that best meets their desires and needs.

Rosen and Venkatesh's study suggests that many sex workers find appeal in sex work because it allows for them to control their own work. Because some sex workers face tenuous housing circumstances or have challenging family demands, sex work is appealing because of its mobility and malleability. Sex work accommodates the individual's need to relocate, allows for the individual to determine the duration of engagement in sex work, and gives the individual full control over work schedules. In addition to the authority which the sex worker can exercise over the mobility and timing of the work, the sex worker also has the power to decide what kind of services are offered, how much to charge, and who the clients are. Because of the nature of the work, having control over these aspects can be extremely important to the sex worker and allows sex workers to believe that they have agency in their occupation.

Many sex workers do not rely solely on sex work to earn income. Because sex workers often experience unstable living circumstances, many come in and out of sex work intermittently. Depending on the current patterns of their lives, it is common that sex workers alternate between prostitution and formal employment throughout their career. While it is found that limited education, resources, time, and job opportunities are often associated with an individual's engagement in sex work, the extent of individual rationality and intent in the decision to do the work cannot be dismissed. Even as economic and social structures influence the decision to enter and stay in sex work, it has been found that sex workers deliberately opt to engage in the work after consideration of the different costs and benefits of their limited options and the compatibility of these options with their social and economic circumstances. For many of these individuals, sex work offers certain elements of agency and control, such as flexibility, mobility, and independence, which are, considering their social locations, valuable additional benefits of the work. Despite this "bounded rationality" within which many sex workers choose to do sex work, the deliberate nature of the decision-making process in which these individuals engage is a powerful illustration of agency (Rosen & Venkatesh 2008).

While economic gain is a huge motivating factor for many sex workers, the personal experience of empowerment and sexual liberation plays an equally powerful role in the sex worker's choice to stay in the industry. Recognizing that agency can and is exercised in nontrafficked prostitution validates the sex worker's right to sexual freedom and supports the sex worker's sense of autonomy and self-determination. The decriminalization of prostitution maintains the sex worker's right to legal protection, supports comprehensive and relevant public health strategies, protects the right of individuals to engage in work that suits their financial needs and circumstances, and allows individuals who want to pay for certain goods and services to exercise their right to do so.

DECRIMINALIZATION OF PROSTITUTION

There are several arguments for the decriminalization of prostitution, including destigmatization of sex workers, protection of the sex worker's right to autonomy, a more encompassing and effective public health approach, and an expanding societal repertoire of acceptable and viable means of income earning (Hayes-Smith & Shekarkhar 2010).

The decriminalization of prostitution would encourage the destigmatization of sex workers by removing legal barriers to selling and buying sexual services, normalizing prostitution as a labor, and ending the penalizing of women engaging in prostitution. In removing legal barriers to selling and buying sexual services, law enforcement, one can argue, would become relatively more accessible to sex workers, and sex workers would be more likely to seek police protection in the event that an offense is committed against them during the course of their work. Decriminalizing prostitution would normalize this type of sex work by framing the work in the context of any other labor, thereby encouraging legal, economic, and social institutions to perceive and respond to the prostitute as a worker rather than a victim and/or criminal.

In addition, the decriminalization of prostitution would protect the sex worker's autonomy by recognizing nontrafficked prostitution as legitimate work, thereby honoring the sex worker's agency and free will to earn income through the sale of sexual services. The recognition of nontrafficked prostitution as similar to any other labor practice encourages an empowering perception of the prostitute as it encourages a view of the sex worker like any other worker in the labor market—an individual who makes a conscientious and deliberate choice in the selection of and tenure in an occupation. Furthermore, when the consensual nature of nontrafficked prostitution is recognized, the spectrum of choice in sex work can be explored in relation to the unique sex worker, allowing for understanding of individual agency.

It is particularly arguable that the destigmatization of sex workers through the decriminalization of prostitution would also remove the stigmatization of sex workers in the health-care industry. Owing to predominant assumptions of the association between sexually transmitted diseases and prostitution (Crago 2008), policies that scapegoat sex workers for the HIV/AIDS epidemic, such as the George W. Bush administration's Anti-Prostitution Pledge, are made into law (Hayes-Smith & Shekarkhar 2010). Considering that politics and public health are inextricably intertwined, it can be expected that the vicious cycles of misguided institutional initiatives, stereotypes, and biases held by medical practitioners will be continually reinforced so long as sex work is criminalized. The criminalization of prostitution not only severely undercuts the sex worker's access to adequate and dignified health care but reduces the sex worker's sense of power and extent of positive civic participation on an institutional level.

Related to this political marginalization is the social and geographic isolation of sex workers. The study by Hayes-Smith and Shekarkhar (2010) reveals that sex workers tend to reside in more rural areas and are thus less likely to seek police protection, because of fear of prosecution and legal punishment. This heightened risk of jeopardizing their social and economic livelihoods is an illustration of disempowerment, as sex workers are faced with the dilemma of sacrificing their right to legal protection or maintaining their financial and economic livelihoods. Moreover, the social and geographic marginalization of prostitutes strips away a crucial facet of their identities as active and participatory citizens.

There is also a strong argument that the criminalization of prostitution hinders effective public health approaches. It has been found that sex workers who conduct their work in a regulated setting, as opposed to sex workers who conduct their work on the streets, are significantly less likely to be infected with or exposed to HIV/AIDS. In regulated contexts, those who are engaged in prostitution demonstrate a relatively greater initiative and concern for preventative health practices, and these practices are enforced on multiple levels of the industry (Hayes-Smith & Shekarkhar 2010). What these findings suggest is that the decriminalization of prostitution could effectively encourage proactive health practices and awareness, thereby influencing the creation of formalized health systems that would work to expand accessibility to medical intervention and care and remove barriers to comprehensive health care for sex workers.

Arguably the most overlooked benefit of the decriminalization of prostitution is economic growth. Segal (2013) contends that the decriminalization of this work would allow for taxation of the labor, increasing the revenue of the local economy. With the decriminalization of prostitution, the local economy would also experience increased revenue from tourism and the creation and/or enhancement of the labor of other participants in the industry. Lifting the stigma and sanctions of prostitution would allow for the development of additional lines of work within the industry that may not be as feasible in the context of criminalization. Jobs such as drivers, bodyguards, agents, and assistants are a few examples of opportunities that can become available and that would arguably have greater economic viability after decriminalization. Related to the creation of new or additional job opportunities is the increased attraction that businesses in red-light districts may gain from the decriminalization of prostitution (Segal 2013). With the economic and social legitimation of prostitution, businesses that are within the same vicinity or that interface with the local sex work industry, such as taxicab services, could experience a gain in revenue from higher customer traffic. The potential economic growth of the decriminalization of prostitution could manifest in the form of job creation or stimulation of business for existing services or establishments that interact with the sex work industry on some level.

Similarly, the decriminalization of prostitution could create savings, particularly those related to the costs of arrests and prostitution prosecutions (Segal 2013). There would be a reduction in the arrests of sex workers and those who participate in the industry, which would reduce court costs and decrease prosecutions of sex work–related activities. Sex workers would have access to legal protections, and there might be improvements in safeguards and reductions in sex workers' social, economic, and cultural vulnerability and their experiences of violence and isolation that might stem from the stigmatization and criminalization of prostitution.

Reducing the stigmatization of those who participate in the industry would greatly enhance the human capital of the sex worker. Through the legitimation of sex work, the sex worker would exercise agency doing work that most suits the individual's circumstances and that brings the greatest return for the investment of time and skills. The decriminalization of prostitution would reduce the rate of arrests, which would contribute not only to savings in the local economy but to the sustainment of financial and domestic stability, which are most drastically disrupted when the sex worker experiences incarceration. Incarceration creates multiple barriers for the sex worker, an obvious one being that the individual's pursuit of economic gain is halted. Another barrier of incarceration involves the challenges that may come when an individual with a criminal record seeks formal employment. More important, the trickle-down effects of incarceration on family cycles severely undercut the human capital of sex workers. Because incarceration diminishes or disrupts the sex worker's capacity to provide adequate and stable child care, it also reduces the sex worker's sense of contribution to generational success. With less than one-third of children from unstable households pursuing higher education (Segal 2013), it is a given that the human capital of children of sex workers will be diminished if sex work remains illegal. Conversely, the decriminalization of prostitution would reduce the rate of incarceration of sex workers, thereby increasing the economic and domestic stability of the sex worker and sustaining, if not expanding, the capacity of sex workers both to maintain a sense of self-worth and to actively participate in the economic, social, and cultural spheres of society.

Decriminalizing prostitution makes comprehensive and culturally responsive health care approaches more feasible and viable. It promotes risk- and harm-reduction health practices and encourages early health interventions, increasing the amount of savings that could be gained from preventative health strategies (Segal 2013). Such trends—prevention education and proactive health-care practices—may also encourage the lowering of health insurance premiums, allowing for individuals to increase their spending in different markets, thereby increasing overall revenue.

More directly, destigmatizing and decriminalizing prostitution increase the earning potential and client base of the sex worker (Segal 2013). By removing the risk of prosecution for participation in the sex work industry, there is likely to be an enhanced level of safety and normalization in being a customer of the services offered by the work itself, the surrounding or related businesses of the work, or both. The accessibility of the industry could expand clientele, attracting more customers and bolstering the earning potential of sex workers.

IMPLICATIONS

The criminalization of prostitution has many social policy, social program, and criminal justice implications, including the misdirection of resources, corruption within criminal justice systems and faulty convictions, gaps in global health approaches, confounding of data and statistics surrounding trafficking and sex work, and, most of all, disempowerment of sex workers and particularly women (Bouhours et al. 2012; Crago 2008; Hayes-Smith & Shekarkhar 2010; Shields 2012).

The criminalization of prostitution leads to the misdirection of resources by collapsing all sex trades, whether consensual or coerced, into the category of "trafficking." This overgeneralization is facilitated by moral panic, which rationalizes the view that all who are involved in any type of sex work are victims of a "wrong" or "immoral" industry. By applying a blanket category of "trafficking" over all sex work, the risk of misdirecting resources away from those who they are intended to serve—actual victims of human trafficking—heightens. In a study by Bouhours et al. (2012), anecdotes suggest that some individuals claim to be victims of human trafficking in order to obtain resources such as housing, free education, and other services. This is, arguably, manageable when a criminal justice system classifies all sex work as "trafficking." Additionally, the criminalization of prostitution shifts governmental focus and funding away from programs, services, or resources for other real victims of sex trafficking and other demanding social issues. Similarly, it can lead to the corruption of segments of criminal justice systems. For example, a study conducted in Bangladesh reveals that a majority of sex workers report that they have experienced sexual assault or some form of physical abuse by law enforcement, and one-third of sex workers in Bangladesh are pressured to pay a portion of their earnings to police officers (Crago 2008). In this context, sex workers often have little or no access to legal protection and have limited means by which they can seek legal retribution. The dilemmas of working in a stigmatized industry and being faced with corrupt law enforcement can add an array of risks to the sex worker, particularly pertaining to their safety and agency.

Since recent crackdowns on human trafficking in Cambodia, many cases of bribery and human trafficking convictions based on dubious or absent evidence have been reported. It was found that, from officers to judges, very few have knowledge of what legally constitutes "trafficking," and instead, many rely on sensationalized images and ideas surrounding the complex industry in their enforcement of antitrafficking laws. As a consequence, many who express consent and free will in their decision to enter into sex work are wrongfully convicted. Bribery is not only exercised frequently and even admitted to by court officials but also often successful in shortening a convict's sentence and, in many cases, exonerating the person in cases of suspected trafficking (Bouhours et al. 2012).

The criminalization of prostitution can reinforce and promote gaps in global health approaches as well as misconceptions about global health issues. As moral panic contaminates dominant medical ideologies and approaches, sex workers are often scapegoated for health epidemics, such as HIV/AIDS, and as a consequence, global health policies are passed that stigmatize sex workers (Crago 2008; Hayes-Smith & Shekarkhar 2010). With much of the international legislation including stipulations that dictate that HIV/AIDS strategies be funded only in countries where anti-prostitution laws are in effect (Crago 2008), sex workers' access to essential health-care resources is severely limited. In many countries police view condoms as contraband, resulting in the arrest and prosecution of sex workers (Shields 2012). The risk of being caught carrying condoms can greatly discourage the use of protection by the sex worker. This increases the level of potential risk for the sex worker in terms of sexually transmitted diseases. It can also be argued that the risk of prosecution (or even the threat of it) increases the likelihood of bribery by law enforcement. Scapegoating and stigmatizing sex workers and criminalizing the carrying of condoms can lead to a number of negative international consequences, starting with the absence of relevant education and formalized systems to encourage preventative health-care practices and informed decisions among sex workers and extending to global health disparities and the disproportionate distribution of power, resources, and access across nations.

An equally concerning consequence of the criminalization of prostitution is that it encourages improper data collection and analysis practices (Bouhours et al. 2012). By collapsing consensual sex work with sex trafficking, statistics that are produced around these subjects can be significantly confounded. In failing to distinguish between prostitution and sex trafficking, data related to sex work are unreliable and run the risk of promoting misguided policies and initiatives. As many social programs provide services or resources and receive funding based on the implications of such data, it is crucial that the data are valid, and particularly that definitions of prostitution and trafficking are operationalized.

Finally, the criminalization of prostitution disempowers individuals, particularly women, who make up a majority of sex workers. Both the moral panic that surrounds human trafficking and the conflating of prostitution with trafficking demonize consensual labor, stigmatize workers, and classify willing and conscientious individuals as victims. On a micro level, the vilifying of consensual sex work can lead sex workers to be thought of as dirty or having low morals or values. On a macro level, the vilifying of consensual sex work encourages both the scapegoating and the social, cultural, and political isolation of sex workers. This vilification diminishes sex workers' individual capacity to sustain a sense of self-esteem and to secure a sense of power in social, cultural, and political contexts. Stigmatization of sex workers bars individuals from fair access to resources and opportunities and can be argued to be undercutting the dignity and perceived human capital of the individual. This stigma discourages active civic participation and engagement by the sex worker in sociopolitical sphere.

Classification of willing and conscientious sex workers as victims disempowers individuals, in that it does not recognize or allow for the exercise of agency by individuals who engage in sex work. The failure to recognize the nature and extent of consent in prostitution leads to the victimization of sex workers, which, as is often the case with victimization, renders the individual in question "helpless" or "exploited." These labels disregard the individual's capacity to exercise self-determination in sex work and, by extension, police how women can and should express and utilize their sexuality. The degree to which women's agency and personal power are suppressed owing to the criminalization of prostitution is extensive, in that women who engage in sex work are predominantly considered to be victims and thereby must be "protected" from "exploitation" vis-à-vis laws that make prostitution illegal. Such a paternalistic approach of criminal justice systems and policies stems from sexism, a system of oppression that has historically disapproved of women's sexual liberation and that continues to police women's behavior and sexual conduct in social, economic, cultural, and political contexts.

The authors argue that it is imperative that the distinction between prostitution and sex trafficking be made on both a micro and an institutional level to ensure that resources are distributed in a fair and relevant manner, strategize toward the decriminalization of prostitution, and, most of all, restore and protect women's agency in sex work and in the social, economic, cultural, and political spheres of society.

DISCUSSION QUESTIONS

1. Describe the difference between sex trafficking and sex work.
2. Do you agree with the authors' position that sex work and sex trafficking should be considered two separate issues?
3. Provide the arguments for and against the decriminalization of sex work.

REFERENCES

Bouhours, T., R. Broadhurst, C. Keo, and B. Bouhours. 2012. *Human Trafficking and Moral Panic in Cambodia: The Unintended Consequences of Good Intentions.* http://papers.ssrn.com/sol3/papers.cfm?abstract_id=2190704.

Crago, A. 2008. *"Our Lives Matter": Sex Workers Unite for Health And Rights.* New York: Open Society Institute.

Hayes-Smith, R., and Z. Shekarkhar. 2010. "Why is prostitution criminalized?" An alternate viewpoint on the construction of sex work. *Contemporary Justice Review* 13 (1): 43–55.

Hoang, K. K. 2011. "She's not a low-class dirty girl!" Sex work in Ho Chi Minh City, Vietnam. *Journal of Contemporary Ethnography* 40 (4): 467–96.

Lindsey, L. L. 2010. *Gender Roles: A Sociological Perspective.* Boston: Pearson.

Rosen, E., and S. A. Venkatesh. 2008. "A 'perversion' of choice": Sex work offers just enough in Chicago's urban ghetto. *Journal of Contemporary Ethnography* 37 (4): 417–41.

Schatz, M. C. S., and R. Furman. 2003. Sexual trafficking of women: Strategies for developing trauma recovery response teams. *Social Development Issues* 24 (2): 60–67.

Shields, A. 2012. *Criminalizing Condoms: How Policing Practices Put Sex Workers and HIV Services at Risk in Kenya, Namibia, Russia, South Africa, the United States, and Zimbabwe.* http://www.opensocietyfoundations.org/sites/default/files/criminalizing-condoms-20120717.pdf.

PART 3

Examples and Contexts of Transnational Sex Crimes

CHAPTER 8

Sexual Violence Against Political Prisoners

AN EXAMINATION OF EMPIRICAL EVIDENCE IN EL SALVADOR AND PERU

▸ *MICHELE LEIBY*

WHY DO SOLDIERS COMMIT SEXUAL violence in times of war? The media, human rights advocacy groups, and even many academics often assert uncritically that sexual violence is a weapon of war. However, given that sexual violence varies considerably in frequency, form, perpetrator, and victim both across and within armed conflicts (Cohen 2013; Leiby 2011; Wood 2006, 2009), it is unlikely that such assertions are universally true. To fully understand its causes, careful attention must be paid to document the patterns of sexual violence in war and what those patterns reveal regarding the motives behind these crimes. In this vein, this chapter provides a first attempt at rigorous, comparative analysis of the patterns of sexual violence during the civil wars in El Salvador (1978–1992) and Peru (1980–2000). The data reveal that Salvadoran and Peruvian state armed forces, particularly police and military units, engaged in the frequent sexual abuse of male and female political prisoners, targeted individually or collectively for their perceived or real opposition to the state. The evidence suggests that these acts of violence were not merely the unavoidable consequence of the chaos of war but rather part of an explicit or implicit strategy to defeat the armed opposition.

A WEAPON OF WAR? UNDERSTANDING
STATE-PERPETRATED SEXUAL VIOLENCE

What does it mean to call sexual violence a strategic weapon of war? To be considered a weapon of war, sexual violence must be "used as part of a systematic political campaign which has strategic military purposes" (Skjelsbaek 2001:213). Such violence, regardless of its frequency or form, is employed purposefully, with the knowledge and consent of commanding officers, to advance the armed group's political and military objectives (Cohen, Hoover Green, & Wood 2013; Gutiérrez & Wood 2013; Leiby 2011).

Studies purporting sexual violence to be a strategic weapon of war emerged, in large part, in response to the atrocities committed in Bosnia-Herzegovina and Rwanda in the early 1990s. While the severity of sexual violence in these cases certainly warrants close examination, focus on these two conflicts has resulted in monocausal theories of sexual violence as a weapon of ethnic cleansing or genocide (Allen 1996; Bloom 1999; Mullins 2009; Sharlach 2000).

If we think more broadly, sexual violence has a number of perverse benefits as a potential weapon of war: it is relatively cheap and easy to use; it can boost the morale and unity of armed groups (Cohen 2013); and it can supplement the incomes of combatants. Perhaps most important, in societies with deeply held social mores about women's honor and purity, sexual violence may be a particularly effective repressive and demoralizing weapon (Allen 1996; Bastick, Grimm, & Kunz 2007). Because of the intimate nature of the attack on a person's understanding of self, sexual violence can be an effective method of neutralizing political opponents without killing them. As one report describes: "with the help of different torture methods, the authorities seek to remove any human, reliable, or mutual relationship and thereby bring the prisoner into a state of extreme physical and psychological regression, where it is no longer possible to relate to the body, to the world outside or to other people" (Agger & Jensen 1986: 307).

Sexual violence may be used as a form of state terrorism to induce fear widely throughout the civilian population. As the state increases its repressive campaign against civilians, the fear of being targeted will dissuade a potential recruit from joining the ranks or providing aid to the armed opposition (Valentino 2004). Similarly, the state may use sexual violence against suspected "enemies of the state" to punish them for their opposition activities. Potential targets could include members of armed rebel groups, opposition political parties, or "subversive" community organizations, as well as those who support them. By targeting individuals for their participation in dissident organizations, states effectively signal to potential recruits their fate if they behave similarly and may induce some subversives either to abandon or to betray the opposition (Kalyvas 2006). Whether the violence is targeted or indiscriminate in scope, the effect is the same: it undermines the ability of armed opposition groups to recruit and retain members or supporters.

In addition to undercutting the source of strength of the rebels, the state may also use sexual violence to collect intelligence on the opposition movement. The state may employ sexualized torture techniques during the interrogation of a suspected guerrilla to gather information about the identity of rebels, the location of their camps, or their military strategies, as was recently reported at the U.S. detention facilities at Guantanamo Bay in Cuba, Bagram airbase in Afghanistan, and Abu Ghraib in Iraq. Accounts suggest that detainees were subjected to a multitude of sexual abuses during interrogation and detention, ranging from being stripped and photographed nude to forced masturbation, rape, sodomy, and simulations of electric shock torture (Human Rights Watch 2004a, 2004b; Leonning & Priest 2005).

The remainder of this chapter examines a unique dataset on wartime sexual violence in El Salvador and Peru to document and understand the state's use of such violence against political prisoners. The civil wars in El Salvador and Peru present a unique opportunity for comparative analysis of the causes of wartime sexual violence. Despite significant differences between the two cases (see table 8.1), both the Salvadoran and Peruvian armed forces engaged in frequent sexual attacks—humiliation, torture, and rape—against political prisoners. Two instrumental functions for these abuses are explored: (1) to undercut popular support for opposition organizations and control the population, and (2) to acquire "actionable intelligence" on opposition organizations.

PATTERNS OF SEXUAL VIOLENCE AGAINST POLITICAL PRISONERS

Data used in this study were collected over the course of nineteen months from the archived human rights denunciations of two nongovernmental

TABLE 8.1   Comparative Data on Civil War in El Salvador and Peru

POTENTIAL CAUSES OF SEXUAL VIOLENCE	EL SALVADOR	PERU
Regime type	Authoritarian, military-dominated	Electoral democracy until 1992
International constraints on state behavior	Moderate-high	Low
Conflict type	Counterinsurgency; no ethnic dimension	Counterinsurgency; some ethnic dimension
Insurgency	FMLN, estimated 6,000–15,000 armed forces	
Limited violence against civilians	SL, estimated 2,000–8,000 armed forces	
Frequent and severe violence against civilians		
Political violence	Estimated 75,000 dead;	
most lethal violence perpetrated by state	Estimated 69,000 dead;	
most lethal violence perpetrated by rebels		
Sexual violence, general	Low frequency; highly asymmetrical	Moderate frequency; asymmetrical but less so than in El Salvador
Sexual violence against detainees	Moderate-high frequency (as % of all state SV)	Moderate-high frequency (as % of all state SV)

Source: Cunningham, Gleditsch, & Salehyan (2009) for estimates of number dead.

human rights organizations in El Salvador—the Office of Legal Aid of the Archbishop (TL) and Christian Legal Aid (SJC)—and the Truth and Reconciliation Commission (CVR) in Peru. Approximately seven thousand testimonies of violence were read and coded to create a database on state-perpetrated violence during the Salvadoran and Peruvian civil wars. In addition to eleven forms of nonsexual political violence (not the focus of the present analysis), the database covers eight forms of sexual violence: rape, gang rape, sexual torture, sexual mutilation, sexual humiliation (such as forced nudity), attempted and threatened acts of sexual violence, and unspecified forms of sexual violence.

General Characteristics

In both conflicts sexual violence was but one form of repression used by the state. According to the human rights denunciations collected for this study, sexual violence constituted approximately 1 percent and 5 percent, respectively, of all state-perpetrated violence during the Salvadoran and Peruvian civil wars. Because it is difficult (and perhaps impossible) to accurately approximate the overall frequency of sexual violence, caution should be used when drawing inferences regarding these figures (for a complete discussion of obstacles in estimating the level of sexual violence in El Salvador and Peru, see Leiby 2011, 2012).

Despite the difficulty in estimating the overall frequency of wartime sexual violence, there is ample documentation that state security agents in both countries often used sexual violence against political prisoners. Of the more than seven hundred acts of sexual violence recorded in the database, a large percentage of them—56 percent in El Salvador and 42 percent in Peru—were perpetrated inside state-run detention facilities against political prisoners. These crimes occurred in both formal and informal prisons on military bases and in police stations. In both countries the most frequent forms of sexual violence used against detainees were sexual humiliation (42 percent), rape and gang rape (23 percent), sexual torture (21 percent), and attempted or threatened acts of sexual violence (11 percent). Although forced abortion and sexual mutilation were reported to have occurred in both countries, this does not appear to have been a pattern of abuse within detention facilities.

In both countries, sexual violence against political prisoners was heavily concentrated in urban centers, notably San Salvador (51 percent of all such cases in El Salvador) and Lima (34 percent of cases in Peru). In addition, sexual violence in detention centers was significantly more frequent during periods when the states' counterinsurgency strategies emphasized population control measures, such as the detention, interrogation, and abuse of suspected "terrorists." In Peru in the early 1990s, for example, President Fujimori redirected the state's counterinsurgency efforts to include more targeted operations that distinguished among friendly, neutral, and enemy populations.

Fujimori established a new special-operations intelligence group (known as GEIN) within the National Counter-terrorism Directorate (DINCOTE) whose sole mission was to identify members of the Shining Path (SL) and gather intelligence that would lead to the capture of their leader, Abimael Guzmán. During this period the overall level of violence against civilians fell (CVR 2004). However, at the same time, sexual violence, particularly against political prisoners, rose markedly. In fact, almost half of all detention-related sexual offenses during the civil war occurred during Fujimori's presidency. This could indicate that counterterror police forces were ordered to commit sexual violence or that they were given carte blanche to use whatever means necessary in the pursuit of Peru's "public enemy #1."

The level of sexual violence in El Salvador similarly correlates with changes in the state's counterinsurgency strategy. The most significant shift came in 1984 after a visit by then U.S. vice president George H. W. Bush, who threatened the withdrawal of military aid, particularly air support, if the Salvadoran armed forces did not improve their human rights record. Knowing that such a withdrawal would almost certainly mean defeat, the state avoided the kind of wholesale and highly visible community massacres that characterized the early 1980s (Peceny & Stanley 2010). Careful to avoid international scrutiny, the state moved its repressive operations behind closed doors. This change in policy resulted in a decrease in the level of lethal violence but at the same time led to an increase in the arbitrary detention, torture, and sexual abuse of individuals suspected of "subversion." That the armed forces' repertoire of violence shifted so quickly (and in response to a vital security concern) suggests that commanders had at least some knowledge of and control over their subordinates' behavior.

Victims

Included in the database are 291 unique victims, each of whom suffered at least one form of sexual abuse while in state custody. According to the data, 66 percent of victims of sexual violence in Salvadoran detention facilities were men. This is significantly higher than is commonly thought and significantly higher than that reported in Peru (32 percent). This finding is confirmed by the nongovernmental Human Rights Commission of El Salvador (CDHES). In a unique study of torture at La Esperanza men's prison between January and August 1986, the CDHES found that 76 percent of the 434 prisoners interviewed had suffered one or more forms of sexual violence. According to the testimonies, the most common forms of sexual violence were forced nudity (58 percent), genital beatings (20 percent), electric torture (14 percent), threats of rape (15 percent), and rape (0.5 percent) (CDHES 1986).

As is often the case, men in Peru and El Salvador were more likely to be viewed as political threats and as a result, were more likely to be detained by the state and subsequently subjected to sexual violence. While the exact proportion of male-female victims may vary owing to reporting biases, the data reveal that men are much more likely to be the victims of sexual violence than is recognized by the academic or policy literatures.

Both male and female victims were often young (between 20 and 30 years old), unmarried, and either a recent graduate or current university student. Students and teachers made up more than one-third of the political prisoners subjected to sexual violence. As rebel groups frequently recruit members from high schools and universities, it is unsurprising that the state would target this subgroup of the population for repression.

Sexual violence was often reserved for prisoners who were accused of being members of or collaborating with "terrorist" or "subversive" organizations. Individuals could come under the suspicion of the state for belonging to an opposition political party, a labor union, or any number of community-based groups thought to be fronts for rebel organizing. Thirty-eight percent of victims of sexual violence in detention were accused of being terrorists; however, only 6 percent actually confessed to being members of the Farabundo Martí National Liberation Front (FMLN) or Shining Path. While political prisoners certainly have no incentive to declare an association with armed guerrilla groups, it is quite likely that this figure reflects the states' indiscriminate antiterrorist policy, which failed to distinguish between legal and illegal opposition organizations.

Lastly, victims of sexual violence in detention centers were very often the targets of repeated abuse by the state. Twenty percent of victims reported having previously been the victims of human rights abuse or knowing someone who was. As it is statistically improbable that an individual would be victimized more than once by chance, this kind of repeated abuse may suggest an intentional targeting on the part of the state.

Perpetrators

The state armed forces perpetrated the vast majority of all wartime sexual violence in El Salvador and Peru (97 percent and 88 percent, respectively). Within the state armed forces, however, there is great variation in the frequency and repertoire of violence perpetrated by each security sector. As expected, units charged with internal security and population control, including the National Guard (GN) and Treasury Police (PH) in El Salvador, as well as the National Police and special operations counterterror police forces in El Salvador and Peru, were the most frequent perpetrators of sexual violence against political prisoners. Police forces committed 70 percent of all such offenses, more than half of which were perpetrated by specially trained counterterrorist squads. In comparison, the national armies of El Salvador and Peru committed 28 percent of sexual violence against detainees. Based on reported cases, sexual violence of any form was not a significant component of the repertoires of violence of the air force, navy, or state-sponsored paramilitary groups in either country.

Both the regular army and police forces were more likely to engage in sexual humiliation than any other form of sexual violence (39 percent and 43 percent of all sexual abuses perpetrated by the military and police, respectively). Beyond sexual humiliation, the army was much more likely to rape or gang rape detainees, while police officers committed various forms of sexual torture, including blunt genital trauma, electrical torture, and genital cutting.

Context

As this chapter focuses solely on sexual violence within detention centers, one might assume that most, if not all, acts of sexual violence occurred during the interrogation of "suspects." However, only 36 percent and 23 percent of all reported acts of sexual violence in El Salvador and Peru, respectively, were committed in an explicit effort to acquire information or coerce a confession from the victim. The case of Claudia from Peru is emblematic of this pattern (all names have been changed):

> [One night] in October in 1983 at 9 pm, 20 soldiers entered the house when I was alone with the kids. They interrogated my older daughter, Julia,

who was 13 at the time. . . . They took me from the house in my pajamas, put me in the armored truck and tied me up. We arrived at the prison at 11pm. The next day, they took me from the room where I was detained and transferred me to another room. . . . Three soldiers interviewed me. They said I had to collaborate with them. They asked me if I knew any terrorists, and where they were. I said I don't know anything. They accused me of being a terrorist and inserted a pipe into my genitals. Then they brought my daughter into the room, right in front of me and threatened to "enjoy" her if I didn't cooperate. Two of the soldiers raped me from behind. (CVR n.d.: testimony 200012).

In El Salvador another victim, who refused to give his name, was captured by armed men (some in military uniform, others in plainclothes) while waiting for the bus outside of the National University (UNES). The men threw the victim into the back of their car and immediately began asking him questions about the guerrillas. They accused him of being a terrorist and beat him in the stomach with their guns. They took him to a police station (the victim did not know where he was) and put him in an interrogation room. The room was covered in human waste. The men stripped him and left him in the room naked. After a while a uniformed officer entered, removed his belt, and tied it around the victim's testicles. They blasted loud music into the room and began to beat him again—in the stomach, neck, and head. Each time he refused or did not answer satisfactorily their questions, they would beat him again and tighten the belt another notch (SJC n.d.).

Even sexual humiliation, an offense not currently recognized by the International Criminal Court as a war crime or a crime against humanity, can be used to dehumanize prisoners and to "prep" them for interrogation. In one such case in El Salvador, armed men in civilian clothes abducted Juan, his father, and his brother from their home and took them to the local PH station. When they arrived at the station, the three men were separated. The officers stripped Juan and forced him to wear a pair of women's underwear, mocking him and calling him a faggot. Afterward they sent him to the interrogation room. They asked him the same questions over and over again. *What is your name? Where do you live? Who do you work for? Do you know Alesandro, Nerio, or Josef?* The officers accused Juan of being a member of the Armed Liberation Forces (FAL, one of the guerrilla groups unified under the FMLN banner) and threatened to kill him and his mother if he did not confess and give them the names of his leaders (TL n.d.). Stripping prisoners is a common tactic used by the police to underscore the detainee's vulnerability and in this case attack the victim's identity as a heterosexual man, both of which serve to disarm and disorient the prisoner, making him more malleable.

Despite these cases, the vast majority of sexual violence in detention centers were *not* perpetrated during interrogation sessions. Instead, as the examples below demonstrate, state armed actors used sexual violence as a common form of punishment, often alongside other forms of physical and psychological torture. In this context sexual violence can so thoroughly dehumanize and terrorize victims that they (and those to whom they serve as witness of the state's power and brutality) withdraw from political and social life.

In one case GN agents in uniform and civilian clothes broke into Alejandro's house in Santa Ana and detained him, accusing him of being a commander of the People's Liberation Forces (FPL, another guerrilla group within the FMLN) and committing crimes of treason against the state. They took him to the central base of the GN in San Salvador. The next morning they began to interrogate him. They said he was in charge of distributing weapons to the various fronts in the war. He denied their accusations. They stripped him, tied a bucket of water around his penis, and beat him all over his body. They blindfolded him and tied his hands behind his back, submerging his head in water and demanding that he confess to his crimes. One of them said, "Don't bother with this motherfucker, we already know everything we need to know. We have been following you for 5 years" (CDHES 1986:102). The next day the torture and questioning resumed. They shocked him with 320 volts of electricity on his tongue and ears and he passed out. After reviving him, they shocked him again, this time on his penis and anus.

In his testimony, Alejandro stated that unlike others in the community who were also detained, but who were targeted collectively because they lived in La Palma, he was singled out for the worst forms of torture because the authorities suspected him of being a guerrilla commander. As his testimony reflects, Alejandro was sexually victimized during police interrogation. However, he insists the attack was designed not to elicit information but to destroy him. According to his testimony, this method of torture was effective: after only two days of detention and torture at the GN base, he began to lose track of time; he began to lose his mind and would have said anything for them to stop the abuse (CDHES 1986:102–9).

The case of Leonardo in Peru reflects a similar pattern of dehumanization and punishment of political opponents. Leonardo was at a meeting of the leftist political party United Left (IU) on October 16, 1988, when he was arrested and accused of being a member of the Shining Path. "The government always said that all leftist organizations and political opposition groups were terrorist organizations, but that wasn't so. In fact, a lot of members of these groups also had problems with the Shining Path" (CVR n.d.: testimony100403). Leonardo was blindfolded and taken by plainclothes officers of the Peruvian Investigative Police (PIP, a branch of the National Police) to the local PIP station. While detained, he was subjected to severe psychological and physical torture. Officers threatened to capture his parents and treat them the same way if he did not cooperate with them. Colonel Castro and Captain Reyes oversaw the torture of Leonardo and actively participated in what they called "the butterfly"—where the prisoner is forced to stand with his hands tied behind his back, is submerged in water, and then is electrocuted on his tongue, armpits, and testicles. They threw freezing water on him and stuck pins underneath his fingernails (CVR n.d.: testimonies, 100403, 100471, 100472).

Despite significant differences in the domestic and international political environment, as well as the strength, tactics, and goals of the insurgency, the Salvadoran and Peruvian military and police engaged in a clear pattern of frequent sexual abuse against political opponents and detainees. These abuses ranged from forced nudity to rape and sexual torture. They were perpetrated against men and women, teachers and students, and others suspected of supporting the FMLN or SL. They were perpetrated during interrogation and/or torture sessions.

DISCUSSION: CONSIDERING STATE STRATEGY AND PERPETRATOR MOTIVES

What accounts for these patterns of sexual abuse in El Salvador and Peru? What motivates state armed actors to rape, torture, or otherwise sexually victimize prisoners in times of war? Is wartime sexual violence a strategic weapon of war?

Attempts to prove the "weapon of war" thesis face several challenges (see Agirre Aranburu 2012 for a full discussion). Among the most difficult is the absence of evidence of direct orders or a military policy to commit sexual violence. However, the lack of such evidence does not preclude the possibility of a state strategy. Requiring definitive proof of this kind sets an unachievable standard and unnecessarily privileges state impunity.

I argue that when there is a clear pattern of sexual violence occurring at times and places and in contexts that appear beneficial to the state's goals; when sexual abuse is targeted against particular subgroups of the population, perpetrated in state-controlled detention centers, often with the express knowledge or participation of high-ranking officers (as in the case of Leonardo, described above); *and* when these crimes go uninvestigated and unpunished, it is untenable to suggest that leaders had no knowledge of and did not benefit from the continued practice of sexual violence. According to the evidence presented, the sexual abuse of political prisoners in El Salvador and Peru was *either* explicitly ordered by the politico-military command *or* permitted under a doctrine of total warfare, wherein "anything goes" in the state's fight against "terrorism." In both scenarios, sexual violence can be seen as a strategic weapon of war, used to advance the state's interests and goals.

While the conclusions drawn from such work must be considered preliminary, attempts like this one to better document and examine the variable patterns of wartime sexual violence are essential to efforts to hold perpetrators (direct and indirect) accountable for their crimes and to prevent such crimes from occurring in the future.

DISCUSSION QUESTIONS

1. What accounts for these patterns of sexual abuse in El Salvador and Peru?
2. What motivates state armed actors to rape, torture, or otherwise sexually victimize prisoners in times of war?
3. Is wartime sexual violence a strategic weapon of war?

REFERENCES

Agger, I., and S. B. Jensen. 1986. The psychosexual trauma of torture. In *International Handbook of Traumatic Stress*, ed. J. P. Wilson and B. Raphael, 685–702. New York: Plenum Press.

Agirre Aranburu, X. (2012). Beyond dogma and taboo: criteria for the effective investigation of sexual violence. In *Understanding and Proving International Sex Crimes*, ed. M. Bergsmo, A. Butenschøn Skre, and E. J. Wood, 267–94. Beijing: Torkel Opsahl Academic EPublisher.

Allen, B. 1996. *Rape Warfare: The Hidden Genocide in Bosnia-Herzegovina and Croatia.* Minneapolis: University of Minnesota Press.

Bastick, M., K. Grimm, and R. Kunz. 2007. *Sexual Violence in Armed Conflict: Global Overview and Implications for the Security Sector.* Geneva: Geneva Centre for the Democratic Control of Armed Forces.

Bloom, M. 1999. War and the politics of rape: Ethnic versus non-ethnic conflicts. Unpublished manuscript.

Cohen, D. 2013. Explaining rape during civil war: Cross-national evidence, 1980–2009. *American Political Science Review* 107 (3): 461–77.

Cohen, D., A. Hoover Green, and E. Wood. 2013. *Wartime Sexual Violence: Misconceptions, Implications and Ways Forward.* USIP special report No. 323. Washington, D.C.: United States Institute for Peace.

Comisión de Derechos Humanos de El Salvador (CDHES). 1986. *La tortura actual.* San Salvador, El Salvador: CDHES.

Comisión para la Verdad y Reconciliación (CVR). 2004. *Hatun Willakuy: Version abreviada del informe final de la Comisión de la Verdad y Reconciliación.* Lima, Peru: Comisión de Entrega de la Comisión de la Verdad y Reconciliación.

——. n.d. *Collection of Individual Testimonies, No. 200012, 100409, 100471, 100472.* Lima, Peru: Centro de Información para la Memoria Colectiva y los Derechos Humanos.

Cunningham, D. E., K. S. Gleditsch, and I. Salehyan. 2009. *Non-State Actor Data: Case Description Notes.* http://privatewww.essex.ac.uk/~ksg/eacd.html.

Gutiérrez Sanín, F., and E. Wood. 2013. What should we mean by "pattern of political violence"? Repertoire, targeting, frequency, and technique. Unpublished manuscript.

Human Rights Watch (HRW). 2004a. *Enduring Freedom: Abuses by U.S. Forces in Afghanistan.* New York: HRW.

——. 2004b. *The Road to Abu Ghraib.* New York: HRW.

International Criminal Court (ICC). 2000. *Rome Statute of the International Criminal Court, pt. 2, art. 8(2) (e) (vi).* http://untreaty.un.org/cod/icc/index.html.

Kalyvas, S. 2006. *The Logic of Violence in Civil War.* Cambridge: Cambridge University Press.

Leiby, M. 2011. State-perpetrated wartime sexual violence in Latin America. Ph.D. dissertation, available from ProQuest Dissertations & Theses database (UMI No. 3473625).

——. 2012. The promise and peril of primary documents: Documenting wartime sexual violence in El Salvador and Peru. In *Understanding and Proving International Sex Crimes*, ed. M. Bergsmo, A. Skre Butenschøn, and E. J. Wood, 315–66. Beijing: Torkel Opsahl Academic EPublisher.

Leonning, C. D., and D. Priest, D. 2005. Detainees accuse female interrogators: Pentagon inquiry is said to confirm Muslims' accounts of sexual tactics at Guantanamo. *Washington Post*, February 10, A01.

Mullins, C. 2009. "We are going to rape you and taste Tutsi women": Rape during the 1994 Rwandan genocide. *British Journal of Criminology* 49 (6): 719–35.

Peceny, M., and W. D. Stanley. 2010. Counterinsurgency in El Salvador. *Politics and Society* 38 (1): 67–94.

Sharlach, L. 2000. Rape as genocide: Bangladesh, the former Yugoslavia and Rwanda. *New Political Science* 22 (1): 89–102.

Skjelsbaek, I. 2001. Sexual violence and war: mapping out a complex relationship. *European Journal of International Relations* 7 (2): 211–37.

Socorro Jurídico Cristiano (SJC). n.d. *Collection of Individual Testimonies: No. 26.7.3.* Boulder: University of Colorado, Archives Department.

Tutela Legal (TL). n.d. *Collection of Individual Testimonies: No. 10.1.13.* Boulder: University of Colorado, Archives Department.

Valentino, B. 2004. *Final Solutions: Mass Killing and Genocide in the 20th Century.* Ithaca, N.Y.: Cornell University Press.

Wood, E. 2006. Variation in wartime sexual violence. *Politics and Society* 34 (3): 307–41.

——. 2009. Armed groups and sexual violence: When is wartime rape rare? *Politics and Society* 37 (1): 131–62.

CHAPTER 9

Conflict and Postconflict Sexual Violence in Africa

CASE STUDIES OF LIBERIA, NORTHERN UGANDA, AND EASTERN DEMOCRATIC REPUBLIC OF CONGO

▸ HELEN LIEBLING

THE CONSEQUENCES OF CONFLICT AND postconflict sexual violence have often been misunderstood. Typically research has conceptualized the effects in terms of an individual manifestation of psychological trauma and physical injuries. The corresponding responses have therefore often been confined to a medical model. This chapter, based on research carried out with survivors of conflict and postconflict sexual violence in Liberia, former child abductees in northern Uganda, and women and girls bearing children from rape in eastern Democratic Republic of Congo (DRC), argues for an alternative understanding and response. First, it views conflict and postconflict sexual violence as gendered; that is, women, men, and children all endure these experiences, and their responses are different. Second, it argues that beyond the individual's trauma, the impact of conflict and postconflict sexual violence affects whole communities and identities. Third, it recognizes a strong desire for justice and social support among survivors whose fulfillment is vital to their recovery. Finally, it recognizes high levels of resilience among survivors. In light of these perspectives, the chapter argue that for conflict and postconflict responses to be effective, they must go beyond a purely individualistic and medical conceptualization of needs and be holistic in nature. This includes being gendered and culturally sensitive, addressing justice and social support as well as health needs, and building on the resilience of sexual violence survivors and their communities.

LIBERIA

In 2008 a study was carried out by Isis-Women's International Cross-Cultural Exchange (Isis-WICCE), an international women's nongovernmental organization based in Kampala, in collaboration with the Women in Peace Building Network, West African Network for Peace Building, and the Ministry of Gender and Development in Liberia and focused on women survivors of the 1989–2003 conflict (Isis-WICCE 2008; Kinyanda et al. 2010; Liebling-Kalifani & Baker 2010b). The study found that women and girls used their bodies for "safe passage" at checkpoints. Rape accounted for 73.9 percent of sexual violence; women survived attempted rape (17 percent), sexual comforting, and defilement (38 percent) sex in exchange for food (28 percent), forced incest (5 percent), abduction with forced sex (8 percent), and insertion of objects into the vagina (20 percent). As many as 62.5 percent of women and girls experienced sexual torture; this included sexual abuse, gang rape (14 percent), opening of the stomachs of pregnant women, genital mutilation, early forced marriages, and pregnancies. A woman interviewee from Maryland County said, "Four soldiers raped me . . . they threatened me that if I refuse, they will kill men with my children. I accepted because I wanted to save my children and I knew they were serious . . . other women were raped, mutilated and then killed . . . for me, to survive together with my children" (Isis-WICCE 2008:120).

The research found evidence of extensive physical, psychological, and sexual torture inflicted on both women and men during the conflict. Further it was found that violence was gendered. Significantly more men survived physical torture, whereas significantly more women and girls survived psychological and sexual torture and sexual violence. However, it is important to note that the issue of sexual violence being perpetrated against men during conflict and postconflict settings is an underresearched area (Henttonen, et al. 2008; Liebling & Baker 2010). Johnson et al. (2008) found higher levels of sexual violence in Liberia among former combatants—42.3 percent in women and 32.6 percent in men. Lawry (2009) also found that 42 percent of women combatants and 32 percent of male combatants in Liberia were survivors of sexual violence. Studies have reported that owing to the stigma and shame of experiences and the resulting underreporting, the actual figures are likely much higher (Governance and Social Development Resource Centre 2009; Liebling-Kalifani 2010).

As a result of sexual violence and torture during the conflict, women and girls suffered severe reproductive and psychological health problems, as well as surgical complications. Those who had objects forcibly and fully inserted in their vagina frequently acquired traumatic vesicle or rectal-vaginal fistulae. Isis-WICCE (2008) revealed that women and girls were infected with sexually transmitted diseases, including HIV/AIDS, and left with serious and urgent reproductive health problems. Although 68.5 percent of women had at least one gynecological complaint, 50 percent had no access to health care. Younger women up to the age of 24 were more likely to get a gynecological problem due to their increased vulnerability. Common problems reported included abnormal vaginal bleeding (9.5 percent), abnormal vaginal discharge (31.8 percent), infertility (22.1 percent), incontinence of urine (21.6 percent), and chronic abdominal pain (37.1 percent). Other complications included incontinence of feces due to fistulae, sexually transmitted diseases, perineal tears, genital sores, sexual dysfunction, and unwanted pregnancies.

Further, because of their experiences, women survivors were discriminated against, marginalized, and sexually assaulted after the conflict had ceased. Many were widowed and became heads of households and were found to be more vulnerable in terms of poverty, human insecurity, and sexual abuse.

Women's experiences of sexual violence during the conflict also affected their psychological health. Isis-WICCE (2008) found that a considerable proportion of the population in Liberia suffered war-related torture/trauma: 27 percent lost a spouse, 62.5 percent of the women had personal experience of sexual torture, at least two-thirds of respondents experienced physical torture, and 80 percent suffered at least one form of psychological torture during the conflict. Approximately 69 percent of respondents reported that psychological symptoms affected their ability to work; 42.8 percent had psychological distress scores suggestive of a mental disorder, 12 percent had alcoholism, which was twice as high as in men, 14.5 percent had attempted suicide, and 17.9 percent had experienced homicidal thoughts. The same study found that significantly more men than women used addictive substances to try to cope with their experiences, including cigarettes (15.1 percent), alcohol (29.2 percent), marijuana/opium (10.1 percent), cocaine (9.6 percent), and sniffing petrol or solvents (10.7 percent). Sexual violence and torture of women and girls and the associated stigma and shame exacerbated the psychological impact. The psychological consequences of sexual violence and torture were severe, and the stigma experienced increased the silence, as a male counselor interviewed in Monrovia described: "One of the women I have been counseling was raped by 7 to 10 soldiers every night for two weeks. . . . She now feels useless and wanted to commit suicide. She could not tell her husband and the children" (Isis-WICCE 2008:119).

In terms of justice, a culture of partial justice and impunity for the powerful was long marked by the prewar system and had been one of the primary catalysts for the civil war. According to one survey (Liberian CJS Report 2002), 56 percent of those who had been arrested and forwarded to court believe that the court had not been fair to them, citing reasons such as partiality of judges (41 percent), interference by government officials (24 percent), no opportunity for legal representation (18 percent), and jury manipulation (6 percent). Thus 59 percent of these respondents were not satisfied with the outcome of the cases. Overall 61 percent of respondents said they had little or no confidence in the courts to render justice, as Smidt (2004) states: "The rebels and fighters killed and raped, but who has come to our aid? They just go free. I saw him, the boy that killed my child. I know who he is and I will never forget him. He had small earrings in his right ear. And nothing happens to him. We are still living with the same people, we see them every day. They see us. There is no justice in Liberia."

Despite the end of the conflict, rates of sexual violence in Liberia remain high. The government action plan of 2006 to prevent and respond to sexual violence against women called for a strengthening of the justice system, but implementation takes time. Significant changes were made to legislation, which expanded the definition of rape so that now any form of sexual penetration is considered rape under Liberian law. The age of consent has also been raised to 18 years. The new laws have established harsher punishment for perpetrators and abolished bail for rape cases. Despite these steps, the judicial system has yet to adopt these changes, so the new laws have made little difference. Perpetrators are still rarely convicted, and rape still tends to be dealt with privately. Most victims never press charges. According to the Association of Female Lawyers of Liberia, there is a conspiracy of silence and denial within the community and families involved. The judicial system is an ongoing source of frustration. A Médecins Sans Frontières/Doctors without Borders (MSF) report in

2009 noted that health workers acknowledge that impunity may affect the way a rape survivor deals with trauma after a sexual attack. "If they know the perpetrator and justice is not done, they feel afraid and powerless," said a MSF psychologist. "Justice is also a way of telling the victims that it is not their fault" (MSF 2009:30). As most rapes are committed by people known by the survivor, impunity also means that survivors may be at risk of repeated attacks.

During the war women were subjected to distinct abuse for reasons linked specifically to their gender. Rebel fighters often raped women and killed men on a systematic basis. More women and girls have survived than were killed, yet with tremendous wounds to their bodies and minds and assaults on their dignity, their feelings of self-worth, and their future. In contrast, there seem to be no consequences for the perpetrators (Smidt 2004).

NORTHERN UGANDA

"We all accept that sexual violence during the time we were in captivity was the most common phenomenon. Normally in captivity the person who abducts you is the one who you are forced to accept as your husband until the person is dead. That is what we experienced as young girls in captivity and this made many of us produce young children during these experiences" (Liebling & Baker 2010:7, quoting a woman during a focus group held in Orom).

British Academy–funded research examined the governance of sexual violence in a district that suffered serious abuses during the twenty-three-year Lord's Resistance Army rebellion, and which has ongoing high levels of local perpetrator sexual violence (Liebling 2012a; Liebling & Baker 2010; Liebling-Kalifani & Baker 2010a). In total fifty-one men and forty-seven women abductees were interviewed in groups and individually in four parishes in Orom subcounty, Kitgum, northern Uganda; as well as six women survivors in Kitgum Town. Each interviewee was asked about his or her experience of sexual violence and of justice and health provision. Also eighty-five semistructured interviews were carried out with police and health officials and nonstate providers that examined their training, facilities, use of women officials, and success in bringing sexual violence cases to a conclusion.

The research found that the poorly resourced state health system struggled to respond to the severe and widespread health needs of survivors of sexual violence. This was due to the following:

- *Low levels of access to health care:* Survivors reported experiencing fear, stigma, and shame and were reluctant to report assaults. They lacked trust in services to provide confidentiality and support, found health staff absent from clinics, or, when referred to Kitgum District Hospital, were unable to afford transport and treatment.
- *Poor health facilities:* For those few participants who did manage to access health care, it usually comprised basic treatment with post-exposure prophylaxis, as a preventative for HIV infection, and/or Panadol for pain. There are no medical doctors at Orom clinic, while the district hospital has only one medical superintendent. There are no specialist doctors such as gynecologists or surgeons, and few victims received any psychological support.
- *Lack of support and training for staff:* Staff had themselves experienced sexual violence during and since the insurgency. They faced lack of support, staff shortages, low salaries, and poor working conditions and required trauma counseling services to be provided for their own experiences.

With respect to justice provision, survivors, criminal justice professionals and key informants suggested that the criminal justice system failed to provide justice for the survivors of sexual violence in Kitgum because of the following:

- *Low level of reporting:* A culture of responding to sexual violence through local negotiation between families (of both accused and survivor) undermines the law's deterrent effect. Though the law regards aggravated rape as a capital offense and less serious cases as liable to life imprisonment, offenders know that most cases will be settled locally. Should a case enter the criminal justice system, bribes ensue (to the police, police doctor, magistrate, etc.) to ensure that the case falters. This bypassing of the criminal justice system is further aggravated by the survivor's own shame and fear (e.g., of the husband divorcing his wife); the distance and expense of getting to the police, police doctor, and court; and a lack of trust in the police.

- *Understaffed, undertrained, and underresourced police:* Even if cases are reported, there are very few police and even fewer women police officers to respond to survivors. The police are short of transport and unable to take survivors and the accused to the central police station, police doctor, and court. Hence cases collapse owing to the failure to obtain a doctor's report within the crucial forty-eight hours post-rape or because witnesses and survivors fail to appear in court. There is limited space for interviewing survivors in police stations, and officers have received little training in handling cases of sexual violence and are therefore poor at gathering evidence of crimes of sexual violence.

- *Failure of court cases and the court system:* Of those cases reported to the police, few end up with successful prosecution. Some fail as the case is prolonged and survivors give up; others are dropped because of bribery of officials. Even those that make it to court often fail, as files are lost, witnesses fail to appear, and evidence offered by the police is inadequate. The courts suffer from understaffing, and normally there is only one senior magistrate to hear "simple" cases of rape.

EASTERN DEMOCRATIC REPUBLIC OF CONGO

"I am a woman with a bad reputation. I am a women without value, they look down on me, are disgusted with me. How can I get rid of this bad reputation?" (Liebling & Slegh 2012:3, quoting Marianne, an 18-year-old survivor interviewed in Goma).

British Academy–funded research carried out in August 2011 examined women's and girls' experiences of bearing children from rape and the health and justice service responses for survivors in Goma, eastern DRC. The researchers listened to over 110 people in individual interviews and focus groups carried out in Goma town and Bweremana, a rural area (Liebling & Slegh 2012; Liebling, Slegh, & Ruratotoye 2012).

Women and girls experienced various forms of sexual violence, including gang rape and rape. Of those interviewed individually, approximately 81 percent were younger than 18 when they were raped. They were raped in a variety of locations (e.g., in a forest, on the family farm, going to the market, traveling to or from work, at home, at an internally displaced persons camp, going to or from school). Women were also forced to witness violence and torture. Some survivors were abducted and others raped by a perpetrator who had a military weapon, although the majority of girls interviewed reported being raped by civilians. Many were raped by men who could not be identified. Though most adult women reported rapes by armed groups or soldiers, the research concluded that although sexual violence increased dramatically during the war, it has now "contaminated" communities and homes, particularly for girls less than 18.

Families, relatives, and communities, including other children, mocked the children born from rape. As other studies have found, they were stigmatized along with their mothers, considered outcasts, harassed, beaten and rejected (Ward & Marsh 2006; Women for Women International 2010). Survivors had conflicting emotions toward their children, viewing them as potentially helpful for society but also as a constant reminder of the traumatic rape and social rejection they continued to suffer. Survivors described their children as depressed, not at peace, angry, and outcasts, who were unable to attend schools and therefore lacked skills and employment and were greatly at risk of becoming street children. Women and girls reported extreme poverty leading to an inability to continue with school and to work, resulting in a lack of means to earn a living or to pay education fees. There were strong feelings that unless survivors and their children were accepted, cared for, and assisted, this would lead to serious problems in eastern DRC.

Survivors reported a serious impact on their reproductive health as a result of rape, including vesicovaginal fistula, sexually transmitted diseases, abnormal bleeding, pains, cysts, HIV infection, AIDS, and disabilities. It is dangerous for young girls to deliver a child when their bodies are not yet mature, and this can result in rupture of the uterus and death of the child. Additional health risks were associated with illegal abortions and malnutrition as an indirect consequence of being unable to eat and therefore being unable to breastfeed their babies.

Women and girls described emotional effects, which had a negative impact on their sense of self. Owing to a lack of trust in others, particularly men, survivors mainly kept their experiences to themselves. They reported psychological effects normally associated with traumatic experiences, including depression, suicidal behaviors, anger, flashbacks, anxiety, disturbed sleep, withdrawal and avoidance, sexual concerns, and identity problems. The consequences for teenage girls included a premature separation from childhood as they became overloaded with responsibilities.

The relationship survivors have with their child is extremely complex, and they described feelings of "love and hate," which intensified their and their child's psychological distress.

The poorly resourced health system struggled to respond to the serious health needs of rape survivors and their children. The vast majority of survivors failed to access urgent health care within the required seventy-two- and forty-eight-hour time frame, including emergency contraception and postexposure prophylaxis, as a preventative for HIV infection. For those few who did seek treatment, it was sometime later or during delivery, and they reported a lack of adequate treatment. Any free treatment stopped after delivery, when women needed it most. Survivors experienced fear and shame and were reluctant to report assaults as they lacked trust in services to provide confidentiality and support. Also they were unable to access treatment, particularly in rural areas, because of poverty, lack of transport, and long distances to services. There were few hospitals to treat rape mutilations and fistula for women who could prove rape; and as abortion is illegal, this led to unsafe and restricted choices for women and young girls. Although some survivors received valuable counseling in listening houses, there was a lack of skilled, coordinated, and culturally sensitive responses for their serious mental health needs and also for those of their children. Health staff and counselors described a severe lack of salaries, poor working conditions, and a lack of support and training to support survivors and their children. Many counselors had experienced rape themselves and were overburdened. They had no protection for the risks that their role entailed or support structures in place for dealing with stress and therefore were at a great risk of burn-out.

In the context of impunity as well as the stigma experienced, the majority of survivors saw little to be gained from reporting rapes, particularly adult women, who preferred to remain silent. Young women frequently did not perceive that a crime had been committed, and there was ignorance and confusion about the justice procedure. A culture of sexual exploitation, including frequent rape of young girls, has become "normalized." There is social pressure from family and communities on survivors to remain silent, although in some cases family members report on behalf of their daughters. The challenges survivors face include stigmatization, social rejection, and fear of the impact of reporting. Poverty and lack of funds to pay for bribes during the legal process limited the success of reporting. In some instances families came to an agreement whereby the perpetrator pays a fine to the survivor's family. However, recent changes in the law deemed it illegal to resolve rape cases through traditional community practices, and survivors are encouraged to report through the state. However, when survivors report rape, neither the state nor the community response results in a positive outcome, and the perpetrator is rarely punished.

The police, prisons, and judicial systems suffer badly from a lack of funding and struggle with overwhelming logistical problems. Even if cases are reported, there are few skilled police and a lack of women officers to respond to survivors. For the minority of cases that reached judgment, the government or perpetrator provided no compensation or reparation. The lack of trust in the process is one of the most important factors making survivors reluctant to report cases. Survivors experience the process as traumatizing, increasing their shame, and carrying personal risk for themselves and professionals involved, including attacks, death threats, and intimidation.

CONCLUSION

Research carried out in Liberia, northern Uganda, and eastern Congo reveals that sexual violence perpetrated in conflict and postconflict settings causes devastating effects on individual survivors as well as whole communities. Sexual violence results in extensive damage to survivors' psychological, reproductive, and gynecological health. Survivors' shame and stigma is exacerbated by the severe social rejection of communities, particularly for women and girls who become pregnant from rape, former abductees, and those with HIV infection. Many resultant health problems are not treatable by the grossly overstretched and underresourced health-care systems. Further, it is argued that sexual violence is not solely a war crime. Although it is extremely prevalent during conflict, it has contaminated the domestic sphere with high levels of sexual inequalities and domestic and sexual violence evident in postconflict settings.

Despite recent awareness by criminal justice systems of the importance of tackling sexual violence, the needs of conflict and postconflict survivors worldwide are poorly understood, and services offered to them are rarely viewed and practiced in a gendered or holistic manner (Jewkes 2007).

Sexual violence was experienced simultaneously as a violation of the survivor's body and rights. It left the survivor in need of both a health and a justice response. As the two are connected in the experience of the survivor, they go hand in hand in terms of service responses required. Therefore there is real value in promoting increased collaboration between health and justice services (Liebling & Baker 2010:52).

Services tend to be time limited and based on a "medicalization of distress" rather than a considered understanding and approach based on survivor's own views, experiences, and needs as well as their strengths and resilience (Almedom & Glandon 2007; Liebling-Kalifani 2010; Liebling-Kalifani & Baker 2010a). Although research indicates that survivors have psychological effects that can be partly understood within what has been termed a "complex post-traumatic stress disorder" model (Herman 1992), it is argued that their trauma is a "normal" not "pathological" response and requires recognition as "normal" by others (Liebling-Kalifani 2010; Liebling-Kalifani & Baker 2010b; Summerfield 1997; Tal 1996). It is recommended that the effects of conflict and postconflict sexual violence be understood as gendered; that is, although women, men and children endure these experiences, their responses are different. Women survivors reconstruct their identities by taking on male roles, becoming heads of households, peace building, and engaging in collective and political activities. Women's ability to voice their experiences and form groups as a political act of resistance results in a shared identity and a decrease in the trauma experienced. In contrast, men largely turn their trauma inward, using strategies such as alcohol and drug use in an attempt to "manage" their distress (Isis-WICCE 2008; Liebling-Kalifani & Baker 2010a). The gendered differences in the nature of the effects of conflict and postconflict sexual violence have been reported in other parts of the world (McDevitt 2009), and service responses need to be sensitive to gender differences in their design and delivery.

Research demonstrates that beyond the individual survivor's trauma, conflict and postconflict sexual violence affects whole communities and identities. The effects can be understood as a collective/communal destruction of cultural identity, not an individualistic manifestation of psychological symptoms. The types of sexual violence and atrocities carried out caused destruction of cultural norms and respectability codes important within African communities. This can be conceptualized as a breakdown of cultural identity, manifested in physical, psychological, and social effects that are integrated and inseparable, not split between mind/body and society (Liebling-Kalifani 2010).

What emerges from the research is a strong desire for justice among survivors. Despite the gross level of human rights abuses and torture of women, men, and children during conflict and postconflict periods, there has been a failure to address the injustices and provide even adequate social support. Justice for survivors of sexual violence still looks a long way off, and yet its fulfillment is vital to their recovery (Liebling 2012b; Liebling-Kalifani & Baker 2010a; Ullman 1999).

Despite the suffering endured, survivors are not merely passive victims. On the contrary, women in particular have been active campaigners for peace and reconciliation. Feminist analysis of women's roles by Anthias and Yuval-Davis (1989), Lovell (2003), Liebling-Kalifani (2010), and Liebling-Kalifani & Baker (2010a), for example, enables us to view women's contributions during and postconflict as active agents. It is therefore argued that despite the devastating effects of sexual violence, it is evident that survivors demonstrate resilience (Almedom & Glandon 2007), resistance, and power during the conflict and after it ends.

The question of who delivers health and justice services for sexual violence survivors and how, from a development point of view, is about the quality, equity, and efficacy of the health-service provision and policing received by the population. It requires an in-depth and gendered analysis of the postconflict state and its political context, capabilities, functions, and cultural legacies. Further, it requires health and justice service provision that conceptualizes conflict and postconflict sexual violence as gendered and incorporates a holistic and resilience framework for understanding and addressing survivor's needs. The most appropriate developmental approach to the delivery of health and justice services in these contexts is one that recognizes the differing nature of states and the presence of multiple providers whose services are layered to meet differing contingencies.

A multilayered approach that uses nonstate agencies appears to be the only solution when the state is deemed unable to provide services in the medium term, even with donor aid. Of course practical difficulties arise concerning the African state's capacity to undertake a steering function of ensuring the quality, efficacy, and accountability of all health and justice services. It may also require local partnerships, which include nongovernmental and community-based organizations that utilize the expertise of survivors, to prove that hybrid and multilayered governance can provide effective, sustainable, and locally accountable health and justice before states will think in terms of radical changes to their national strategies.

DISCUSSION QUESTIONS

1. Discuss the similarities and differences between each nation based on the type of sexualized violence and responses to it. What can we learn from this comparison?
2. The author concludes by suggesting a multilayered approach that uses non-state agencies. Discuss what an approach such as this would look like.

REFERENCES

Almedom, A. M., and D. Glandon. 2007. Resilience is not the absence of PTSD any more than health is the absence of disease. *Journal of Loss and Trauma: International Perspectives on Stress & Coping* 12 (2): 127–43.

Andermahr, S., T. Lovell, and C. Wolkowitz. 1997. *A Concise Glossary of Feminist Theory*. London: Hodder Arnold.

Anthias, F., and N. Yuval-Davis. 1989. Introduction. In *Woman-Nation-State*, ed. N. Yuval-Davis and F. Anthias. Cambridge: Macmillan.

Governance and Social Development Resource Centre. 2009. *Conflict and Sexual Violence and Domestic Violence Against Women*. Birmingham, UK. http://www.gsdrc.org/docs/open/HD589.pdf.

Herman, J. L. 1992. *Trauma and Recovery: The Aftermath of Violence: From Domestic Abuse to Political Terror*. New York: Basic Books.

Henttonen, M., C. Watts, B. Roberts, F. Kaducu, and M. Borchert. 2008. Health services for survivors of gender-based violence in northern Uganda: A qualitative study. *Reproductive Health Matters* 16 (31): 122–31.

Isis-WICCE. 2008. *A Situation Analysis of the Women Survivors of the 1989–2003 Armed Conflict in Liberia: An Isis-WICCE Research Report*, in collaboration with Ministry of Gender and Development, Liberia and WANEP/WIPNET, Liberia. Kampala, Uganda: Isis-WICCE.

——. 2009. *Management of Medical and Psychological Effects of War Trauma: Training Manual for Operational Health Workers: Liberia Version*. Unpublished and adapted training manual.

Jewkes, R. 2007. Comprehensive response to rape needed in conflict settings. *Lancet* 369 (9580): 2140–41.

Johnson, K., J. Asher, S. Rosborough, A. Raja, R. Panjabi, C. Beadling, and L. Lawry. 2008. Association of combatant status and sexual violence with health and mental health outcomes in post conflict Liberia. *Journal of the American Medical Association* 300 (6): 676–90.

Kinyanda, E., V. Nakiboneka, R. Ojiambo-Ochieng, J. Were-Oguttu, V. Gayflor, H. Liebling-Kalifani, and I. Diawara-Howard. 2010. Prevalence and correlates of psychological distress as seen in post-conflict Liberia. *African Journal of Traumatic Stress* 1 (2): 96–102.

Lawry, L. 2009 *Association of Combatant Status and Sexual Violence with Health and Mental Health Outcomes in Post-Conflict Liberia*. http://www.jama.com.

Liberian Criminal Justice Report. 2002. *Report on Survey of the Public's Perception of the Operations and Effectiveness of Criminal Justice Institutions in Liberia*. Monrovia.

Liebling, H. 2012a. The Hidden Consequences of Rape and Sexual Violence. *UNA-UK New World*, Autumn and Winter special edition.

——. 2012b. Experiences of a young girl abducted by the Lord's Resistance Army, Northern Uganda. *Psychology of Women Section Review* 14 (1): 44–48. British Psychological Society, Leicester.

Liebling, H., and B. Baker. 2010. *Justice and Health Provision for Survivors of Sexual Violence: A Case Study of Kitgum, Northern Uganda*. Saarbrücken, Germany: LAP Lambert Academic Publishing.

Liebling, H., and H. Slegh. 2012. *Thematic Article on Women and Girls Bearing Children from Rape for the Post-2015 Global Development Areas for UNICEF and UN Women*. New York: Women's Refugee Committee.

Liebling, H., H. Slegh, and B. Ruratotoye. 2012. Women and girls bearing children through rape in Goma, Eastern Congo: Stigma, health and justice responses. *Itupale Online Journal of African Studies* 4:18–44.

Liebling-Kalifani, H. 2010. Research and intervention with women war survivors in Uganda: Resilience and suffering as the consequences of war. In *War, Medicine and Gender: The Sociology and Anthropology of Structural Suffering*, ed. H. Bradby and G. Lewando-Hundt. Surrey, UK: Ashgate Books.

Liebling-Kalifani, H., and B. Baker. 2010a. Justice and health provision for survivors of sexual violence in Kitgum, northern Uganda. African Journal of Traumatic Stress, 1, 1, 22–31.

———. 2010b. Women war survivors of sexual violence in Liberia: Inequalities in health, resilience and justice. *Journal of International Social Research*, Woman Studies Special Issue, 3 (13): 188–99.

Lovell, T. 2003. Resisting with authority: Historical specificity, agency and the performative self. *Theory, Culture & Society* 20 (1): 1–17.

McDevitt, A. 2009. *The Impact of Conflict on Women's Education, Employment and Health Care*. Birmingham, UK: Governance and Social Development Resource Centre.

Médecins sans Frontières. 2009. *Shattered Lives: Immediate Medical Care Vital for Sexual Violence Victims*. Brussels: Médecins sans Frontières.

Smidt, H. 2004. *Liberia: Women Still Suffer and Wait for Justice*. World Council of Churches. http://www.oikoumene.org/en/news/newsmanagement/eng /a/browse/4/article/1722/liberia-womenstillsuff.html?tx_ttnews%5Bcat% 5D=84%2C35&cHash=1a758b00c6http://www.oikoumene.org/en/news /newsmanagement/eng/a/browse/4/article/1722/liberia-womenstillsuff .html?tx_ttnews%5Bcat%5D=84%2C35&cHash=1a758b00c6.

Summerfield, D. 1997. Trauma is a dangerous label for a normal reaction: Challenging Western wisdom. *Recovery* 1 (January/February): 9–10.

Tal, K. 1996. *Worlds of Hurt: Reading the Literatures of Trauma*. Cambridge: Cambridge University Press.

Ullman, S. E. 1999. Social support and recovery from sexual assault: A review. *Aggression and Violent Behavior* 4 (3): 343–58.

UNIFEM. 2000. *Progress of Worlds Women 2000*. http://www.unifem.undp.org /progressww/2000/ 10/01/03

———. 2004. *Rebuilding of Liberia Must Involve Full Participation of Women*. Reporting on conference presentation by Noeleen Heyzer, executive director of UN Development Fund for Women. http://www.unifem.org/news_events /story_detail.php?StoryID=128http://www.unifem.org/news_events/story _detail.php?StoryID=128.

Ward, J., and M. Marsh. 2006. Sexual violence against women and girls in war and its aftermath: realities, responses and required resources. Briefing Paper. Brussels.

Women for Women International. 2010. Briefing on women's status in DRC: July 2010. *The Democratic Republic of Congo Survey: Stronger Women: Stronger Nations*. London: Women for Women International.

CHAPTER 10

Donor Dollars and Ministerial Mindsets

CONSTRAINTS ON NGO RESPONSES TO RAPE IN CAMBODIA

▸ *CATHERINE BURNS AND KATHLEEN DALY*

IN MARCH 2013 THE ORGANIZATION UN Women declared "an historic global agreement [had been] reached . . . to prevent and end violence against women and girls" (UN Women 2013). Its "global blueprint" is said to provide a "roadmap" for redress by framing violence against women as a human rights violation that requires a rule of law response. In much of the Western world, these ideas dominate the international community's response to sexual violence in fragile and postconflict countries: funds should be directed to "rule of law" and "best practice" reforms. Although framing violence against women as a human rights violation has gathered momentum, rule-of-law responses to violence have also been challenged.

In the past decade we saw a shift in thinking by the scholarly community and donor bodies away from conventional criminal justice responses and toward customary dispute resolution mechanisms, at least for some offenses (Chirayath, Sage, & Woolcock 2005; Samuels 2006; World Bank 2012). This shift does not include responses to rape, which is considered too serious for informal justice (Harper 2011; Wojkowska 2006). We examine how this dynamic is unfolding in Cambodia in the responses by international and local nongovernmental organizations (NGOs) to everyday rape. (By everyday rape, we mean rape not occurring as part of war or conflict, although many recognize a continuum between every-day and extraordinary violence against women [Arthur 2010:10]). The criminal justice system in Cambodia is dysfunctional and beyond the reach of most citizens, but international and local NGO staff promote it as the optimal response. Why do NGOs hold steadfastly to this position when most Cambodians prefer customary justice practices, even for rape? What constraints, limitations, and opportunities are operating on NGOs in the local environment that emphasize criminal justice and discourage informal justice? Drawing on interviews with NGO staff, we address these questions and their implications for rape survivors' access to justice.

Our analysis draws from Weinstein and colleagues (2009:28), who consider dilemmas in responding to "atrocity crime" in Iraq, Cambodia, and Uganda. It is well-known that trials in transitional justice contexts are limited, both as a deterrent and in building peace, although they are preferred by the international community. In Uganda, for example, Weinstein et al. suggest that both the government and many people wanted to see peace negotiations and amnesties rather than trials. The authors ask, "Do we abandon victims if we argue for a response that addresses the greater good of a community?" (32). They raise questions about the "beneficiaries [and] priorities [of international criminal law], and the reactionary, if not parochial nature of the human rights field" (28). Although our focus is on everyday violence, similar questions are raised about the role and priorities of the international community and the impact of human rights on framing response to violence against women. Added to this mix is government and NGO dependence on international donors.

CAMBODIA IN CONTEXT

Cambodia is one of the poorest countries in the world: 80 percent of people live in rural areas, and about one-third live below Cambodia's poverty line (Asian Development Bank 2012:4–5). Its legal system, developed under the Kingdom of Cambodia from 1993, loosely mirrors Cambodia's history, in its combination of French-based civil law, elements of common law, and informal justice. The latter include village- and commune-level customary dispute resolution mechanisms (*somroh somruel*) that draw from precolonial Buddhist and Khmer legal traditions. These informal justice mechanisms aim to improve poor people's access to justice and the efficiency of the courts by alleviating the backlog of cases. They also address the critical shortage of legal professionals resulting from the complete destruction of the legal system and an educated class under the Khmer Rouge in 1975–1979.

Although there has been significant funding and reform of the judicial system, the challenges are so great that most donors have disengaged

(Popovic 2009:17). The United Nations Development Programme (UNDP) faced difficulties working with the Ministry of Justice in implementing its Access to Justice program and withdrew in 2010 partly as a result (Popovic 2009:7). An early project, the Judicial Mentor program, failed to increase average salaries of judicial officers beyond US$20 per month or to provide basic legal infrastructure (Olivella 2003:4). Despite the injection of almost $3 million, the UNDP evaluation of its Access to Justice in Cambodia program reported that "none of the project outputs to improve government responses on the supply side of justice were achieved, [and] . . . the quality of judicial decisions was . . . too poor to serve as a reference in the future" (UNDP 2007:1).

CRIMINAL JUSTICE AND SOMROH SOMRUEL

For rape victims, engaging the criminal process is expensive and time consuming. All costs of the investigation and of collecting and processing evidence are borne by the complainant: fuel for a police vehicle (if available), food, medical examinations, transporting witnesses to court, payments to process documents, payments to schedule hearings, and so forth. Accessing the courts may require one to two days of travel from rural areas, and a public trial amplifies the shame experienced by rape victims and reduces their future marriage prospects. Legal aid is scarce, particularly in remote areas, and defendants who have the financial means will likely be freed before or during trial. Judicial officers lack gender sensitivity and have a poor understanding of the law (O'Connell 2001). For these reasons, most criminal cases, including those of gender-based violence, are addressed by a local customary dispute mechanism called somroh somruel (Yrigoyen Fajardo, Kong, & Phan 2005).

Somroh somruel is generally affordable, accessible, familiar, swifter, and more likely to result in a financial payment, which is negotiated rather than imposed by outsiders. Either party may ask the village head or commune chief to resolve a conflict and convene meetings in his home (almost all are male) until agreement reached. Discussion centers on the amount of money to be paid and a promise not to offend again. If a solution cannot be reached, the matter may proceed to the police. Attributions of guilt and blame tend to be avoided because the fundamental goal is restoration of social harmony. The same process is used in rape because most offenders are known to the victim and live nearby (EcpatCambodia 2012).

Somroh somruel is the preferred dispute resolution mechanism, but it is not a panacea. Cambodian NGO staff almost invariably note that resolution, particularly if the rape resulted in a pregnancy, may include marriage between victim and offender, and that police are able to generate income in the form of bribes from both parties. Some also note that it is families, not victims, at the center of negotiations. In addition, human rights advocates and development practitioners identify a lack of accountability, transparency, and predictability in the decision-making process; they view it as noncompliant with international human rights standards. Women's rights advocates emphasize the patriarchal structures of traditional cultures, limited participation of women in decision making, and gendered and wealth power differentials that make a fair resolution difficult. Others argue that informal justice is fundamentally inequitable, offering substandard justice for the poor (Ramage et al. 2008; Swaine 2003; Wojkowska 2006). However, because there is donor and government interest in improving access to justice for the poor and vulnerable, conditional formal support exists for somroh somruel. In 2005 it was legislated as an appropriate response for domestic violence, which is classified a "minor misdemeanor or petty crime," in contradistinction to "severe" cases of rape in marriage.

FOREIGN AID

The foreign-aid environment was created by the temporary governance of Cambodia under the United Nations Transition Authority Cambodia (UNTAC) during 1992–1993. To rebuild the country, large amounts of aid flowed in: more than US$3 billion during 1992–1995 (Nagasu 2004:3). Total foreign aid continues to increase at a rate higher than the developing country average, at just over $1.2 billion in 2011; it is almost half Cambodia's annual budget (Khieng 2013). Cambodia is widely recognized as aid dependent. Some go further by saying it is donor driven (Khieng 2013; Nagasu 2004) and a "donor's playground" (Fforde & Seidel 2010).

Cambodian NGOs emerged under UNTAC, and many were specifically created by donors to deliver donor-initiated and -funded social services. According to the most recent 2011 estimate, there are approximately 1,350 active NGOs that deliver a vast number of diverse social services beyond the capacity or interests of the government (Khieng 2013). A survey of NGOs in Cambodia found that 57 identified a gender-based violence program (personal communication, Khieng 2012).

UNDERSTANDING NGO COMMITMENT TO CRIMINAL JUSTICE: AN APPARENT CONTRADICTION

In previous research, we investigated the degree of support for somroh somruel by those working in gender-based violence programs, by carrying out interviews with twenty staff working for international and local NGOs (see Burns & Daly 2014 for detail on methods used). All were familiar with somroh somruel, although not through direct experience. Opinions varied on the appropriateness of somroh somruel in responding to rape: six were against it; six expressed tentative interest; four saw it more positively as having potential to be more victim-centered than a court process; and four gave no opinion. A contradiction emerged in the findings. Although all were critical of Cambodia's formal criminal justice system, particularly its systemic corruption, most believed it was the right response to rape. What explains this?

For many, it was simply that "rape is criminal law so it must go to the courts, not somroh somruel" (interview #8). It is important to emphasize that this is a relatively new idea in Cambodia. The 2005 law on domestic violence, coupled with an NGO educational campaign to implement it, has strengthened the view that the legitimate and modern response to rape is through criminal law.

For others, support comes from significant investment (professional and organizational) in criminal justice, coupled with conventional understanding of "justice." For example, the country director of a policing-focused NGO, which is attempting to establish a "one-stop shop" for victims, explained, "The biggest justice challenge for the girls is that they're going to be mediated out at the village level rather than seeking services. That's our biggest challenge" (interview #6). Likewise, a legal aid lawyer expressed frustration when somroh somruel derails court cases mid-proceedings: "In some cases, the perpetrator's family goes over to the victim's family to pay compensation to close the case. . . . When the negotiation is over, they are [found] sitting outside court, and they tell the lawyer they won't proceed with the case. . . . Sometimes the other party doesn't pay, and then they come back to us asking for further legal assistance!" (interview #17).

Prosecution is perceived as a deterrent and a strong reason to support formal legal mechanisms. The Cambodian director of an NGO umbrella group said: "NGOs cannot get involved [in somroh somruel] because it's illegal. . . . The victim may get money from the offender, but then [the offenders] do it again and again. Somroh somruel does not solve the problem" (interview #14).

A Cambodian country director of another NGO made a similar point, arguing further that cases must be brought to court to address corruption:

> It is not going to help because he'll just do it again. . . . [The women] must stand up. We explain that the strength comes from the woman herself first and that there is a system [of local authority being established that] you can trust and you will benefit from. You have to put them in jail. . . . The Ministry of Women's Affairs is very strong. They have a network to . . . connect with the police, judge, court. So that's why we have to go through [the system]: many people together to deal with and stop corruption. (interview #9)

There are many complexities in addressing corruption, which we cannot address here. However, the goals and priorities of ministries and NGOs, which align with human rights concerns, may compromise rape survivors' (and their families') interests and raise ethical questions. We turn next to how human rights ideas have shaped the thinking of the NGO staff and the landscape of international responses to violence against women.

HUMAN RIGHTS

A commitment to human rights is a commitment to legalism, specifically, Western ideas of law and justice. NGO staff recognized the gap between human rights aspirations and the reality facing rape survivors in Cambodia, but ultimately they equated human rights with legal mechanisms of formal justice redress. An NGO researcher who had lived in Cambodia for seven years said, "Rape is far too serious a crime to ever leave the justice system and go for something like [somroh somruel] when you have a justice system. The justice system . . . is the primary institution to provide redress . . . what [somroh somruel does] is remove the seriousness of how the crime is perceived." Despite the emphasis on using the justice system in responding to serious crime, the human rights advocate shifted her position later in the interview by acknowledging that "So many cases are lost in corruption and malpractice. . . . Many [victims] talked about how vulnerable they felt with the police and the court, and we must remember that we're talking about people who are extremely vulnerable in the sense that they're basically illiterate. It's very difficult for them and frightening to go to the authorities, the police and to the court" (interview #3).

Her shift in perspective shows the tension between how a "community" may see the seriousness of rape and how an individual experiences justice: whose rights are promoted and whose are sacrificed in the push toward formal justice? A U.S.-trained academic social worker, who advocates for a client-centered approach to services, explained:

> Human rights NGOs have good intentions, but they pressure survivors to go to court. They think the best way to help is to put them through the legal services. But girls are reluctant to go to court. They don't want to confront the perpetrator, make their story public, lose time and money. . . . I used to work with survivors of rape and sexual violence, they think why not get compensation now [through somroh somruel] and keep quiet. (interview #20)

These two NGO staff members show the problems of applying human rights ideals in responding to rape in Cambodia. Where, we may ask, did these ideals come from? Why do they hold such sway?

Beginning in the 1980s the global campaign to end violence against women gathered momentum, with increasing acceptance of the idea that "women's rights are human rights." The international community's response to violence against women is now largely directed by UN Women, established in 2010. It supports and assists intergovernmental bodies' formulation of policies, international standards, and norms, and governments' adoption and enactment of legal reforms in alignment with international standards. Such standards and norms are articulated (among other places) in guidelines for program planning and design, which emphasize the "powerful role" of the justice sector (Thomas, Young, & Ellingen 2011:6), explicitly rejecting alternative dispute resolution mechanisms. Thomas et al. (2011) refer to informal justice throughout the text, highlighting a negative assessment. For example, "it is important to note that . . . restorative justice mechanisms can be detrimental in cases of violence against women" (8);

"informal justice mechanisms pose many risks to women and girl victims of violence" (10); "restorative practices, which can minimize the effect that violence has in women's lives, can perpetuate discrimination, and can risk women and girls giving up their individual rights so as to preserve harmony within a social group" (24). No research evidence or citations are given. We argue that this reiteration of Western values and norms within an emerging international regime to end violence against women sits uncomfortably with the need to address local circumstances. The possibility of survivors' individual rights being sacrificed to broader justice principles becomes even more apparent in the Cambodian context of a dysfunctional criminal justice system.

What is the source of authority for international standards and norms? In the Thomas et al. (2011) guidelines, fifteen of the twenty contributors were lawyers; at least five were from the United States, and the publication was endorsed by the Advocates of Human Rights. A legal orientation dominates donor-initiated programs and government development policy. The United Nations is the biggest multilateral donor that focuses on gender equality in Cambodia (Bottomley et al. 2012:30), and its programs on violence against women are coordinated by UN Women, using its international standards and norms. In this context, it would be difficult to find support for a project that challenges such standards.

Our point is not that international standards and norms should be undermined. Rather, drawing from Hafner-Burton and Ron (2009:393–94), by conceptualizing violence against women solely within a global human rights framework, we obscure the local significance of community as social identity and as a means of survival. This stifles consideration of alternative perspectives and approaches to justice and threatens to displace resources that might be directed to more innovative or locally appropriate responses, even in the interim period of establishing a functioning criminal justice system. In short, a human rights framework "offers a discourse of both freedom and domination" (Evans 2005:1049).

DONOR DEPENDENCE

In Cambodia's donor-driven aid environment, the government and NGOs largely comply with top-down directives. In relation to everyday rape, the result is that programs redirect victims away from customary dispute mechanisms toward a criminal justice response. It is not the government or NGOs who approach a donor with a project. Rather, donor interests or experts initiate and drive the development program from conception to delivery (Dosch 2012:1074; Nagasu 2004:1).

For government, this is not entirely or necessarily a reflection of ineptitude. It may utilize existing aid arrangements and an apparent lack of capacity to maximize foreign aid opportunities that align with donors' projects (Nagasu 2004:4). At the same time, an exodus of donor dollars from the justice sector suggests that the government's strategy might backfire after consistent failure or low ministerial commitment.

The impact of a ministry's dependence on funding was emphasized by one interviewee, whose NGO wanted to close an orphanage when child abuse allegations emerged. She explained that the raid was scheduled, but they then had to fight the ministry to get approval because the international donor was going to be in-country. "We're like, are you kidding?! It's very very donor centric here" (interview #6). The orphanage was an early example of "volun-tourism," a new, multibillion-dollar global volunteering industry, which has contributed to a significant increase in the number of Cambodian "orphans" (70 percent of whom are said to have a parent) and unregistered orphanages (Ruhfus 2012).

For NGOs, donor dependence affects their activities in three ways: NGO services cluster in areas limited to donor priorities and interests, though these may not accord with the perceived needs of the NGOs; original NGO goals or priorities may be diverted to enhance funding opportunities; and aspirations to play an expanded role in civil society are constrained.

Donors generally contribute to specific projects and personnel costs, but little to a NGO's operating costs. Additional donors are needed to cover any shortfalls. One effect is competition among NGOs and a regional-sectoral clustering in areas where donors dominate; this creates "aid darlings" (where aid is most concentrated) and "aid orphans" (where aid is needed yet missing). According to the country director of a policing affiliated NGO, police training programs are a "darling": "Twenty different organizations are turning out 20 different training programs. There's a big push to get one standardized program; but it's been 6 years, and they still haven't been able to do it. . . . No NGO wants to give that up because it's a huge source of funding" (interview #6). Everyday

rape does not motivate donors. However, according to the same interviewee, "everyone loves trafficking. It's very sexy, very cool," with these
implications:

> In the Cambodian context, it [trafficking] is not happening nearly as much
> as [donors and therefore NGOs] want. . . . They really want that to be a big
> issue here. And what do you really call trafficking? . . . A lot of NGOs have
> to say it's a trafficking case because of their donors, but it's not trafficking.
> It's exploitation, it's awful; but it's not trafficking. You have the internation-
> al donors who are insisting on trafficking and so NGOs create trafficking
> cases. . . . It's a complete misdirection of funding. (interview #6)

Available statistics show that rape is far more widespread than trafficking, but few NGOs focus on the rape of adults (over 18 years). Rape cases
are captured by NGOs that provide services in the areas of trafficking,
domestic violence, and the protection of children—all donor-funded programs that reflect priorities of the international aid community. Cambodian NGO reports on gender-based violence and violence against women
overwhelmingly focus on domestic violence and trafficking. There has been
no targeted research on rape and appropriate justice responses. Universal
"best practice" criminal justice responses are assumed to be optimal.

To accommodate donor objectives, NGOs may need to adjust their priorities and programs and accept new projects. Khieng (2013) argues that
such alignment with donor interest has a "goal displacement effect" on the
NGO. To illustrate, aid dependency derailed a once prominent NGO with
considerable experience researching and working directly with gender-
based violence. As a result of their need to attract funding, they turned
away from this work to assist reforms on women in politics. They became
project focused, preoccupied with writing reports for donors, and, in the
eyes of one interviewee, Cambodia lost their accumulated expertise and
leadership role in the area of sexual violence.

NGO dependence on donor funding may constrain engagement in
long-term, policy agenda-setting activities. Despite a recent shift in the
international development community encouraging the participation of
NGOs in planning processes, one NGO country director confirmed that
this was inhibited by donors who had little interest in funding policy work.
What attracts funding, she says, is results in service and project delivery.

However, "Cambodia is changing," she argues, "and what we need now is strategic work rather than the service delivery" (interview #4).

OPENINGS AND OPPORTUNITIES

There is more to the Cambodian story than the hegemony of human rights ideals and the dominance of donors. Openings and opportunities are emerging. These have resulted from two shifts in the international dialogue on aid effectiveness: increased recipient country ownership of development programs and increased participation of civil society organizations, including NGOs. To achieve the first, donor partners of the Organization for Economic Co-operation and Development (OECD) are now obligated to provide more funding through government institutions. This means less direct donor funding to NGOs. The pressure on NGOs to find alternative income is increasing and may encourage some to turn to the government as a funding source. In the past government funding was extremely limited, generally forthcoming when foreign development partners provided government grants stipulating collaboration with NGOs to implement programs (Khieng 2013). Although there is greater NGO competition for funding, NGOs have new opportunities to shape government policies and initiate programs where NGOs see the need. As one NGO country director explained, "So far gender-based violence is all about trafficking and domestic violence. Unless other aspects get on the agenda, there's no funding" (interview # 4).

Cooperation between donors and NGOs in agenda-setting work has been encouraged, albeit inadvertently, by the difficulties donors have had in working with the government. Before meeting with the government, donors and NGOs now get together to strategize. A subgroup of all UN bodies, bilateral donors, and NGOs working on gender-based violence meets monthly. Its consultations with the Minister of Women's Affairs on the Second National Action Plan to Prevent Violence Against Women, 2013–2017, put gender-based violence in urban areas on the government agenda.

Increasing involvement of NGOs in policy making has been embraced by some, particularly those with a degree of donor independence, like interviewee #4 above. This interviewee regards the opportunity to make a more significant contribution through policy input as a more effective way to address "aid orphans" than service delivery in the changing aid environment. Once on the agenda, it is more likely to attract the attention of donors and other government ministries.

CONCLUSION

Cmiel (2004) invites us to ask difficult questions of human rights. Ours are: What if responses framed by universal human rights are not the best way to address everyday rape in countries where the justice system is dysfunctional and customary law is preferred? What if most victims and their families prefer to use an informal justice mechanism instead? There is a need to investigate the unintended negative consequences of encouraging formal justice—which is distant both in geography and global ideal for most Cambodians—and discouraging locally based practices of somroh somruel.

We see several ways forward, guided in part by the interviews. First, we agree that pressure to improve the criminal justice system is vital to providing appropriate legal redress, as one justice pathway. We also advocate client-centered and community-based responses to survivors, and we think that this can be extended to address survivors' justice interests. The existing informal justice pathway is far from perfect, but so too is the existing criminal justice system. The legal implications that complicate NGO engagement with somroh somruel in cases of rape cannot be ignored. NGOs might continue to provide the same services, including legal advice and support, but consider more carefully the range of needs and options available to their clients, rather than encouraging them to engage formal justice. Some NGOs might work to support and improve customary practices in ways that do not compromise their own legal position, that is, by not working directly on particular cases, but with the village or commune leaders and local communities to improve an understanding of rape, its causes, and its effects. Agenda-setting forums might also offer opportunities to extend research on somroh somruel in responding to rape, with greater attention to the experiences of those who have used it.

To return to Weinstein et al.'s (2009) question, "Do we abandon victims if we argue for a response that addresses the greater good of a community?" Our answer is that if, by community, is meant an (inter)national body upholding symbolic universal principles, then our answer is yes, victims are abandoned. If, by community, is meant a local basis of identity, support, and survival, then our answer is no, they are not.

DISCUSSION QUESTIONS

1. What are the constraints on NGOs, in countries like Cambodia, in developing and promoting alternative justice responses to rape?
2. If you were to work for an NGO in a country like Cambodia, what activities would you promote to reduce rape and develop justice responses to rape?
3. When one informant said that trafficking was "very sexy," what does this imply for how NGOs set priorities?
4. What are the limits of a human rights framework in responding to rape and violent crime in fragile and postconflict societies?

REFERENCES

Arthur, P. 2010. Introduction: Identities in transition. In *Identities in Transition: Challenges for Transitional Justice in Divided Societies*, ed. P. Arthur, 1–14. Cambridge: Cambridge University Press.

Asian Development Bank. 2012. *Cambodia Country Poverty Analysis*. Manila: Asian Development Bank.

Bottomley, R., U. Leang, C. Urashima, and B. Prak. 2012. *Monitoring Aid Effectiveness from a Gender Perspective, Country Report Cambodia*. Phnom Penh: ActionAid.

Burns, C., and K. Daly. 2014. Responding to everyday rape in Cambodia: Rhetorics, realities and somroh somruel. *Restorative Justice: An International Journal* 1 (2): forthcoming.

Chirayath, L., C. Sage, and M. Woolcock. 2005. Customary law and policy reform: Engaging with the plurality of justice systems. Background paper for the World *Development Report 2006: Equity and Development*. http://siteresources. worldbank.org/INTWDR2006/Resources/477383–1118673432908 /Customary_Law_and_Policy_Reform.pdf.

Cmiel, K. 2004. The recent history of human rights. *American Historical Review* 109 (1): 117–35.

Dosch, J. 2012. The role of civil society in Cambodia's peace-building process: Have foreign donors made a difference? *Asian Survey* 52 (6): 1067–88.

End Child Prostitution, Pornography and Trafficking (ECPAT) Cambodia. 2012. *NGO Joint Statistics Project: Quarterly Trend Monitoring Brief on Sexual Traf- ficking, Sexual Exploitation and Rape in Cambodia, April–June 2012.* http: //www.ecpatcambodia.org/index.php?menuid=1&rp=126.

Evans, T. 2005. International human rights law as power/knowledge. *Human Rights Quarterly* 27 (3): 517–43.

Fforde, A., & K. Seidel. 2010. *Donor Playground Cambodia? What a Look at Aid and Development in Cambodia Confirms and What It May Imply.* http://www .boell.de/sites/default/files/Donor_Playground_Cambodia_Study.pdf.

Hafner-Burton, E., and J. Ron. 2009. Seeing double: Human rights impact through qualitative and quantitative eyes. *World Politics* 61 (2): 360–401.

Harper, E. 2011. *Customary Justice: From Program Design to Impact Evaluation.* Rome: International Development Law Organization.

Khieng, S. 2013. Funding mobilization strategies of nongovernmental organiza- tions in Cambodia. *Voluntas: International Journal of Voluntary and Nonprofit Organizations.* doi: 10.1007/s11266–013–9400–7.

Nagasu, M. 2004. *Ownership in Cambodia: Review of Process of Preparing Poverty Reduction Strategy Paper.* http://www.grips.ac.jp/forum/pdf04/CAownership .pdf.

O'Connell, D. 2001. *Rape and Indecent Assault: Crimes in the Community.* Phnom Penh: LICADHO.

Olivella, S. F. 2003. *Judicial Mentoring: A Strategy for Capacity Development of the Judiciary in Cambodia.* Asia-Pacific Rights and Justice Initiative, Case Studies on Access to Justice by the Poor and Disadvantaged. Bangkok: UNDP.

Popovic, V. 2009. *The Asia-Pacific Rights and Justice Initiative, Cambodia Country Assessment.* Bangkok: UNDP.

Ramage, I., G. Pictet, C. Sophearith, and A. Jorde. 2008. *Somroh Somruel and Vio- lence Against Women.* Phnom Penh: Domrei.

Ruhfus, J. 2012. Cambodia's orphanage business. *Huffington Post.* http://www .huffingtonpost.com/juliana-ruhfus/cambodias-orphanage-busin_b _1616255.html.

Samuels, K. 2006. *Rule of Law Reform in Post-Conflict Countries: Operational Ini- tiatives and Lessons Learnt.* World Bank, Social Development Papers, Conflict Prevention and Reconstruction, Paper No. 37.

Swaine, Aisling. 2003. *Traditional Justice and Gender Based Violence: Research Report.* New York: International Rescue Committee.

Thomas, C., L. Young, and M. Ellingen. 2011. *Working with the Justice Sector to End Violence Against Women and Girls*. UN Women and the Advocates for Human Rights. http://www.endvawnow.org/uploads/modules/pdf/1325624043.pdf.

United Nations Development Programme, Democratic Governance Thematic Trust Fund. 2007. *DGTTF Cambodia 2007: Access to Justice*. http://www .undp.org/content/dam/aplaws/publication/en/publications/democratic -governance/dgttf-/access-to-justice-in-cambodia/DGTTF-Cambodia-1%20 pager.pdf.

UN Women. 2013. *UN Women Urges Implementation of Historic Global Agreement to End Violence Against Women and Girls*. March 20, UN Women Press release. http://www.unwomen.org/en/news/stories/2013/3/un-women-urges -implementation-of-historic-global-agreement-to-end-violence-against- women-and-girls.

Weinstein, H. M., L. E. Fletcher, P. Vinck, and P. N. Pham. 2009. Stay the hand of justice: Whose priorities take priority? In *Localizing Transitional Justice: Interventions and Priorities After Mass Violence*, ed. R. Shaw and L. Waldorf with P. Hazan, 27–48. Stanford, Calif.: Stanford University Press.

Wojkowska, E. 2006. *Doing Justice: How Informal Justice Systems Can Contribute*. United Nations Development Programme, Oslo Governance Centre, Democratic Governance Fellowship Programme.

World Bank. 2012. *The World Bank: New Directions in Justice Reform*. Companion Piece to the Updated Strategy and Implementation Plan on Strengthening Governance, *Tackling Corruption*. http://www-wds.worldbank.org/external /default/WDSContentServer/WDSP/IB/2012/09/06/000386194_2012090 6024506/Rendered/PDF/70640oREPLACEMoJusticeoReformoFinal. .pdf.

Yrigoyen Fajardo, R. Z., R. Kong, and S. Phan. 2005. *Pathways to Justice: Access to Justice with a Focus on Poor, Women, and Indigenous Peoples*. Phnom Penh: United Nations Development Program Cambodia/Ministry of Justice, Royal Government of Cambodia.

CHAPTER 11

Sexual Abuse Within Institutional Contexts

▶ *ANNE-MARIE MCALINDEN*

THIS CHAPTER ADOPTS A CROSS-NATIONAL comparative perspective on institutional child sexual abuse. It seeks first to provide a critical overview of a range of high-profile inquiries and official reviews into allegations of institutional child abuse and the dominant transnational themes arising from them. It also seeks to highlight the dynamics of what I have previously termed "institutional grooming" (McAlinden 2006) and the features of the organizational environment that both facilitate institutional child sexual abuse and help mask its discovery or disclosure. In so doing, the analysis examines the tension between what others have termed "preferential" or "situational" sexual offending—that is, whether offenders deliberately set out to gain employment that affords access to children or whether the motivation to sexually offend emerges only after they become ensconced in an institutional environment. Finally, the chapter concludes by offering some suggestions for combating institutional grooming and sexual abuse.

PUBLIC INQUIRIES AND OFFICIAL REVIEWS: KEY THEMES

Over the past two decades, high-profile cases of institutional child abuse have emerged in an array of jurisdictions, including the United States (John Jay College 2004, 2011), Canada (Law Commission of Canada 2000), Australia (Parliament of Victoria 2013), the Netherlands (Commission of Inquiry 2011), and England and Wales (Waterhouse 2000). These cases have stemmed from a variety of secular and religious organizations in both residential and nonresidential settings, including care homes, nurseries, and schools. In the religious context, public and political concerns have been dominated by a string of allegations against the Catholic Church (Keenan 2011), though abuse is by no means confined to this particular religious context. While the term "institutional child abuse" encompasses a range of abusive and harmful behaviors toward children (e.g., physical, emotional, and sexual abuse and neglect), and indeed typically more than one form of abuse is highlighted in the resulting public inquiries or reviews, the focus throughout this chapter is on institutionalized forms of child sexual abuse.

Efforts to address institutional child sexual abuse have drawn from a range of legal frameworks. Australia and Canada, for example, have used a mixture of public apology, reparation, compensation, and truth commission as responses to clerical sexual abuse as well as institutional child abuse against indigenous peoples (Llewellyn 2002; Nagy & Sehdev 2012). In the United States victims have sought redress via the civil courts, where many parishes have gone into bankruptcy, paying out large sums of victim compensation (Robert, 2011). The dominant model for responding to institutional child sexual abuse in many jurisdictions, including the United Kingdom and the Republic of Ireland, however, is the judge-led public inquiry, with the attendant possibility of subsequent prosecutions, compensation, and public apology.

The Republic of Ireland has been one of the most prolific jurisdictions in responding to allegations of institutional child sexual abuse within the Catholic Church, with four high-profile inquiries within six years (Murphy, Buckley, & Joyce 2005; Commission of Investigation 2009, 2011; Commission to Inquire into Child Abuse 2009). The Ryan Report, whose five volumes took nine years to produce, highlighted the fact that the abuse of children (physical, sexual, emotional, and neglect) and the failure of church and state authorities to adequately respond to the problem were *systemic* in Irish child-care institutions (Commission to Inquire into Child Abuse 2009: vol. 4, paras. 6.09–6.18).

Collectively, the inquiries and reviews have highlighted a range of global themes relating to the occurrence and dynamics of institutional child sexual abuse, including the following:

- The abuse normally took place over a number of years, and its extent went unrecognized for some time.
- Usually more than one victim was involved, and often more than one offender.

- There was often a culture of acceptance or disbelief where other staff ignored signs of abuse or were afraid to challenge inappropriate behavior or act on initial suspicions.
- Many complaints were not formally reported, and victims were afraid to disclose the abuse.
- When they did disclose, no action was taken, because there was either a conspiracy to keep allegations quiet or a ready acceptance of the denial by the alleged perpetrator in order to protect the reputation of the institution.
- There were poor internal management and external governance frameworks in place, including the absence of an effective system for complaints. (McAlinden 2006, 2012:157)

The latter criticisms have been made in particular within the context of sexual abuse within churches or faith communities (Berry 1992; Francis & Turner 1995). These factors are confirmed by the general literature on child sexual abuse, which suggests primarily that the complaints appear to be of a sexual nature, involving both boys and girls, and that the majority have not been reported (Barter 1999; Gallagher 1998). Many of these themes, including delays in disclosure, a culture of silence, and denial and minimization of allegations, relate directly to the process of "institutional grooming" and will be returned to below.

As Parton (2004) notes in the context of the United Kingdom, however, many of the major public inquiries over the past few years have made similar recommendations for effecting legislative or policy change that have not always been acted on. This is due to a complex interplay of factors, including the increased resource implications as well as broader processes of political expediency whereby the state seeks to demonstrate its commitment to handling a problem (Garland 1996) in the aftermath of a particular scandal or crisis. Indeed, concerns about institutional child abuse over time, in tandem with concerns about child sexual abuse more generally, have been a highly contested field that tends to be characterized by extreme positions (Conte 1994; Smart 1999). The waves of panic surrounding high-profile cases result in increased levels of professional intervention principally in the form of reform of regulatory frameworks on pre-employment vetting. These often diminish once the case becomes less prominent in both public and professional consciousness until the next high-profile case emerges and there is a renewed call for intervention.

The drawbacks of the public inquiry model in providing redress for victims of institutional child sexual abuse, particularly in the case of clerical sexual abuse, have been well highlighted in the literature. Their limitations in seeking "truth recovery" (McAlinden 2013) or "justice" for victims (McAlinden & Naylor 2014) are related to denial of victim participation in the broadest sense and passive participation by offenders. Moreover, the institutional gaze of many of these inquiries has been too narrow in focus and has tended to impede a meaningful and effective review of policy and procedures (McAlinden 2010:30; see also Scraton 2004). In essence, the linear focus on accountability and blame for individual acts or omissions within the context of a particular scandal impedes a broader examination of the systemic problems of child-care institutions and the wider policy issues concerning the identification and management of sex offenders within institutionalized contexts.

The limitations of this model have also led to calls for the use of restorative justice as an alternative response to institutional clerical sexual abuse (Gavrielides & Coker 2005; McAlinden & Naylor 2014 Noll & Harvey 2008), with isolated initiatives across the United States, Canada, and the Netherlands (Gavrielides 2012). Within this broader context, "apology" becomes the touchstone of reconciliation and a pivotal means of securing offender redemption as well as accountability and acknowledgment of wrongdoing and "justice" for individual victims (Blecher 2011; Rossner 2013).

INSTITUTIONAL GROOMING AND ABUSE

The inquiries and resulting themes outlined above serve to underscore the existence of what I have previously termed "institutional grooming"—that the unique features of the institutional environment are instrumental in both facilitating institutional child sexual abuse and preventing its discovery or disclosure (McAlinden 2006). Certain forms of employment allow an abuser to access children in a way that would not otherwise be possible. These occupations relate to a wide variety of settings, including not just religious work but also secular work within voluntary organizations, private and public schools, residential homes, and a range of community-based child-care settings, such as nursery schools and foster-care placements.

Children in residential care appear more susceptible to abuse than those within the community and provide a captive vulnerable population for sexual abusers (Utting 1997). This has been attributed to the imbalance of power between adult perpetrators and child victims, which is exaggerated by the offender's "caring role and the children's traumatic or abusive histories" (Erooga, Allnock, & Telford 2012:62). Research has also highlighted the existence of grooming and abuse in relation to specific organizational contexts, such as sport (Brackenridge 2001) or the Catholic Church (John Jay College 2011; McAlinden 2012:170–75). The reality, however, is that probably every profession or organization that has contact with children in terms of their care, education, or social or leisure activities is vulnerable to infiltration by those minded to abuse (Beyer, Higgins, & Bromfield 2005).

While sex offenders are a highly heterogeneous population with diverse motivations and "manipulation styles" (Sullivan & Quayle 2012), there are a number of particular features of the organizational setting that allow "grooming" and other pro-offending behaviors to flourish. It is these unique facets of "vulnerable organizations" (Erooga 2009b: 38), or what Hall terms "the institutional syndrome" (Hall 2000, cited in Erooga 2009b:38), that enable offenders to manipulate perceptions, create opportunities, and prevent suspicion. These particular dynamics include features such as trust, opportunity, anonymity, secrecy, and power. The gaining of trust, or "emotional seduction" (Salter 1995:74), plays a pivotal role in the grooming process with respect to children, their families, and the wider community.

In this sense, while institutional sexual abuse is a subcategory of extrafamilial sexual abuse, the dynamics of organizational abuse have also been said to be akin to abuse within intrafamilial contexts. This has generally been attributed to two main factors: First, the proximate and ongoing relationships between adults and children within an organizational environment, where adults may have sole responsibility for the welfare of children, "often place them *in loco parentis*" (Sullivan et al. 2011:58) and provide enhanced opportunity. Organizational positions facilitate the grooming process in allowing sex offenders to present as nonthreatening so that they can easily build a relationship with a child as peer, father figure, or rescuer (Colton & Vanstone 1996; Leclerc, Proulx, & McKibben 2005). Second, the imbalance of power entrenched within abusive relationships in both settings facilitates access to children and inhibits disclosure.

Institutions can create multiple opportunities for the manipulation and abuse of children and can allow the offender to take on a different persona and remain anonymous in terms of their deviant sexual tendencies.

The organizational culture itself may be conducive to abuse of power, the "corruption of care" (Erooga 2009b:39–40), and erosion of the primary functions of care and protection. Child-care institutions appear to be "especially self-protective, secretive and closed by nature" (McAlinden 2010:30) and strongly discourage the drawing of attention to any deficiencies in policies or procedures. Furthermore, if other staff or local agencies or parents hold these individuals or organizations in high esteem, children may experience added difficulties in both resisting and disclosing the abuse (Gallagher 2000:810). If the offender is in a senior management position, with few checks or balances on behavior, this may give him or her the necessary control over the organizational culture or "the power to betray" (Ben-Yehuda 2001:28).

A small number of inquiries (e.g., Commission to Inquire into Child Abuse 2009: vol. 3, para 9.57) and more recent empirical research (McAlinden 2012:182) have highlighted the overlap between various forms of grooming (such as "peer-to-peer grooming" and "institutional grooming"). They have also underlined the complexity of the "victim-offender continuum" within an organizational context where victims may progress to becoming offenders themselves as sexual and other forms of abuse become part of the organizational culture. The gamut of institutional sexual abuse may variously involve child and adult, victims and perpetrators, as "insiders" or parties to the abusive process, as well as the duplicity and compliance, unwitting or otherwise, of outsiders in failing to acknowledge or act on suspicions of abuse.

This argument also has resonance in relation to the wider processes of social denial (Cohen 2001) concerning allegations of institutional child sexual abuse. This culture of disbelief was evidenced, for example, by the historical reluctance of Irish society to acknowledge clerical sexual abuse in the Republic of Ireland for decades (McAlinden 2013). More recently the collective failures of the authorities, organizations, and the public to act on suspicions of sexual abuse by the late Jimmy Savile and to challenge his behavior were attributed to his celebrity status and his charitable works (Burns & Somaiya 2012). The unprecedented scale of his sexual abuse of children was posthumously traced back at least five decades, involving potentially thousands of children across a range of institutional settings (Boffey 2014).

A further interesting dimension of the literature is whether "professional perpetrators" have different characteristics from those who abuse children outside a professional setting (Sullivan et al. 2010). While research shows that such offenders do not differ significantly from other sex offenders against children (Haywood et al. 1996; Langevin, Cunroe, & Bain 2000), there may a number of notable differences. There is a clear gendered dimension to institutional child sexual abuse, with "a negative, male-dominated culture in residential settings" (Erooga 2009b:43). As with child sexual abuse more generally, the vast majority of offenses are committed by men, with higher rates of male victimization, and with victims also being in the older age range of adolescents rather than young children (Elliott, Brown, & Kilcoyne 1995; Colton 2002). As Mercado et al (2011:56, citing Abel et al. 1994) point out, while those who sexually assault children in a professional context may not be that different from those who abuse outside such contexts, they may "constitute a particular public health danger, given the power entrusted to these individuals and their ready access to children."

PREFERENTIAL VS. SITUATIONAL OFFENDING

The spate of inquiries and reviews into institutional child abuse and the existence of regulatory frameworks on pre-employment vetting highlight the fact that individuals may use their employment as a cover within which to sexually abuse children in their care. The research literature, however, is generally split on whether "professional perpetrators" (Sullivan & Beech 2002) are best categorized as "preferential" or "situational" offenders (Wortley & Smallbone 2006:13–18). That is, while some sex offenders may deliberately set out to gain employment or choose a career that provides contact with children whom they can abuse, for others, the motivation to sexually offend materializes only once an individual has become installed within the institutional environment (John Jay College 2011).

In relation to the former category, sex offenders may become affiliated with youth groups or children's clubs or a range of other professions that allow one-to-one unsupervised contact with children (Powell 2007:22–23, 37–39). Some sex offenders have taken on paid or voluntary work as coaches or assistants in sports clubs, which facilitates particularly close physical contact with children (Brackenridge 2001). The literature suggests that those who deliberately choose careers that provide contact with children account for a sizable proportion of sexual abuse within organizational contexts (Colton & Vanstone 1996; Ritchie 2001; Sullivan & Beech 2004). Smallbone and Wortley (2000), for example, found that

20 percent of extrafamilial offenders reported having accessed children though a child or youth organization, with 8 percent having joined primarily to commit a sexual offense. Sullivan and Beech's (2004) study of forty-one institutional sex offenders, however, reports higher percentages, where for 41.5 percent, abusing children was a partial if not primary motivation for working with children.

As regards the latter category, other sex offenders, however, may be installed in a position of trust with children prior to any clear intention to sexually offend (Finkelhor, Williams, & Burns 1988). Sullivan and Beech (2004) also noted that only 15 percent were motivated to exclusively obtain employment that would provide them with access to children. For these offenders, "the motivation is less tangible and possibly situationally as well as personally derived" (Erooga et al. 2012:52). The opportunistic nature of sexual offending against children means that for many "professional offenders," "the key factor is not the particular sexual attraction but rather the availability and vulnerability of the children" (Erooga 2009b:65) within the institutional environment.

This broad dichotomy between preferential and situational offending was also reflected in the views of professionals who risk assess, treat, or manage sex offenders within the context of my recent multijurisdictional empirical study on "Grooming" (McAlinden, 2012:176–78). A treatment professional in the Republic of Ireland, for example, commented: "All of the offenders, bar none, that I've worked with have all got themselves into situations that definitely are a back door, or a side door . . . into having access to children." This pattern of offending was related to an "approach-explicit" pathway (Ward & Hudson 1998) and more ingrained and predatory forms of sexual offending against children. An independent interviewee in England and Wales explained further: "The entrenched child sex offender, i.e., somebody whose needs, so emotionally, socially, sexually, are only met by children is more likely . . . to be involved in institutional [sexual] abuse, just simply because they will seek an environment where there is the ability to access victims."

For other interviewees, however, institutional child sexual abuse was "very situation specific" and linked to organizational risk factors. As noted above, other sex offenders may be installed in a position of trust with children prior to the crystallization of any motivation to sexually offend. Situational risk factors were succinctly attributed by a Scottish voluntary sector interviewee to "a pressured environment . . . the element of solo working . . . [and] the lack of physical boundaries" between children and the staff responsible for their care. It is this blurring of organizational roles and physical boundaries that may serve to normalize the onset of physical and later sexualized contact with children. As discussed in the final section, this divergence in professional views and research findings underlines the importance of developing both external and internal controls on the behavior of potential sex offenders in institutional settings.

CONCLUSION: ENHANCING PROTECTION AND PREVENTION

Many jurisdictions have developed some form of pre-employment vetting or barring to prevent sexual abusers from gaining employment that provides access to children or the vulnerable. The danger, however, is that these legal and policy frameworks have largely been reactive responses to the problem. The principal difficulty with any system of external controls is that it can address only the known, identifiable, and preventable risks and not the unknown, hidden, and therefore most dangerous ones (McAlinden 2010). That is, regulatory frameworks are relevant only when an individual has a clear record of offending or at the very least where there is a history of concerns. Moreover, as Fitch, Spencer, and Hilton (2007) have shown in the case of Europe, there are very limited transnational mechanisms for managing sex offenders, and vetting arrangements are highly inconsistent between jurisdictions, which may allow persistent sex offenders to slip through the net.

The difficulties of early detection of potential risks of sexual harm to children within an institutional environment stem from the fact that emotional congruence with children may at once be indicative of a potential risk to children as well as a desirable characteristic of those most effective in working with children (Sullivan et al. 2011:70). Since sex offenders "share many relevant characteristics with the 'general population'" (Erooga 2009a:4), and there is no typical or "full-proof" profile (Elliott et al. 1995:109), it is difficult to detect potential sex offenders within organizational or other contexts on a proactive basis. It becomes vitally important, therefore, to develop complementary, effective internal supervision and controls on institutional culture and individual working practices in settings that involve "close and contact interaction" with children (Erooga 2009b:65).

One practical means of achieving this is the adoption of broader public health approaches to sexualized violence and abuse (Laws 2000). Such an approach would help raise awareness of child sexual abuse and promote a "politics" (Stanko, 1990) or "culture of safety" (Busch 2002) within wider society as well as organizational contexts specifically. Institutional child sexual abuse, much like intrafamilial sexual abuse, emerges as the confluence of three factors—a motivated offender, a suitable victim, and the lack of an appropriate and capable guardian (McAlinden 2012:195). As Erooga (2009b:28) contends, therefore, "without an appropriate organizational culture of safeguarding, any setting . . . is vulnerable to the corruption of the ethic of care."

In practice, as I have argued elsewhere (McAlinden 2012:276), this broad aspiration of safeguarding could be furthered by enhancing staff training around issues specific to sexual offending behavior, and strengthening external and particularly internal management systems that would maximize "the features that make organizations safer for children" (Beyer et al. 2005:106). This would include, for example, systems of staff support and monitoring to facilitate the early identification and effective management of inappropriate or potentially sexually harmful behavior (Sullivan et al. 2011:70) and an organizational "culture of awareness and vigilance" (Erooga 2009a: 6) that fosters "open and constructive questioning of practice and relationships" (Shaw 2007:150). A multilayered approach to institutional child sexual abuse would offer a more viable means of protecting children and preventing offender by enhancing children's safety while simultaneously reducing the offender's opportunity for abuse.

DISCUSSION QUESTIONS

1. What are the key lessons for polity arising from the range of high-profile cases of institutional child abuse?
2. Why are institutions a situational risk for child sexual abuse?
3. What are the limitations of national and transnational regulatory frameworks in combating institutional child sexual abuse?
4. How can we develop more proactive and effective mechanisms to combat institutional child sexual abuse?

REFERENCES

Abel, G., S. Lawry, E. Karlstrom, C. Osborn, and C. Gillespie. 1994. Screening tests for pedophilia. *Criminal Justice and Behavior* 21:115–31.

Barter, C. 1999. Practitioners' experiences and perceptions of investigating allegations of institutional abuse. *Child Abuse Review* 4:392.

Ben-Yehuda, N. 2001. *Betrayal and Treason: Violations of Trust and Loyalty*. Boulder: Colo.: Westview.

Berry, J. 1992. *Lead Us Not into Temptation: Catholic Priests and the Sexual Abuse of Children*. New York: Doubleday.

Beyer, L., D. Higgins, and L. Bromfield. 2005. *Understanding Organizational Risk Factors for Child Maltreatment: A Review of Literature*. Melbourne: National Child Protection Clearinghouse, Australian Institute of Family Studies.

Blecher, N. J. 2011. Sorry justice: Apology in Australian family group conferencing. *Psychiatry, Psychology and the Law* 18:95.

Boffey, D. 2014. Revealed: How Jimmy Savile abused up to 1,000 victims on BBC premises. *Observer*, January 18.

Brackenridge, C. H. 2001. *Spoilsports: Understanding and Preventing Sexual Exploitation in Sport*. London: Routledge.

Burns, J., and R. Somaiya. 2012. A shield of celebrity let a BBC host escape legal scrutiny for decades. *New York Times*, November 1.

Busch, R. 2002. Domestic violence and restorative justice initiatives: Who pays if we get it wrong? In *Restorative Justice and Family Violence*, ed. H. Strang and J. Braithwaite. Melbourne: Cambridge University Press.

Cohen, S. 2001. *States of Denial: Knowing About Atrocities and Suffering*. Cambridge: Polity Press.

Colton, M. 2002. Factors associated with abuse in residential child care institutions. *Children and Society* 16:33.

Colton, M., and M. Vanstone. 1996. *Betrayal of Trust: Sexual Abuse by Men Who Work with Children: In Their Own Words*. London: Free Association Books.

Commission to Inquire into Child Abuse. 2009. *Report of the Commission to Inquire Into Child Abuse*. http://www.childabusecommission.ie/.

Commission of Inquiry, Sexual Abuse of Minors in the Roman Catholic Church (Deetman Commission). 2011. *Summary of the Report in English*. http://www.commissiedeetman.nl/english-summery.html.

Commission of Investigation. 2009. *Report into the Catholic Archdiocese of Dublin.* Dublin: Department of Justice and Law Reform. http://www.dacoi.ie/.

——. 2011. *Report into the Catholic Archdiocese of Cloyne.* Dublin: Department of Justice and Law Reform. http://www.dacoi.ie/.

Conte, J. R., S. Wolf, and T. Smith. (1989. What sexual offenders tell us about prevention strategies. *Child Abuse and Neglect* 13:293.

Elliott. M., K. Browne, and J. Kilcoyne. 1995. Child abuse prevention: What offenders tell us. *Child Abuse and Neglect* 19:579.

Erooga, M. 2009a. *Towards Safer Organizations: Adults Who Pose a Risk to Children in the Workplace and Implications for Recruitment and Selection.* Executive Summary NSPCC. http://www.nspcc.org.uk/Inform/research/findings/towardssaferorganizationssummary_wdf63929.pdf.

——. (2009b. *Towards Safer Organizations: Adults Who Pose a Risk to Children in the Workplace and Implications for Recruitment and Selection.* London: NSPCC. http://www.nspcc.org.uk/Inform/research/findings/towardssafer organizationsreport_wdf72972.pdf.

Erooga, M., D. Allnock, and P. Telford. 2012. *Towards Safer Organizations II: Using the Perspectives of Convicted Sex Offenders to Inform Organizational Safeguarding of Children.* London: NSPCC.

Finkelhor, D., L. Williams, and N. Burns. 1988. *Nursery Crimes: A Study of Sexual Abuse in Day Care.* Newbury Park, Calif.: Sage.

Fitch, K., K. Spencer, and Z. Hilton. (2007. *Protecting Children from Sexual Abuse: Safer Recruitment of Workers in a Border-Free Europe.* London: NSPCC. http://www.nspcc.org.uk/Inform/publications/downloads/protectingchildrenfromsexualabuseineuropefullreport_wdf54737.pdf.

Francis, P., and N. Turner. 1995. Sexual misconduct within the Christian Church: Who are the perpetrators and those they abuse? *Counselling and Values* 39:218.

Gallagher, B. 1998. *Grappling With Smoke: Investigating and Managing Organised Abuse—A Good Practice Guide.* London: NSPCC.

——. 2000. The extent and nature of known cases of institutional child sexual abuse. *British Journal of Social Work* 30:795.

Garland, D. 1996. The limits of the sovereign state: Strategies of crime control in contemporary society. *British Journal of Criminology* 36:445.

Gavrielides, T. 2012. Clergy sexual abuse and the restorative justice dialogue. *Journal of Church and State* 55:617.

Gavrielides, T., and D. Coker. 2005. Restoring faith: Resolving the Catholic Church's sexual scandals through restorative justice. Working Paper I. *Contemporary Justice Review* 8:347.

Hall, M. 2000. After Waterhouse: Vicarious liability and the tort of institutional abuse. *Journal of Social Welfare and Family Law* 22:159.

Haywood, T., H. Kravitz, L. Grossman, O. Wasyliw, and D. Hardy. 1996. Psychological aspects of sexual functioning among cleric and noncleric alleged sex offenders. *Child Abuse and Neglect* 20:527.

John Jay College 2004. *The Nature and Scope of Sexual Abuse of Minors by Catholic Priests and Deacons in the United States, 1950–2002*. Washington, D.C.: United States Conference of Catholic Bishops.

——. 2011. *The Causes and Context of Sexual Abuse of Minors by Catholic Priests in the United States, 1950–2010* Report presented to the United States Conference of Catholic Bishops by the John Jay College Research Team. Washington, D.C.: United States Conference of Catholic Bishops.

Keenan, M. 2011. *Child Sexual Abuse and the Catholic Church: Gender, Power and Organizational Culture*. New York: Oxford University Press.

Langevin, R., S. Curnoe, and J. Bain. 2000. A study of clerics who commit sexual offenses: Are they different from other sex offenders? *Child Abuse and Neglect* 24:535.

Law Commission of Canada. 2000. *Restoring Dignity: Responding to Child Abuse in Canadian Institutions*. Law Commission of Canada.

Laws, D. R. 2000. Sexual offending as a public health problem: A North American perspective, *Journal of Research and Treatment* 8:243.

Leclerc, B., J. Proulx, and A. McKibben. 2005. Modus operandi of sexual offenders working or doing voluntary work with children and adolescents. *Journal of Sexual Aggression* 11:187.

Llewellyn, J. 2002. Dealing with the legacy of native residential school abuse in Canada: Litigation, ADR and restorative justice. *University of Toronto Law Journal* 52:253.

McAlinden, A. 2006. "Setting 'em up": Personal, familial and institutional grooming in the sexual abuse of children. *Social & Legal Studies* 15:339.

——. 2010. Vetting sexual offenders: State over-extension, the punishment deficit and the failure to manage risk. Social & Legal Studies 19:25.

——. 2012. "Grooming" and the sexual abuse of children: Institutional, Internet and familial dimensions. Clarendon Studies in Criminology. Oxford: Oxford University Press.

——. 2013. An inconvenient truth: Barriers to truth recovery in the aftermath of institutional child abuse in Ireland. *Legal Studies* 33:189.

McAlinden, A., and B. Naylor. 2014. *Restoring Trust: Public Inquiries as Mechanisms for Achieving Justice for Victims of Institutional Child Abuse.* In press.

Mercado, C. C., K. Terry, and A. D. Perillo. 2011. 'Sexual abuse in the Catholic Church and other youth serving organizations. In *International Perspectives on the Assessment and Treatment of Sexual Offenders: Theory, Practice and Research,* ed. D. P. Boer, R. Eher, L. A. Craig, M. H. Miner, and F. Pfäfflin. Chichester, UK: Wiley-Blackwell.

Murphy, F. D., H. Buckley, and L. Joyce, L. 2005. *The Ferns Report, Presented by the Ferns Inquiry to the Minister for Health and Children.* Dublin: Government Publications.

Nagy, R., and R. K. Sehdev. 2012. Introduction: Residential schools and decolonization. *Canadian Journal of Law and Society* 27:67.

Noll, D. E., and L. Harvey. 2008. Restorative mediation: The application of restorative justice practice and philosophy to clergy sexual abuse. *Journal of Child Sexual Abuse* 17:377.

Parkinson, P., K. Oats, and A. Jayakody. 2009. *A Study of Reported Sexual Abuse in the Anglican Church.* http://www.apo.org.au/research/study-reported-child-sexual-abuse-anglican-church.

Parliament of Victoria. 2013. *Betrayal of Trust: Inquiry into the Handling of Child Abuse by Religious and Other Non-government Organizations.* http://www.parliament.vic.gov.au/.

Parton, N. 2004. From Maria Colwell to Victoria Climbié: Reflections on public inquiries into child abuse a generation apart. *Child Abuse Review* 13:80.

Powell, A. 2007. *Paedophiles, Child Abuse and the Internet* Oxford: Radcliffe Publishing.

Ritchie, G. 2001. *Study on Disqualification from Working with Children Within the EU.* London: Institute of Advanced Legal Studies.

Roberts, T. 2011. Milwaukee Eighth Diocese to file for bankruptcy. *National Catholic Reporter,* January 5.

Rossner, M. 2013. *Just Emotions: Rituals of Restorative Justice.* Oxford: Oxford University Press.

Salter, A. 1995. *Transforming Trauma: A Guide to Understanding and Treating Adult Survivors of Child Sexual Abuse.* Newbury Park, Calif.: Sage.

Scraton, P. 2004. From deceit to disclosure: The politics of official inquiries in the United Kingdom. In *Crime, Truth and Justice: Official Inquiry,*

Discourse, Knowledge, ed. G. Gilligan and J. Pratt. Cullompton, Devon: Willan Publishing.

Shaw, T. 2007. *Historical Abuse Systemic Review: Residential Schools and Children's Homes in Scotland 1950–1995* Edinburgh: Scottish Government. http://www .scotland.gov.uk/Publications/2007/11/20104729/0.

Smallbone, S. W., and R. K. Wortley. 2000. *Child Sexual Abuse in Queensland: Offender Characteristics and Modus Operandi.* Brisbane: Queensland Crime Commission.

Smart, C. 1999. A history of ambivalence and conflict in the discursive construction of the "child victim" of sexual abuse. *Social & Legal Studies* 8:391.

Stanko, E. A. 1990. *Everyday Violence.* London: Virago.

Sullivan, J., and A. Beech. 2002. Professional perpetrators. *Child Abuse Review* 11:153.

——. 2004. A comparative study of demographic data relating to intra- and extra-familial child sexual abusers and professional perpetrators. *Journal of Sexual Aggression* 10:39.

Sullivan, J., A. R. Beech, L. A. Craig, and T. A. Gannon. 2011. Comparing intra-familial and extra-familial child sexual abusers with professionals who have sexually abused children with whom they work. *International Journal of Offender Therapy and Comparative Criminology* 55:56.

Sullivan, J., and E. Quayle. 2012. Manipulation styles of abusers who work with children. In *Creating Safer Organizations,* ed. M. Erooga. New York: Wiley.

Truth and Reconciliation Commission of Canada. 2012. *Truth and Reconciliation Commission of Canada: Interim Report.* http://www.attendancemarketing .com/~attmk/TRC_jd/Interim_report_English_electronic_copy.pdf.

Utting, W. 1997. *People Like Us: The Report of the Review of the Safeguards for Children Living Away From Home.* London: HMSO.

Ward, T., and S. M. Hudson. 1998. A model of the relapse process in sexual offenders. *Journal of Interpersonal Violence* 13:700.

Waterhouse, R. 2000. *Lost in Care.* London: HMSO.

Wortley, R., and S. Smallbone, eds. 2006. *Situational Prevention of Child Sexual Abuse, Crime Prevention Studies,* vol. 19. Monsey, N.Y.: Criminal Justice Press, and Cullompton, Devon: Willan Publishing.

CHAPTER 12

Child Sexual Abuse in the Catholic Church

▸ *KAREN J. TERRY*

MANY INSTITUTIONS AND ORGANIZATIONS HAVE come under scrutiny in the past decade after reports surfaced about child sexual abuse by adults within those organizations. Several high-profile cases in the United States were reported in schools (such as the esteemed private schools Horace Mann and Poly Prep), universities (Penn State), social organizations (the Boy Scouts of America), and sports (including USA hockey, swimming, gymnastics, weightlifting, and tennis). Yet no organization has been scrutinized more than the Catholic Church.

Child sexual abuse within the Catholic Church dominated media attention in the United States beginning in 2002, when the *Boston Globe* began covering the abuse allegations of serial predator John Geoghan in the Boston Archdiocese (*Boston Globe* 2004). At the height of this media attention, the United States Conference of Catholic Bishops created a charter that aimed to understand and address this problem. The charter established two entities, the Office of Child and Youth Protection and the National Review Board, which were charged with overseeing research on the abuse crisis. As part of their mandate, they commissioned researchers at John Jay College to conduct two studies. The first, *The Nature and Scope of Sexual Abuse of Minors by Catholic Priests and Deacons: 1950–2002* (hereafter referred to as the *Nature and Scope* study), provided information about the extent of the abuse crisis, the distribution of offenses nationally and over time, the priests against whom allegations were made, the minors they abused, the Church's response to the allegations, and the financial impact of the crisis (John Jay College 2004, 2006). The second study, *The Causes and*

Context of Sexual Abuse of Minors by Catholic Priests in the United States, 1950–2010 (hereafter referred to as the *Causes and Context* study), analyzed the conditions that permitted abusive behavior in the Catholic Church to persist, integrating research from sociocultural, psychological, situational, and organizational perspectives (Terry et al. 2011). Together, these studies provide critical information about the extent of abuse in the United States; an overview of the abusers, victims, and incidents; and explanations of factors correlated to the abuse crisis.

Though abuse in the Catholic Church in the United States became worldwide news, similar patterns of abuse were evident in Canada at the same time (Kenny 2012). These garnered far less media attention but resulted in inquiries and investigations into the abuse problem by the Canadian Conference of Catholic Bishops (CCCB 1992). And it was only years later that the focus on abuse in the Catholic Church shifted to Europe and other Western countries (Pew Research Center 2010). Academics and commissions began assessing the extent and effects of victimization and responses to it in Australia (Family and Community Development Committee 2013), Belgium (Aertsen 2014), England (Gilligan 2014), Ireland (Commission of Investigation into Catholic Diocese of Cloyne 2011; Commission of Investigation into Catholic Diocese of Dublin 2009; D'Alton, Guilfoyle, & Randall 2013; Keenan 2011; McAlinden 2006, 2012), and the Netherlands (Deetman et al. 2011), among others. Scholars and the media also began to draw attention to the role of the Vatican in the abuse crisis (Pew Research Center 2010), with the United Nations publishing a scathing attack on the Church (United Nations 2014). Conferences on sexual abuse in the Catholic Church have also recently become more global rather than U.S.-centric, and by 2011 such conferences even included participants from Asia, Latin America, and Africa (Glatz 2013; International Institute for the Sociology of Law 2014).

This chapter provides an overview of what is known about sexual abuse in the Catholic Church. The primary focus is on the extensive studies of abuse in the United States, including the findings of the two national studies sponsored by the U.S. Conference of Catholic Bishops, followed by a summary of the findings about abuse in other Western countries. The chapter concludes with suggestions for future research and policy perspectives related to the abuse crisis.

EARLY STUDIES ON ABUSE IN THE CATHOLIC CHURCH

Prior to 2002 few scholars empirically evaluated the prevalence or etiology of sexual misconduct by Catholic priests. Most of the early studies were based on samples that were small, were not random, focused on select clinical centers or dioceses, and had limited generalizability. Some scholars, such as Andrews (1999) and Flynn (2000), collected self-reports from parishioners to understand who was abused and the impact of this abuse. Others, such as Goetz (1992), collected self-reports of pastors to find out how many had committed acts of sexual misconduct with adults. Many of these early scholars (e.g., Fones et al. 1999; Irons & Laaser 1994; Mendola 1998) evaluated small samples of priests who were treated or referred for treatment. Loftus and Camargo (1993) conducted a larger study with a clinical sample of 1,322 priests and brothers, which found that 27.8 percent reported having engaged in a sexual relationship with an adult woman while 8.4 percent reported sexual misconduct with a minor. In another study with a nonclinical sample, Anthony Sipe (1990) concluded that 2 percent of priests engage in pedophiliac behavior, 4 percent are sexually preoccupied with adolescent boys or girls, and 20 to 40 percent engage in sexual misconduct with adults. To further understand the types of victims priest abusers target, Ukeritis (2005) studied seventy-four clergy who had abused children and found that approximately 38 percent primarily abused children age 13 or younger while 62 percent abused adolescents between ages 14 and 18.

Some scholars attempted to estimate the prevalence of child sexual abuse in the Catholic Church. Based on data from the St. Luke Institute (a treatment facility for priests), Plante (2003) estimated that three thousand priests committed sexually abusive acts against twenty-four thousand victims over the past fifty years. In its literature review, the Catholic League for Religious and Civil Rights (2004) estimated that between 1 and 2 percent of priests had abused children. At the behest of the Vatican, several scholars also attempted to place the issue of sexual abuse and the clergy into a broader perspective. Kafka (2004) stated that priest offenders differ significantly from offenders in the general population (based on clinical samples), and that the typical child sexual abuser in the Catholic Church is a diocesan priest who is an ephebophile.

As the high-profile cases of abuse by Gauthe, Porter, and Geoghan emerged, several journalists began investigating abuse within the Catholic

Church as well. According to Jenkins (1996), the media emphasis on sexual abuse by priests led to a public image of the "pedophile priest" and portrayed abuse as a Catholic problem. Based on his coverage of the Gilbert Gauthe case in Louisiana from 1984 to 1992, Jason Berry (1992) claimed that four hundred priests and brothers had sexually abused children and that the Church spent more than $400 million in legal, medical, and psychological expenses. *New York Times* journalist Laurie Goodstein (2003) wrote an investigative article that stated that by the end of 2002, more than 1,205 priests had abused 4,268 victims. She found that most of the abuse had occurred in the 1970s and 1980s, most victims (80 percent) were male, and nearly half were under the age of 12.

THE *NATURE AND SCOPE* STUDY

Because of their limited scope, the early studies on sexual abuse in the Catholic Church did not provide a complete understanding of the prevalence of abuse and the nature of the offenses. The mandate for the *Nature and Scope* study was to determine the extent of the sexual abuse of minors by Catholic priests nationally from 1950 to 2002. Specifically, the bishops needed more knowledge about the offenses (including the number of and nature of the offenses, when and where the offenses were committed, and during what activities); the priests who abused (including their age at the time of abuse, date of ordination, length of time ordained prior to first allegation of abuse, job description/duties at the time the abuse occurred, number of victims, actions taken against the priest, and background of the priest); and the victims (including age when abused, gender, family situation (who they were living with), grooming behavior that occurred before/during the abusive relationship, length of time between the abuse and when the abuse was reported, and to whom the abuse was reported) (Terry 2008).

The John Jay research team gathered information about every allegation of sexual abuse of a minor by priests and deacons in the United States from existing files at all Catholic dioceses (districts of the Catholic Church that are supervised by bishops), eparchies (eastern rite districts that are similar to dioceses), and religious communities. The research team developed three separate surveys and sent them to all dioceses and eparchies in the United States, as well as 140 religious orders of men. Identities of all priests and victims were confidential, and the researchers employed a double-blind procedure to ensure the anonymity of the subjects. Overall, 97 percent of all dioceses and eparchies (representing 99 percent of all diocesan priests) and 63 percent of all religious communities (representing 84 percent of religious priests) responded.

The results of the *Nature and Scope* study showed that 4,392 priests sexually abused nearly 11,000 children between 1950 and 2002, which was equivalent to 4 percent of priests in ministry during that time having allegations of abuse. Data collected over the following decade by researchers at the Center for Applied Research of the Apostolate (CARA) indicate that the number has increased: 5 percent of priests in ministry since 1950 have allegations of abuse against approximately 15,000 victims. The John Jay data, supported by subsequent data from CARA, show that abuse incidence peaked in the 1970s and early 1980s. This distribution was consistent across all regions of the Catholic Church in the United States, as well as in all sizes of dioceses (the U.S. Catholic Church is divided into fourteen regions, averaging just over a dozen dioceses per region). Figure 12.1 shows the abuse distribution from 1950 to 2002.

There was a significant delay in reporting of offenses, and many victims waited decades to report their abuse to the dioceses. In the years of the

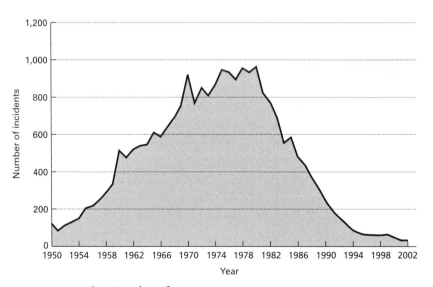

FIGURE 12.1 **Abuse Incidents from 1950 to 2002**

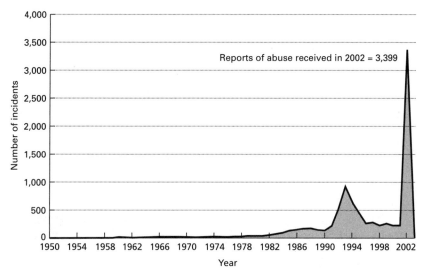

FIGURE 12.2 **Abuse Incidents by Year of Report**

high-profile cases of abuse that were published in the media—Gauthe in 1985, Porter in 1993, and Geoghan in 2002—reports increased, with the largest number of cases reported in 2002. Figure 12.2 shows the distribution of reports from 1950 to 2002. Though many reports are still being made today, most of the abuse being reported occurred decades ago. The peak of abuse cases that are being reported today remains in the late 1970s–early 1980s.

For all cases of abuse reported to the dioceses by 2002, the majority of abusers (69 percent) were diocesan priests, and most were either serving as a pastor (25 percent) or associate pastor (42 percent) at the time of the abuse. This is important in that pastors and associate pastors generally have high levels of discretion in their parishes, have little direct supervision of day-to-day activities, and usually live in a parish residence alone. The priest abusers committed numerous and often multiple types of sexual offenses, ranging from touching outside the clothes to penetration. Abuse occurred most often in the home of the priest (41 percent), though it also occurred in high frequency in the church (16 percent), the victim's home (12 percent), a vacation house (10 percent), school (10 percent), and a car (10 percent).

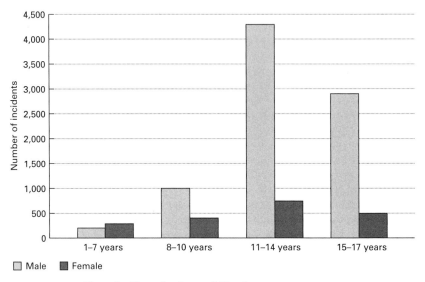

FIGURE 12.3 **Abuse Incidents by Age and Gender**

The majority of abusers (56 percent) had one victim (often with multiple incidents of abuse), though 3.5 percent of abusers were responsible for abusing 26 percent of the victims. These "career criminals" were unique in their number and types of victims as well as the duration of their abusive careers. The large majority of victims (81 percent) were male, and victims were most commonly (51 percent) between the ages of 11 and 14. Figure 12.3 shows the gender and age distribution of the victims.

Despite the high number of male victims, most of the career criminal priests were "generalists," victimizing children and adolescents of various ages and/or genders rather than targeting a specific type of victim. They tended to have a very long abusive career: those with ten to nineteen victims abused over a mean period of 18.0 years, and those with twenty or more victims abused over a mean period of 22.5 years. They began abusing within the first year after ordination and continued throughout much of their time in ministry.

The most common Church response to allegations of abuse was evaluation and treatment of the priest. Data show that 1,624 priests received treatment between 1950 and 2002 for sexually abusing minors, and most of

TABLE 12.1   Diocesan Response to Priests Who Abused Minors, by Decade
(in percent)

DIOCESAN RESPONSES	DISTRIBUTION BY DECADE OF FIRST REPORT				
	1950–1979	1980–1989	1990–1999	2000–2003	TOTAL %
Reprimanded and returned	34.8	12.4	4.8	3.8	8.8
Referred for evaluation	33.0	50.7	45.6	28.0	40.4
Suspended	6.4	7.6	6.8	8.1	7.3
Administrative leave	6.0	8.9	11.9	16.3	12.0
Resigned or retired	5.2	4.8	8.7	11.6	8.5
Reinstated	3.0	1.7	1.6	1.4	1.7
Treatment	2.2	4.6	3.6	2.2	3.2
No action taken	3.7	2.4	6.5	14.7	7.7

those priests received more than one type of treatment. There was a rise in the use of treatment in the 1980s, particularly with specialized sex offender treatment programs, which is consistent with the response to sex offenders in the general population.

As indicated in table 12.1, treatment was not the only action taken. (The table shows the types of actions clustered by the decade in which the report was made, as opposed to when the abuse actually occurred.) The actions are not mutually exclusive, and in some cases multiple actions were taken with an individual priest. Of importance, however, is the change in response by decade. Before 1980 a reprimand and return to duty was as likely as a referral for evaluation by a professional. From the 1980s forward the likelihood of a reprimand and return to duty decreased, and the likelihood of being put on administrative leave or suspended increased. The elevated percentages for the category of "no action taken" were most often a result of accusations against priests who were not in active ministry at the time of the report. Because of the delay in reporting, the later the decade of the report, the more likely the abuser was no longer in active ministry.

Few cases of child sexual abuse by priests were processed through the criminal justice system. Data indicate two primary reasons for this: (1) bishops were more likely to take action to help the abusers (such as with treatment) rather than punish them, and (2) there was a substantial delay in the reporting of most offenses. Many abuse cases were reported after the statute of limitations had expired, and often decades after the abuse occurred. Traditionally, statutes of limitation in most states were approximately five to seven years after the incident occurred, or a limited amount of time after the abused child has reached the age of majority. Thus, rather than being processed through the criminal justice system, most abusive priests were handled by the dioceses.

THE *CAUSES AND CONTEXT* STUDY

While the *Nature and Scope* study provided a snapshot of the problem of sexual abuse of minors by Catholic priests, it raised many questions. Specifically:

- What factors could explain the peak of abusive behavior in the 1970s? Were the contributing factors that led to the increase in abuse incidents in the 1960s and the subsequent decline in the 1980s in society generally or in the Catholic Church?
- Are priest abusers unique, either to other priests or to nonclergy sexual abusers, and are there risk factors that might identify potential offenders?
- How has seminary education and training changed over this time period?
- What role did the Church leadership play in addressing the abuse crisis, and when?
- What role did opportunity and situation play in the abusive behavior?
- Why was the harm of sexual abuse not understood?

The *Causes and Context* study provided a unique opportunity to collect data from a variety of sources on the sexual abuse of minors over a sixty-year period. The researchers began by analyzing existing longitudinal data sets of various types of social behavior (including crime, divorce, and premarital sex) to provide a historical framework (see Gfroerer & Brodsky 1992; Goldstein 1999; Hofferth, Kahn, & Baldwin 1987; Norton & Moorman 1987). Next, they evaluated seminary documents outlining the history and development of a curriculum on human formation throughout the century. This included information on the priests' personal formation, with an emphasis on sexuality and preparation for celibacy. The study methodology also included surveys conducted of various groups within the Catholic Church, such as bishops and other diocesan leaders; vicars general; victim assistance coordinators; priests with allegations of abuse and a comparison sample of priests in active parish ministry who had not been accused (the identity and behavior survey); and a group of "priests with integrity" who served in some capacity to assist victims of abuse. Finally, the researchers collected clinical data from three treatment centers. The clinical data were on four groups of priests: those with allegations of abuse against minors, those with allegations of other sexual misconduct, those with behavioral or mental health problems, and a normative sample. Data included psychological history and testing, as well as information from in-depth clinical interviews.

The findings of the *Causes and Context* study indicated that there is no single cause of the sexual abuse crisis. Instead, it was caused by a complex interaction of psychological, developmental, organizational, cultural, and situational factors. Consistent with literature about sex offenders in the general population, the *Causes and Context* data show that priests who sexually abused minors constituted a heterogeneous population who abused for myriad reasons.

The longitudinal data analysis indicated that the rise in abuse cases in the 1960s and 1970s was consistent with the rise in other types of "deviant" behavior in that time period in the United States, such as drug use and crime, as well as changes in social behavior, such as an increase in premarital sexual behavior and divorce (Terry et al. 2011). Factors that are unique to the Catholic Church, such as an exclusively male priesthood and the commitment to celibate chastity, did not change during the increase, peak, and decrease in abuse incidents and thus are not causes of the abuse crisis.

Seminary education changed significantly over the period of study, and the *Causes and Context* findings indicate that patterns of abuse behavior varied by decade of ordination. The majority of abusive priests were ordained prior to the 1970s, and more abusers were educated in seminaries in the 1940s and 1950s than at any other time period in the study. There was a significant expansion of seminaries in this postwar period, and prior to the 1970s the curriculum focused almost entirely on spiritual development.

There was little or no human formation component to the education, and as such seminarians were not being adequately prepared to live a life of chaste celibacy. Human formation training evolved from the 1980s onward, and while there is no indication that this is a cause of the decrease in abuse of minors, it is consistent with the drop in allegations of abuse.

The clinical data provided a wealth of information about the population of priests who were referred for treatment. The data indicate that priests with allegations of sexually abusing minors were not significantly more likely than other priests in the sample to have personality or mood disorders or a lower IQ, as shown by the MCMI, MMPI, and WAIS tests. The clinical data also showed that few abusers were driven by sexual pathologies, as only 5 percent of the priests with allegations of abusing children were diagnosed with pedophilia.

Most priests who had allegations of sexual abuse against minors had exhibited indiscriminate sexual behavior and could be identified as "generalists" rather than "specialists" in regard to their victim choice. Eighty percent of the priests who abused minors also had participated in sexual behavior with adults, and few targeted a particular age and/or gender of child to abuse. Priests who had participated in sexual behavior prior to ordination were more likely to participate in sexual behavior after ordination, but that behavior was with adults and not minors. Sexual identity did not predict abuse of a minor; priests who had same-sex sexual experiences either before seminary or in seminary were more likely to have sexual behavior after ordination, but this behavior was most likely with adults. Many abusers educated in early cohorts had a "confused" sexual identity; however, this was not evident in later cohorts, and sexual identity did not predict abuse of a minor.

The clinical history data as well as the identity and behavior survey and interview data indicate that the priests' personal vulnerabilities, in combination with situational stresses and opportunities, increased the risk of abuse. Many of the abusers had poor psychosexual development or other weaknesses (such as emotional congruence with children or adolescents), **had** intimacy deficits (including few close peers and weak family bonds), experienced increased stressors from work (for example, having recently received more responsibilities, such as becoming a pastor), and had opportunities to abuse (such as unguarded access to minors in their role as pastors). Access to victims played a critical role in victim choice.

Few significant differences were found between the locations and situations in which boys and girls were abused, but priests had more access to boys until recently (primarily because parishes permitted girls as altar servers after 1983). Priests who abused minors exhibited behavior consistent with child sexual abusers in general society. In particular, the priests who sexually abused minors "groomed" their victims and justified and excused their own behavior, often shifting responsibility to the victims or others.

Most of the abuse incidents that have been reported occurred decades ago. Though abuse does still occur in the Catholic Church, analyses show that it is at a significantly lower rate now than at the peak of the abuse crisis in the 1970s. Most of the incidents of sexual abuse of minors by priests that are being reported today continue to fit into the distribution of abuse incidents concentrated in the mid-1960s to mid-1980s. This delay in reporting led to an unfortunate reality: few cases of child sexual abuse by priests were processed through the criminal justice system. Most victims came forward to report abuse years after the statute of limitations had expired, and often decades after the abuse occurred.

The *Causes and Context* study assessed the diocesan responses to abuse from 1985 onward. It was in 1985 that the high-profile case of Gilbert Gauthe led to national discussions about sexual abuse, and by 1985 nearly every diocese in the United States had experienced cases of sexual abuse of minors by priests. The questions of how to understand the act of sexual abuse of a minor by a priest and how to respond to the victim, the family and the parish were presented for regular discussion in bishops' meetings from that point onward. Legal advisers and insurers counseled the development of explicit policies, but in many dioceses there was not a thorough recognition of the problem or implementation of policies. Based on written documents from that time, the bishops were focused primarily on the well-being of the priests who had abused, not the harm they had caused their victims.

In 1993 the American bishops endorsed the "Five Principles" in response to the sexual abuse of minors. These principles stated that diocesan leaders should (1) respond promptly to all allegations of abuse where there is reasonable belief that abuse has occurred; (2) relieve the alleged offender promptly of his ministerial duties and refer him for appropriate medical evaluation and intervention if such an allegation is supported by sufficient evidence; (3) comply with the obligations of civil law regarding reporting of the incident and cooperating with the investigation; (4) reach out to the victims and their families and communicate sincere commitment to their spiritual and emotional well-being; and (5) deal as openly as possible, within the confines of respect for privacy of the individuals involved, with members of the community. The implementation of the principles, however, was uneven among dioceses and delayed in most.

In response to the *Causes and Context* surveys, bishops who held positions through the early 1990s stated that they had made several efforts to remove abusive priests from ministry, but many of these efforts were not successful. In particular, they noted that some of the psychological treatments for abusive priests were not always successful, the Church had inadequate processes to help priests leave the priesthood, and the canon law processes for suspension were complex and took years to complete. Most bishops focused on canonical processes or helping the priests overcome their problems through rehabilitative processes rather than turning to outside sources such as the criminal justice system. Generally, until the 2000s diocesan leaders tended to view the sexual abuse of minors through the lens of human failure and sin rather than as a criminal act. Those bishops who came to their positions after 2000 explained the sexual abuse crisis and the Church response to it in a far wider and evolving framework. They were more likely to focus on societal issues and faulty seminary teaching and formation programs as contributors to the sexual abuse crisis. They were also more likely to acknowledge the significant harm to the victims that resulted from the abusive acts by the priests.

ABUSE IN THE CATHOLIC CHURCH: A GLOBAL ISSUE

While the Catholic Church in the United States has been scrutinized in the media for more than a decade, the focus on abuse in the Catholic Church in most other countries has come more recently. This focus has primarily been on English-speaking and European countries, though individuals from the Catholic Church in Africa, Asia, and Latin America are starting to discuss abuse and responses to it as well. Most of the information about abuse in the Catholic Church worldwide has been published through governmental inquiries and commissions, or through journalistic accounts in the media. Few scholars have yet published research studies on the extent of abuse and factors associated with it, though several studies are currently ongoing.

Like its U.S. counterpart, the Catholic Church in Canada has been responding to abuse allegations for decades. The CCCB created an ad hoc committee in 1989 to investigate allegations of abuse that occurred in the 1970s and 1980s. The mandate of the committee was to develop guidelines and policies for responding to and caring for victims of abuse by priests; responding to those priests who abused; breaking the cycle of abuse; and preventing future acts of abuse. In 1992 the committee published a report, *From Pain to Hope*, outlining these guidelines (CCCB 1992), which bear striking similarity to the Five Principles published by the USCCB.

Though abuse occurred in multiple provinces—resulting, for example, in a $40 million settlement by the government to survivors in Ottawa and Toronto—the province of Newfoundland experienced particularly high rates of abuse and was one of the catalysts for the creation of the Ad Hoc Committee. In Newfoundland the Christian Brothers religious order at the Mount Cashel orphanage allegedly abused more than 300 boys during the 1970s and 1980s. Allegations against the Christian Brothers led to a Royal Commission investigation, which found that officials covered up abuse cases and had transferred abusive priests rather than disciplining them (Hughes 1991).

The Christian Brothers, whose order originated in Ireland, were also the subject of inquiry there. Known for their extensive use of corporal punishment, they reportedly abused many of the children in their schools. The Irish government established a commission to investigate allegations against the Christian Brothers and published a five-volume report outlining the physical, sexual, and emotional abuse and neglect of thousands of children (Ryan 2009). The Ryan Report, as it is colloquially called, found that 90 percent of the witnesses interviewed experienced physical abuse, and nearly half experienced sexual abuse. The victims were both male and female, and they said the abuse often took place during excursions or other outings (Ryan 2009). Girls in particular were made to feel responsible for the abuse that happened to them, by both the abusers and those to whom they reported abuse.

The Ryan Report was only one of several inquiries into abuse by Catholic priests in Ireland, though it is the most extensive of the reports published. Between 1990 and 2010 the government issued inquiries into six individual dioceses—Cloyne, Dublin, Ferns, Limerick, Raphoe, and Tuam—to review the extent of and responses to abuse cases there. Each of these inquires was initiated after a high-profile abuse case within the diocese, and the subsequent reports reached similar conclusions. Namely, the reports blamed high levels of secrecy by leaders of the Church, protection of the institution from scandal, protection of the Church's reputation and assets, and little attention to the harm caused to victims (Commission of Investigation into Catholic Archdiocese of Dublin 2009).

In one of the few published academic studies on abuse in the Catholic Church outside of the United States, Keenan (2011) discusses the long-term effects that sexual abuse has on survivors within the Irish Catholic Church, and also the organizational and cultural factors that allowed such abuse to continue. Keenan attributes the abuse crisis in the Church to a complex interaction of factors that include priestly formation, clerical culture, organizational structure, and sexuality. She notes that these factors combine to create high-risk situations for abuse to occur, and that to reduce opportunities for abuse the Church needs significant institutional reform. Though her recommendations are similar to those made in the reports resulting from the governmental inquiries, she takes her critical analysis further by discussing the need to reconsider the role of women in the Church and the role of celibacy for priests.

The government in Australia has taken a more comprehensive approach to its review of abuse, including the abuse by Catholic priests in a broader inquiry about abuse in religious and other organizations. In its report, *Betrayal of Hope*, the Family and Community Development Committee (2013) was tasked with investigating three things: how organizations respond to allegations of abuse within the organizations; whether these organizations have policies or systemic practices that discourage the reporting of abuse; and what changes in these organizations might help prevent future abuse incidents. The committee's report included findings similar to those in other countries; namely, the organizations needed more appropriate responses to allegations of sexual abuse. They also noted that organizational responses to abuse were particularly egregious between the1950s and 1980s, and that the Catholic Church specifically responded inadequately at that time. The committee said that children were at high risk of abuse in the Catholic Church because of its complex hierarchy and structure, processes for responding to allegations, inherent system of culture and power, teachings and beliefs, and failure to respond appropriately to abuse allegations (Family and Community Development Committee 2013).

In spring 2010, the media began to report on abuse allegations in the Catholic Church in Europe at rates not seen since the crisis erupted in 2002 (Pew Research Center 2010). This coincided with a police raid of the headquarters of the Catholic Church in Belgium ("Popeshuffle" 2010), where they seized documents from a Church commission investigating allegations of abuse. After this raid the director of the commission resigned and no report has yet been released, though the police confiscated several hundred internal documents from the personal residences of current and former archbishops. The following year a commission in the Netherlands released a report chronicling the abuse crisis there and the Church's responses to it (Deetman et al. 2011). This report, while not academic, is one of the few to estimate the scope of the crisis outside of the United States, as the authors state that at least eight hundred priests have sexually abused children since 1945. And while two thousand victims in the Netherlands have come forward, the authors of the report estimate that the extent of victimization is much greater—between ten thousand and twenty thousand victims (Deetman et al. 2011). Also in 2011 the German Bishops' Conference pledged transparency in understanding and responding to abuse and selected an academic group to study the nature and scope of the problem there. However, they controversially canceled the contract, with both sides saying the other was not cooperating (Hans 2013).

The scandal in Germany was particularly contentious, largely because of the potential role Pope Benedict XVI played in the handling of abuse cases there. Prior to his election as pope, then-Cardinal Ratzinger served as the archbishop of Munich and Freising and then as the prefect of the Sacred Congregation of the Doctrine of the Faith (CDF). As a result of his role as prefect of the CDF, he was privy to, and oversaw, more cases of sexual abuse than any other individual in the Catholic Church globally. He restructured the CDF such that it became responsible for reviewing cases of sexual abuse, removing that role from individual dioceses. Though he attempted to improve the response to abuse cases through these structural changes, his tenure as pope was marred by the constant allegations that he was not doing enough to address the problem. In particular, he failed to defrock an abusive priest in the United States who had allegations of abusing hundreds of deaf boys at a Catholic school, and he allegedly covered up cases of abuse in Germany when he was cardinal.

As sexual abuse in the Catholic Church was starting to be viewed as a global crisis, several organizations within and outside the Church began to convene meetings to discuss the issue. These international meetings have drawn on the expertise of professionals, academics, advocates, Church officials, and victims. For example, McGill University's Centre for Research on Religion hosted a conference in 2011, Trauma and Transformation, where experts discussed the sexual abuse crisis and its profound impact on the Church (Centre for Research on Religion 2011). In 2012 psychologist Tom Plante and former OCYP director Kathleen McChesney convened a meeting to discuss the state of the abuse crisis in the United States a decade after the 2002 peak of attention (Plante & McChesney 2012). In 2013 the Centre of Excellence in Policing and Security (CEPS) at Griffith University in Australia hosted a symposium on the redress of harm and the prevention of child sexual abuse within institutions. The goal of the symposium was to convene a group of experts and discuss the scope of the problem, harms caused by abuse, and institutional responses to it (CEPS 2013). This symposium followed the formation of a Royal Commission to address the problem of sexual abuse within institutions, with commission leaders looking to the crisis in the Church as an example of institutional abuse and responses to it (Royal Commission 2013). While this symposium and the related Royal Commission did not focus solely on abuse in the Catholic Church, a conference in Spain in 2014 did exactly that. Convened by a Belgian scholar, this conference drew together empirical scholars from Austria, Belgium, Finland, Germany, Ireland, Spain, the Netherlands, the United Kingdom, and the United States, in the most comprehensive global conference to date discussing abuse in the Catholic Church (IISL 2014). Representatives from each country presented empirical data about the extent of the problem, while other scholars discussed the institutional responses to abuse within that country. The focus was not only on the organizational response but also on the restorative response to victims and their families.

Though these conferences are recent responses to the problem of sexual abuse within the Catholic Church, English-speaking countries worldwide began meeting in 2000 for the annual Anglophone Conference on the Safeguarding of Children. This coincided with a growing awareness about the problem of abuse in the Church and an understanding that the institution needed to create an appropriate response to both abusers and victims. The Anglophone Conference has had an increasingly global presence since

2011, with representation from Catholic churches in Asia, Latin American, and Africa attending for the first time (Glatz 2013). The conference in 2011 was also notable in that it occurred immediately after the release of the *Causes and Context* report, using this as a basis for understanding the problem of abuse in the Church worldwide, and simultaneously with the release of a Circular Letter from the CDF. This circular mandated that all conferences worldwide develop abuse prevention guidelines, and by 2013, 80 percent of the conferences had done so (Conlon 2013).

This was not the first time the Vatican sought direction from external experts, however. In 2003 the Vatican convened a group of experts who presented research findings about the psychological factors associated with child sexual abuse, recidivism studies, the harmful effects of sexual abuse on child victims, and the efficacy of therapy for abusers (Hanson, Pfäfflin, & Lütz 2004). Representatives of the Vatican intended to apply the information provided to them to improve psychological screening of potential offenders, improve seminary training, and respond more appropriately to those harmed by abuse. Like the *Causes and Context* study that was released years later, the Vatican report noted that there is no certain way to screen out potential abusers, and that the situational factors they face in seminary and subsequently after ordination may also play a role in their abusive behavior (Hanson et al.2004).

CONCLUSION

The sexual abuse of minors is a serious societal problem, and one that can lead to substantial and long-term harm to victims. Abuse is not uncommon in institutions where adults form mentoring and nurturing relationships with adolescents, including schools, religious organizations, sports teams, and social organizations. The studies and reports about abuse in the Catholic Church provide a framework for understanding not only the sexual abuse of minors by Catholic priests but sexual victimization of children in other institutions. And while there is no single cause of this abuse or profile of a priest offender, it is clear that the organizational structure and culture allowed for onset and persistence of abuse within the institution.

For nearly a decade the Catholic Church in the United States appeared to be the epicenter of the sexual abuse crisis, yet by 2010 it became apparent the problem was much more widespread. The empirical studies that have been published in the United States can help inform other countries about factors associated with sexual abuse by priests; the spiritual, emotional, and psychological harm caused to victims by this abuse; and the failure of the Church to address the problems in a timely and appropriate manner. The global discussions about abuse in the Catholic Church are helping with the dissemination of information about how to respond to cases of abuse and how to apply best practices for prevention of future cases. The steps taken by scholars, practitioners, church officials, and advocates have led to the implementation of abuse prevention guidelines and safe-environment training programs worldwide. The Church now must continue to work toward helping those who have been harmed for so many years to heal and prevent such abuses to the greatest extent possible in the future.

DISCUSSION QUESTIONS

1. What steps should the individual bishops' conferences take to reduce the risk of sexual abuse for children by Catholic priests? What steps should the Vatican take?
2. What are similarities between abuse cases in the Catholic Church in different countries? What are differences?
3. Based on the empirical evidence collected in the United States, what factors played a key role in the abuse crisis? Do you think these factors also played a role in abuse in the Church in other countries?
4. How is sexual abuse in the Catholic Church similar to sexual abuse within other institutions? What lessons can be learned from the Church about how organizations should respond to abuse?

REFERENCES

Aersten, I. 2014. Sexual abuse in the Roman Catholic Church in Belgium: A study of the phenomenon and response mechanisms. Paper presented at the Workshop on Sexual Abuse in the Church and Other Institutional Settings, Onati, Spain, April 10–11.

Andrews, D. J. 1999. Healing in congregations in the aftermath of sexual abuse by a pastor. Dissertation, Hartford Seminary.

Berry, J. (1992). *Lead Us Not Into Temptation: Catholic Priests and the Sexual Abuse of Children* Champaign: University of Illinois Press.

Boston Globe. 2004. *The Boston Globe Spotlight Investigation: Abuse in the Catholic Church.* http://www.boston.com/globe/spotlight/abuse/.

Catholic League for Religious and Civil Rights. 2004. *Sexual Abuse in Social Context: Catholic Clergy and Other Professionals.* New York: Catholic League for Religious and Civil Rights.

CCCB Ad Hoc Committee on Child Sexual Abuse. 1992. *From Pain to Hope.* Ottawa; CCCB.

Centre of Excellence in Policing and Security (CEPS). 2013. *Looking Back, Looking Forward: The Redress of Harm and Prevention of Child Sexual Abuse.* Brisbane, Australia: Griffith University.

Centre for Research and Religion. 2011. *Trauma and Transformation: The Catholic Church and the Sexual Abuse Crisis.* Montreal: McGill University. http://traumaandtransformation.org/.

Commission of Investigation into Catholic Diocese of Cloyne. 2011. *Cloyne Report.* Dublin: Department of Justice and Equality.

Commission of Investigation into Catholic Archdiocese of Dublin. 2009. *Murphy Report.* Dublin: Department of Justice and Equality.

Conlon, R. D. 2013. When nations get together on child sexual abuse. USCCBlog. http://usccbmedia.blogspot.com/2013/07/when-nations-get-together-on-child.html.

D'Alton, P., M. Guilfoyle, and P. Randall. 2013. Roman Catholic clergy who have sexually abused children: Their perceptions of their developmental experience. *Child Abuse & Neglect* 37:698–702.

Deetman, W., N. Draijer, P. Kalbfleisch, H. Merckelbach, M. Monteiro, and G. de Vries. 2011. *The Sexual Abuse of Minors within the Roman Catholic Church.* Amsterdam: Research Commission on the Sexual Abuse of Minors Within the Roman Catholic Church.

Family and Community Development Committee. 2013. *Betrayal of Trust: Inquiry into the Handling of Child Abuse by Religious and Other Non-Government Organisations.* Victoria, Australia: Parliament of Victoria.

Flynn, K. A. 2000. Clergy sexual abuse of women: A specialized form of trauma. Ph.D. dissertation, Claremont Graduate University.

Fones, C. S. L., S. B. Levine, S. E. Althof, & C. B. Risen. 1999. The sexual struggles of 23 clergymen: A follow-up study. *Journal of Sex & Marital Therapy* 25, 183–95.

Gfroerer, J., and M. Brodsky. 1992. The incidence of illicit drug use in the United States, 1962–1989. *British Journal of Addiction* 87 (9): 1345–51.

Gilligan, P. 2014. Rhetoric, review and recognition: Exploring the failure of the Catholic Church in England and Wales to satisfy survivors of sexual abuse by its clergy. Paper presented at the Workshop on Sexual Abuse in the Church and Other Institutional Settings, Onati, Spain, April 10–11.

Glatz, C. 2013. Meeting on sex abuse expands reach, promoting global approach. *Catholic News Reporter.* http://ncronline.org/news/accountability/meeting-sex-abuse-expands-reach-promoting-global-approach.

Goetz, D. 1992. Is the pastor's family safe at home? *Leadership* 13:38–44.

Goldstein, J. R. 1999. The Leveling of Divorce in the United States. *Demography* 36 (3): 409–14.

Goodstein, L. 2003. Decades of damage: Trail of pain in Church crisis leads to nearly every diocese. *New York Times,* January 12, 1.

Hans, B. 2013. Sex abuse scandal: German Catholic Church cancels inquiry. *Spiegel Online International.* http://www.spiegel.de/international/germany/german-catholic-church-cancels-sex-abuse-scandal-inquiry-a-876612.html.

Hanson, R. K., F. Pfäfflin, and M. Lütz, eds. 2004. *Sexual Abuse in the Catholic Church: Scientific and Legal Perspectives.* Rome: Libreria Editrice Vaticana.

Hofferth, S. L., J. R. Kahn, and W. Baldwin. 1987. Premarital sexual activity among U.S. teenage women over the past three decades. *Family Planning Perspectives* 19 (2): 46–53.

Hughes, S. H. S. 1991. *Royal Commission of Inquiry into the Response of the Newfoundland Criminal Justice System to Complaints.* Newfoundland: Office of the Queen's Printer.

International Institute for the Sociology of Law (IISL). 2014. Workshop on Sexual Abuse in the Church and Other Institutional Settings, Onati, Spain, April 10–11.

Irons, R., and M. Laaser. 1994. The abduction of fidelity: Sexual exploitation by clergy—Experience with inpatient assessment. *Sexual Addiction & Compulsivity* 1:119–29.

Jenkins, P. 1996. *Pedophiles and Priests: Anatomy of a Contemporary Crisis.* Bridgewater, N.J.: Replica Books.

John Jay College. 2004. *The Nature and Scope of Sexual Abuse of Minors by Catholic Priests and Deacons in the United States, 1950–2002.* Washington, D.C.: United States Conference of Catholic Bishops.

——. 2006. *The Nature and Scope of Sexual Abuse of Minors by Catholic Priests and Deacons in the United States, 1950–2002: Supplementary Data Analysis.* Washington, D.C.: United States Conference of Catholic Bishops.

Kafka, M. P. 2004. Sexual molesters of adolescents, ephebophilia, and Catholic clergy: A review and synthesis. In *Sexual Abuse in the Catholic Church: Scientific and Legal Perspectives*, ed. R. K. Hanson, P. Friedmann, and M. Lutz. Vatican: Libreria Editrico Vaticana.

Keenan, M. 2011. *Child Sexual Abuse and the Catholic Church: Gender, Power and Organizational Culture.* London: Oxford University Press.

Kenny, N. 2012. *Healing the Church: Diagnosing and Treating the Clergy Sexual Abuse Scandal.* Montreal: Novalis.

Loftus, J. A., and R. J. Camargo. 1993. Treating the clergy. *Annals of Sex Research* 6:287–303.

McAlinden, A. 2006. "Setting 'em up": Personal, familial and institutional grooming in the sexual abuse of children. *Social & Legal Studies* 15:339.

——. 2012. "Grooming" and the sexual abuse of children: Institutional, Internet and familial dimensions. Clarendon Studies in Criminology. Oxford: Oxford University Press.

Mendola, M. J. 1998. Characteristics of priests and religious brothers for evaluation of sexual issues. Ph.D. dissertation, Antioch University, New England Graduate School.

Mouton, F. R., and T. P. Doyle. 1985. *The Problem of Sexual Molestation by Roman Catholic Clergy: Meeting the Problem in a Comprehensive and Responsible Manner.* Unpublished document written for the USCCB. http://www.bishop -accountability.org/reports/1985_06_09_Doyle_Manual/DoyleManual _NCR_combined.pdf.

Norton, A. J., and J. E. Moorman. 1987. Current trends in marriage and divorce among American women. *Journal of Marriage and the Family* 49:3–14.

Pew Research Center. 2010. *The Pope Meets the Press: Media Coverage of the Clergy Abuse Scandal.* Pew Research Religion and Public Life Project. http://www.pewforum.org/2010/06/11/the-pope-meets-the-press -media-coverage-of-the-clergy-abuse-scandal/.

Plante, T. G. 2003. After the earthquake: Five reasons for hope after the sexual abuse scandal. *America* 190:11–14.

Plante, T., and K. McChesney, eds. 2012. *Ten Years of Crisis: What the Catholic Church Has Learned and Done to Prevent Clergy Sex Abuse Since Dallas.* Santa Barbara, Calif.: Greenwood.

Popeshuffle. 2010. *Economist.* http://www.economist.com/blogs/newsbook/2010 /06/catholic_church?source=features_box_main.

Royal Commission. 2013. *Royal Commission into Institutional Responses to Sexual Abuse.* http://www.childabuseroyalcommission.gov.au/.

Ryan, P. 2009. *The Commission to Inquire into Child Abuse*. Dublin: Department of Justice and Equality.

Sipe, A. W. R. 1990. *A Secret World: Sexuality and the Search for Celibacy*. New York: Brunner/Mazel.

Terry, K. J. 2008. Stained Glass: The nature and scope of sexual abuse crisis in the Catholic Church. *Criminal Justice & Behavior* 35 (5): 549–69.

Terry, K. J., M. L. Smith, K. Schuth, J. Kelly, B. Vollman, and C. Massey. 2011. *Causes and Context of the Sexual Abuse Crisis in the Catholic Church*. Washington, D.C.: United States Conference of Catholic Bishops.

Ukeritis, M. D. 2005. Clergy who violate boundaries: Sexual abuse and misconduct in a sample of Canadian men. Paper presented at the annual meeting of the Religious Research Association, Rochester, N.Y., November.

CHAPTER 13

Sexual Violence By and Against Trans People

▸ *PHOENIX J. FREEMAN*

THIS CHAPTER DISCUSSES GLOBAL ISSUES concerning Western trans people and sexual violence. Limitations of the available data about sexual violence in trans populations are described, and risk factors associated with sexual violence by and against Western trans people are examined. Examples and ideas are provided regarding how sexual violence by and against trans people can be better understood and addressed.

The chapter is based on a research review and almost a decade of my professional and personal experiences as an "out" transman (a transman who is known by other people to be trans). Observations about trans people and sexual violence were made during my research into trans health services. Observations were also made when conducting support work with trans people and while working in the homelessness sector. The remaining observations were made through my personal contact with other trans people.

The definition of sexual violence employed by the World Health Organization (WHO) (Krug et al. 2002:149) is used in this chapter. The Western world is the main focus of the chapter because constructions of "gender," "sex," "sexual orientation," and "trans people" in white-dominated Western cultures can have limited applicability in other cultures (Towle & Morgan 2002).

The term "trans" refers to people who identify as a different gender from the one they were assigned as an infant. A trans person wants to live according to another gender on a permanent or episodic basis. For instance, a female-bodied person might identify as a man and want to live permanently as a man. Another example of a trans person is a man who cross-dresses sporadically and lives as a woman for a few hours at a time. Or a trans person might identify as being neither a man nor a woman and cultivate an androgynous appearance. trans people often refer to themselves using a label such as "cross-dresser," "trans," "transgender," "transsexual," or "person of transsexual history." Two common labels for trans people are "transman" and "transwoman." A transman identifies as a man but was assigned "female" as an infant. A transwoman identifies as a woman but was assigned "male" as an infant. Some trans people want different sex characteristics from those with which they were born (and developed at puberty). A trans person may want to alter all, some, or no sex characteristics. Trans people have the same range of sexualities as the general population. For instance, a trans person may be heterosexual, gay, lesbian, or bisexual. This chapter and many trans people use "cis" to refer to individuals who are not trans. I employ the phrase "general population" to refer collectively to cis and trans people.

GLOBAL ISSUES WITH RESEARCH ABOUT TRANS PEOPLE AND SEXUAL VIOLENCE

Trans populations worldwide endure stigmatization and an increased risk of sexual and other violence. Kidd and Witten (2007) describe transphobic violence as a "global pandemic." Globalized risk factors also increase the likelihood that some trans people will sexually offend. Nonetheless, data available about sexual violence by and against trans people worldwide have shortcomings that obstruct understanding and addressing such offenses.

Inadequate Data

Research about sexual violence worldwide rarely documents whether any research participants are trans (United Nations High Commissioner for Human Rights [UNHCHR] 2011). Data about sexual victimization and offending in trans populations are often only collected when a study's sole focus is trans or LGBTQ people. Furthermore studies concerning trans people and sexual violence overwhelmingly investigate only transphobic violence.

Research about sexual offending by trans people is particularly scarce worldwide and usually examines incarcerated individuals. Often trans sex offenders documented in detail cross-dress, were born physically male, and have killed more than one person, with the modus operandi for these murders relating to their sexual interests (see Lauerma, Voutilainen, & Tuominen 2010; Myers et al. 2008). These individuals would not represent all trans sex offenders—and studies often provide inadequate information to determine whether these cross-dressing offenders identify as trans. The insufficient nontransphobic discussion and research about trans people who are sexually violent may partly reflect people's assumptions that no victim of prejudice would perpetrate violence. It may also reflect people's efforts to avoid further stigmatizing trans people, or to avoid being regarded as transphobic.

Trans populations globally are typically regarded as too small or insignificant to be documented in research about the general population. Researchers frequently classify research participants as male or female without documenting if individuals are trans. Typically basic data about trans populations—such as mean income and mean level of educational attainment—are unavailable. Globally the percentage of people who are trans is also unknown (and this is further complicated by diverse definitions of "trans") (Mitchell & Howarth 2009). However, I have observed trans people being more common than studies estimate. For instance, when attending trans events in Australia I have often seen been more locally based trans people sitting at a table than are estimated to live in the entire city. Insufficient demographic data about trans populations can make it impossible to determine whether criminological data about trans people capture a representative sample of individuals.

Finally, some countries (for instance, Canada) have even less data about their trans populations than other countries (such as the United States) do. Inadequate local research can lead to services and researchers overrelying on foreign data to anticipate or describe issues for their local trans populations.

Divergent Research Foci, Measures, and Methods

Globally most studies about sexual violence by and against trans people are conducted differently from studies of general populations. This can make it impossible to determine whether sexual violence by and against trans people differs from sexual violence by and against cis people.

Studies of general populations often use random-style sampling or representative sampling. In comparison, surveys of trans people typically involve self-selection of respondents and are often advertised via trans or LGBTQ social networks (this often relates to difficulties in locating trans people). Such differences in recruitment methods can make it impossible to determine whether a trans-focused study captures a representative sample of individuals, particularly because trans people do not necessarily know other trans people, and many trans people are heterosexual.

Furthermore, studies of general populations are often conducted on the phone, in person, or via mail (for instance, see Australian Bureau of Statistics [ABS] 2005). In comparison, many recent studies of trans people have been conducted online. Poverty means that fewer trans people may have access to the Internet compared to cis people. Therefore online surveys about sexual violence may not recruit some of the most marginalized trans people.

Some trans studies worldwide survey different age ranges from studies of corresponding general populations. For instance, the U.S. Department of Justice (USDOJ) bulletin on Criminal Victimization (Truman & Planty 2012) focuses on individuals who are least 12 years old, whereas the largest survey of trans people in the United States (Grant et al. 2011) focuses on people who are at least 18 years old.

Studies of general populations worldwide also typically ask individuals whether they have experienced sexual violence (irrespective of motive). However, studies of trans people overwhelmingly only ask individuals if they have experienced sexual violence relating to their gender identity. Such questions can be useful for documenting transphobia but do not capture the total rate of sexual violence against trans people.

Finally, trans studies worldwide often ask research participants about victimization within different time periods from those in studies of corresponding general populations. For instance a major Australian government survey on crime (ABS 2005) asked respondents whether they had endured sexual assault, or attempted sexual assault, within the previous twelve months. In comparison a major survey of Australian trans people (Couch et al. 2007) inquired about lifetime victimization.

Aggregation of Risk Factors

Trans people have diverse personal characteristics, circumstances, and life histories that can affect their likelihood of enduring or perpetrating sexual violence. Unfortunately researchers globally rarely disaggregate such factors when discussing sexual violence in trans populations (the exception being comparisons made between transmen and transwomen). For instance, research may document the disabilities, ethnicities, and annual incomes of trans respondents but not examine whether such factors are associated with higher or lower rates of sexual victimization.

RISK FACTORS FOR SEXUAL VIOLENCE

Trans Victimization

The Universal Declaration of Human Rights states that trans people worldwide are entitled to protection from violence and discrimination (UNHCHR 2011). Nonetheless, trans people across all regions of the world endure discrimination and violence, including sexual violence (Couch et al. 2007:61; Stotzer 2009; Turner, Whittle, & Combs 2009; UNHCHR 2011).

An offender may have one or more motives to be sexually violent to a trans person:

- Transphobia—negative attitudes toward trans people
- Homophobia—negative attitudes toward gay and lesbian people. For instance, a cis man might sexually assault a transwoman on the basis of believing that she is a feminine gay man.
- Sexism—believing that one gender is superior to another gender (for instance, believing that men are superior to women)
- Motivations unrelated to transphobia, homophobia, or sexism. For instance, a child molester might sexually abuse a trans child on the basis of the child's age and vulnerability. Or a transman might sexually assault another transman on the basis of his appearance and vulnerability.

The proportion of trans people who have experienced sexual violence is unknown but probably varies internationally. This is because rates of sexual violence in general populations vary between countries (Krug et al. 2002:150–55). It is also because legislation against transphobic discrimination, hate-violence, and vilification varies internationally. For instance, The Council of Europe (COE) (2011:42) reports that (only) nine of its forty-seven member states have comprehensive antidiscrimination legislation protecting trans people: Albania, Croatia, the Czech Republic, Germany, Hungary, Montenegro, Serbia, Sweden, and the United Kingdom. And U.S. federal legislation includes trans people as a protected group against hate crimes (Matthew Shepard and James Byrd, Jr., Hate Crimes Prevention Act 2009), but Canadian legislation does not (Criminal Code 1985: s318–319).

Globalized issues affecting trans populations put many trans people at increased risk of sexual victimization. For instance, trans-related relationship conflict and inadequate social support can increase a trans person's risk of enduring sexual violence. Relationship conflict can particularly occur when a trans person asserts being trans, is discovered to be trans, or asserts living permanently as another gender. Partnerships with low relationship satisfaction and ongoing conflict are more likely to involve intimate partner violence than other partnerships (WHO and London School of Hygiene and Tropical Medicine 2010:28). If a trans person expresses gender identity to someone who already controls the trans person using sexual violence, this person may respond through further sexual violence. U.S. research also documents that trans people, and young trans people in particular, whose families do not accept their gender identity are more likely to have circumstances and activities associated with enduring sexual violence, including homelessness, engaging in sex work, incarceration, and using drugs or alcohol (Grant et al. 2011:7). Young people in general are at greater risk of sexual violence than older people if they are homeless or engage in sex work (Kushel et al. 2003).

Studies in Northern Ireland (McBride 2013) and the United States (Grant et al. 2011:106–8; Quintana, Rosenthal, & Krehely 2010) document that many trans people's risk of homelessness is increased by employment discrimination and transphobic responses from relatives. Sexual violence can cause homelessness and also result from homelessness (Morrison 2009).

Being perceived to be trans also directly increases the likelihood an individual will experience transphobic sexual violence—a well-known example of this being the rape and murder of Brandon Teena by two cis men (Ohle 2004).

Trans people in the United States have experienced discrimination from services for vulnerable people (Grant et al. 2011; Ray 2006), including homelessness shelters, housing services, legal services, police, and rape crisis centers. Such discrimination can increase the risk of a trans person experiencing and reexperiencing sexual violence. For instance, a transwoman enduring sexual violence from her partner may be at increased risk of revictimization if a domestic violence shelter refuses to assist her.

Additionally, trans people may be more likely to engage in sex work than cis people. For instance, 11 percent of Grant et al.'s (2011:64) Transgender and Gender-Nonconforming survey respondents in the United States reported having engaged in sex work. A post-1980s estimate of the proportion of the U.S. general population who have engaged in sex work could not be located. However, the percentage of women in the general population who currently engage in sex work has been estimated to be far lower than 11 percent in other Western countries; for instance, 0.5% in the UK and 1.4 percent in Germany (European Network for HIV-STD Prevention in Prostitution 2000, cited in Vandepitte et al. 2006).

Trans sex workers face compounded stigmas and safety impediments. Many sex workers, particularly those who engage in substance use and individuals working from the street, are at high risk of experiencing sexual violence (Krug et al. 2002; Neame & Heenan 2003; WHO 2005). Sex workers in many parts of the world also face additional barriers to reporting sexual violence, and obtaining health care after sexual violence, compared with non–sex workers (WHO 2005). For instance, sex workers can endure discrimination from health services and law enforcement, physical and sexual violence from police, sex work being criminalized, and inadequate information about their rights (Quadara 2008; WHO 2005).

Trans people can also be more reluctant to disclose sexual violence to services that could help to prevent their revictimization, such as counseling services and police (Couch et al. 2007; Grant et al. 2011; Mayer et al. 2008; UNHCHR 2011). Victims of sexual violence, in general, have many reasons for being reluctant to disclose their victimization (Australian Law Reform Commission 2010:1193–96), and trans people can have additional trans-related bases for being reluctant to disclose. Trans people may, for instance, anticipate transphobia from services and fear that disclosing sexual violence to services will lead to other people learning they are trans (Couch et al. 2007; Grant et al. 2011; Mayer et al. 2008; UNHCHR 2011).

Because of their poverty and marginalization, many trans people are more likely to be incarcerated than cis people—and incarcerated trans people are at particular risk of experiencing sexual violence compared with the general prison population (National Coalition of Anti-Violence Programs [NCAVP] 2008:45–50; UN 2001; UNHCHR 2011). Just Detention

International explains that "people who are marginalized in the community tend also to be the most vulnerable to abuse while in detention" (NCAVP 2008:45). Furthermore, many prison systems (such as in Canada and the United States) exacerbate trans inmates' risk of being sexually victimized by placing them in men's or women's facilities based on their genitals or legal sex rather than their gender identity and presentation (Mann 2006). However, such policies vary internationally. For instance, trans prisoners in parts of Australia may be placed into single-sex facilities based on their gender identity (Mann 2006).

Finally, other prejudices, such as racism, exacerbate many trans people's risk of enduring sexual violence. For instance, black trans people in the United States report higher rates of employment discrimination, homelessness, housing discrimination, and employment in the "underground economy" (such as sex work and drug sales) than white trans people report (Grant et al. 2011).

Trans Sexual Offending

A person is not prevented from perpetrating sexual violence by being trans or enduring transphobia. For instance, more than one in five (20.5 percent) trans inmates in California's male prisons were registered sex offenders—compared with 14.6 percent of the general male prison population in California (study N = 315 trans inmates) (Sexton, Jenness, & Sumner 2009:38). Individual and social risk factors increase the likelihood that some people will sexually offend, irrespective of being cis or trans. Trans-related factors also increase the likelihood of some trans people sexually offending.

A risk factor for sexual offending by some trans people is their actual or perceived anonymity during social interactions in trans social networks. Among trans people there is wide acceptance of living simultaneously under more than one name, gender, and identity. This reflects the risks associated with being known as trans and the considerable time it can take for a trans person to understand and accept their gender identity. Many trans people also interact online with other trans people, particularly because "out" trans people are relatively sparse. Through online interaction people can, to some extent, conceal their legal identity or perceive they are anonymous. Research demonstrates that people who believe they are anonymous are more likely to commit acts of violence and may be more violent than if they believe their identity is known (Silke 2003; Zimbardo 1969). A trans person who is motivated to be sexually violent may be more likely to offend if the person perceives there is a low likelihood of being identified.

Sexualized interactions in some trans social networks are another risk factor for some trans people sexually offending. Members of some trans social networks explicitly discuss their sexual interests and activities with one another. Sometimes such networks overlap with licit or illicit sex-related social networks. Open discussion of sexuality does not inherently increase the risk of sexual violence being perpetrated. However, when some members of a trans group, particularly dominant members, openly express attitudes of sexual entitlement, this can increase the likelihood of sexual violence being perpetrated. Trans people with a motivation to be sexually violent can more easily identify potential victims and co-offenders when they have opportunity to observe other people's sexual attitudes, behavior, and interests. Potential offenders may also find it easier to overcome any of their own resistance to offending if they witness other people expressing attitudes of sexual entitlement or indifference to sexually abusive behavior.

The online, transnational, sexualized, and relatively anonymous characteristics of social interactions in some trans networks also mean that trans sex offenders can find opportunities to offend globally. Social interactions with such characteristics can, for instance, facilitate trans sex offenders sharing child sexual exploitation material with offenders in other countries and can enable offenders to have contact with potential co-offenders and victims in other countries to which they travel.

Transphobia, and the small size of local trans social networks, also increase the likelihood of sexual violence being perpetrated within trans social networks. Many trans people rely on a relatively dense or small trans social network for support and companionship. Such individuals are more likely to be alienated by their network if they openly disagree with more dominant people in the network, or if they disclose violence perpetrated by other network members. Trans offenders can also strategically employ prejudice to control victims and hide their sexual offending. For instance, I have repeatedly heard offenders in LGBTQ social networks excusing violence by claiming to trans and trans-accepting victims that it is queer or trans—the violence therefore allegedly being acceptable but unfairly stigmatized. I have also repeatedly witnessed trans sex offenders attempt to conceal offending by claiming that their victims, and government authorities who may investigate sexual offending, are "transphobic" for indicating that a trans person could be a sex offender.

Finally, another risk factor for some trans people sexually offending is having sexist and "macho" ideals, social networks, and subjectivities. Many transwomen seek to live a "hypermasculine" life before they have come out as trans (and are still living as men) (for discussion, see Brown 1988; McDuffie & Brown 2010). For instance, one in five respondents to Grant et al.'s (2011:30) U.S. study of trans and gender-nonconforming people (N = 6456) reported a history of military service, which is double the military participation rate of the general U.S. population. Brown (1988) describes "hypermasculine" behaviors as activities such as employment in stereotypically "macho" occupations, risk-taking, sexual activity with women, and perpetrating violence. A person's closest relationships can influence the person's behavior and range of experience, and therefore the likelihood of perpetrating sexual violence (Krug et al. 2002). A trans person who shares "hypermasculine" activities and attitudes with others the person knows may be more likely perpetrate sexual violence and meet potential co-offenders.

DISCUSSION

Sexual violence by and against trans people globally cannot be understood through research that focuses solely on general populations. However, data collection already taking place about sexual violence in the general population could provide valuable data about sexual violence by and against trans people.

The lack of information about trans populations, and the small size of these populations, make it useful to collect data about trans people and sexual violence via large-scale research and reporting systems. Statistics could be collected about sexual violence by and against trans people via hate crime reporting systems, national crime victimization surveys, police statistics about offenders, prison incident reporting systems, and sex offender registries.

Governments rarely collect data about sexual violence by and against trans people. However, federal reforms in the United States now ensure that the USDOJ documents and addresses some forms of sexual violence against trans people. Such reforms are internationally noteworthy. Among other USDOJ changes, the Federal Bureau of Investigation (2012) has added the option of reporting anti-transgender hate crimes (including sexual offenses) to its national Uniform Crime Reporting Program for law enforcement. The U.S. Bureau of Justice Statistics (BJS) has also given individuals the option of disclosing whether they are trans in research that documents inmate sexual victimization, including the National Inmate Surveys (2007, 2009, 2013) and the National Former Prisoner Survey (2008) (see BJS 2008, 2010).

Nongovernmental organizations such as domestic violence agencies, rape crisis centers, and homelessness services could also provide valuable data about sexual violence by and against trans people. Agencies could, for instance, document the number of trans individuals who are victims or perpetrators of sexual violence in their client statistics. Such statistics could be particularly useful in larger cities if made available to other local welfare, health-care, and law enforcement agencies.

Changes to address sexual violence by and against trans people need to encompass justice systems and broader social reform. Transforming prejudiced attitudes, legislation, and policies could decrease the risk trans people face of enduring sexual violence. Increasing trans people's access to informed and accepting health-care, law enforcement, legal assistance, and welfare services could reduce rates of sexual violence in trans populations and help address the ramifications of such violence. International organizations, such as the COE, and national bodies, such as the Australian Human Rights Commission, could be involved in monitoring and increasing trans people's equity of access to justice services. Trans sex offenders' capacities to victimize could be reduced through addressing transphobia and addressing the taboo in trans social networks on discussing sexual offending by trans people.

Some countries have already implemented justice system reforms. Many police services around the world have LGBT liaison officer programs that educate police about trans people and work to increase trans people's trust and confidence in reporting crime. The UK's Crown Prosecution Service (2008) has Hate Crime Scrutiny Panels that review criminal prosecutions of transphobic hate crimes, with the goal of improving case outcomes. The U.S. Code of Federal Regulations (28 CFR §§ 115.41–42 2013) also requires that adult jail and prison inmates are screened upon intake for their vulnerability of being sexually victimized and placed accordingly, with official risk criteria for victimization, including being (or being perceived as) "transgender." Justice systems worldwide may learn how they can better document and address sexual violence by and against trans people in their jurisdictions by examining policies and reforms in other jurisdictions; many reforms that have taken place in one location have not been implemented elsewhere.

All countries need to take significant steps toward understanding and addressing sexual violence by and against trans people. Further data could yield valuable insights for justice agencies and other services. I hope that future research on this topic will consider the methodological opportunities and ethical issues associated with collecting data on this small, stereotyped, and stigmatized population.

DISCUSSION QUESTIONS

1. What trans-specific factors make it challenging to investigate sexual violence in trans populations?
2. How could you design a sexual violence survey for trans people that produces useful data?
3. What could be some benefits and limitations of using foreign research to anticipate the nature and extent of sexual violence in a local trans population?
4. Can you name other minority groups that face any sexual violence–related issues comparable to those faced by trans populations?

REFERENCES

Australian Bureau of Statistics (ABS). 2005. *4509.0 Crime and Safety, Australia*. http://www.ausstats.abs.gov.au/ausstats/subscriber.nsf/0/D68F78EDFB7965 E4CA25715A001C9192/$File/45090_apr%202005.pdf.

Australian Law Reform Commission. 2010. *Family Violence—A National Legal Response*. http://www.alrc.gov.au/sites/default/files/pdfs/publications/ALRC114 _WholeReport.pdf.

Brown, G. 1988. Transsexuals in the military: Flight into hypermasculinity. *Archives of Sexual Behavior* 17 (6): 527–37.

Bureau of Justice Statistics (BJS). 2008. *National Former Prisoner Survey Interview*. http://www.bjs.gov/content/pub/pdf/nfps_2008.pdf.

——. 2010. *Data Collection: National Inmate Survey*. http://www.bjs.gov/index .cfm?ty=dcdetail&iid=278.

Council of Europe (COE). 2011. *Discrimination on Grounds of Sexual Orientation and Gender Identity in Europe.* http://www.coe.int/t/Commissioner/Source /LGBT/LGBTStudy2011_en.pdf.

Couch, M., M. Pitts, H. Mulcare, S. Croy, A. Mitchell, and S. Patel. 2007. *Tranznation: A Report on the Health and Wellbeing of Transgender People in Australia and New Zealand.* http://www.latrobe.edu.au/arcshs/downloads/arcshs -research-publications/Tranznation_Report.pdf,

Criminal Code, R.S.C. 1985.

Crown Prosecution Service. 2008. *Homophobic and Transphobic Crime Toolkit: Good Practice and Lessons Learnt.* http://www.cps.gov.uk/publications/ prosecution/htc_toolkit.html.

Federal Bureau of Investigation (2012). *Hate Crime Incident Report.* http://www .fbi.gov/about-us/cjis/ucr/reporting-forms/hate-crime-incident-report-pdf.

Grant, J., L. Mottet, J. Tanis, J. Herman, J. Harrison, and M. Keisling. 2011. *Injustice at Every Turn: A Report on the National Transgender Discrimination Survey.* http://www.thetaskforce.org/downloads/reports/reports/ntds_full.pdf.

Kidd, J., and T. Witten. 2007. Transgender and transsexual identities: The next strange fruit—hate crimes, violence and genocide against global trans-communities. *Journal of Hate Studies* 6 (1): 31–63.

Krug, E., L. Dahlberg, J. Mercy, A. Zwi, and R. Loano, eds. 2002. *World Report on Violence and Health.* http://whqlibdoc.who.int/publications/2002/9241545615 _eng.pdf.

Kushel, M., J. Evans, S. Perry, M. Robertson, and A. Moss. 2003. No door to lock: Victimization among homeless and marginally housed persons. *Archives of Internal Medicine* 163:2492–99.

Lauerma, H., J. Voutilainen, and T. Tuominen. 2010. Matricide and two sexual femicides by a male strangler with a transgender sadomasochistic identity. *Journal of Forensic Sciences* 55 (2): 549–50.

Mann, R. 2006. The treatment of transgender prisoners, not just an American problem—A comparative analysis of American, Australian, and Canadian prison policies concerning the treatment of transgender prisoners and a "universal" recommendation to improve treatment. *Law & Sexuality* 91:91–134.

Matthew Shepard and James Byrd, Jr., Hate Crimes Prevention Act of 2009, 18 U.S.C. § 249. 2009.

Mayer, K., J. Bradford, H. Makadon, R. Stall, H. Goldhammer, and S. Landers. 2008. Sexual and gender minority health: What we know and what needs to be done. *American Journal of Public Health* 98 (6): 989–95.

McBride, R. 2013. *Grasping the Nettle: The Experiences of Gender Variant Children and Transgender Youth Living in Northern Ireland.* http://www.ofmdfmni.gov .uk/grasping-the-nettle-transgender-youth-living-in-ni.pdf.

McDuffie, E., and G. Brown. 2010. 70 U.S. veterans with gender identity disturbances: A descriptive study. *International Journal of Transgenderism* 12 (1): 21–30.

Mitchell, M., and C. Howarth. 2009. *Research Report 27: Trans Research Review.* http://www.equalityhumanrights.com/uploaded_files/trans_research _review_rep27.pdf.

Morrison, Z. 2009. *Homelessness and Sexual Assault.* http://www.aifs.gov.au /acssa/pubs/wrap/acssa_wrap7.pdf.

Myers, W., A. Bukhanovskiy, E. Justen, R. Morton, J. Tilley, K. Adams, . . . R. Hazelwood. 2008. The relationship between serial sexual murder and autoerotic asphyxiation. *Forensic Science International* 176 (2–3): 187–95.

National Coalition of Anti-Violence Programs (NCAVP). 2008. *Hate Violence Against Lesbian, Gay, Bisexual and Transgender People in the United States.* http://www.ncavp.org/common/document_files/Reports/2008%20HV%20 Report%20smaller%20file.pdf.

Neame, A., and M. Heenan. 2003. *What Lies Behind the Hidden Figure of Sexual Assault? Issues of Prevalence and Disclosure.* http://www.aifs.gov.au/acssa /pubs/briefing/acssa_briefing1.pdf.

Ohle, J. 2004. Constructing the trannie: Transgender people and the law. *Journal of Gender, Race & Justice* 8:237–80.

Quadara, A. 2008. *Sex Workers and Sexual Assault in Australia: Prevalence, Risk and Safety.* http://www.aifs.org.au/acssa/pubs/issue/acssa_issues8.pdf.

Quintana, N., J. Rosenthal, and J. Krehely. 2010. *On the Streets: The Federal Response to Gay and Transgender Homeless Youth.* http://www.americanprogress.org /issues/2010/06/pdf/lgbtyouthhomelessness.pdf.

Ray, N. 2006. *Lesbian, Gay, Bisexual and Transgender Youth: An Epidemic of Homelessness.* http://www.thetaskforce.org/downloads/HomelessYouth.pdf.

Sexton, L., V. Jenness, and J. Sumner 2009. *Where the Margins Meet: A Demographic Assessment of Transgender Inmates in Men's Prisons.* http://ucicorrections. seweb.uci.edu/files/2013/06/A-Demographic-Assessment-of-Transgender -Inmates-in-Mens-Prisons.pdf.

Silke, A. 2003. Deindividuation, anonymity, and violence: Findings from Northern Ireland. *Journal of Social Psychology* 143 (4): 493–99.

Stotzer, R. 2009. Violence against transgender people: A review of United States data. *Aggression and Violent Behavior* 14 (3): 170–79.

Towle, E., and L. Morgan. 2002. Romancing the transgender native: Rethinking the use of the "third gender" concept. *GLQ: A Journal of Lesbian and Gay Studies* 8:469–97.

Trans Media Watch (TMW). 2011. *The British Press and the Transgender Community: Submission to the Leveson Inquiry into the Culture, Practice and Ethics of the Press.* http://www.transmediawatch.org/Documents/Publishable%20 Trans%20Media%20Watch%20Submission.pdf.

Truman, J., and M. Planty. 2012. *NCJ 239437 Criminal Victimization, 2011.* http://www.bjs.gov/content/pub/pdf/cv11.pdf.

Turner, L., S. Whittle, and R. Combs. 2009. *Transphobic Hate Crime in the European Union.* http://www.transgenderzone.com/library/st/pdf/Transphobic _Hate_Crime_in_EU.pdf.

28 CFR §§115.41–42. 2013.

United Nations (UN). 2001a. *A/56/156 Report of the Special Rapporteur on the Question of Torture and Other Cruel, Inhuman or Degrading Treatment or Punishment.* http://www.un.org/documents/ga/docs/56/a56156.pdf.

——. 2011b. *A/66/265 Extreme Poverty and Human Rights: Report by the Secretary General.* http://www.ohchr.org/Documents/Issues/Poverty/A.66.265.pdf.

United Nations High Commissioner for Human Rights (UNHCHR). 2011. *Discriminatory Laws and Practices and Acts of Violence Against Individuals Based on Their Sexual Orientation and Gender Identity: Report of the United Nations High Commissioner for Human Rights: A/HRC/19/41.* http://www2.ohchr. org/english/bodies/hrcouncil/docs/19session/A.HRC.19.41_English.pdf.

Vandepitte, J., R. Lyerla, G. Dallabetta, F. Crabbé, M. Alary, M., A. Buvé. 2006. Estimates of the number of female sex workers in different regions of the world. *Sexually Transmitted Infections* 82 (Supplement III): iii18–iii25.

World Health Organization (WHO). 2005. *Violence Against Women and HIV/ AIDS: Critical Intersections: Violence Against Sex Workers and HIV Prevention.* http://www.who.int/gender/documents/sexworkers.pdf.

World Health Organization and London School of Hygiene and Tropical Medicine. 2010. *Preventing Intimate Partner and Sexual Violence Against Women: Taking Action and Generating Evidence.* http://apps.who.int/iris/bitstr eam/10665/44350/1/9789241564007_eng.pdf.

Zimbardo, P. 1969. The human choice: Individuation, reason and order versus deindividuation, impulse and chaos. *Nebraska Symposium on Motivation* 17:237–307.

CHAPTER 14

The Sexual Abuse of Animals

▸ *JENNIFER MAHER*

THIS CHAPTER EXPLORES THE OFTEN neglected but publicly contentious act of sexual violence against nonhuman animals (hereafter referred to as "animals"). Wider academic literature on sexual offending seldom focuses on interspecies sexual contact, and even less so on animals as "victims." Interest in sexual violence against animals is generally anthropocentric. Animals are victims of sexual violence both by being forced to perform sexual acts (frequently referred to as bestiality) and by being mutilated or killed to fulfill sexual gratification. Beirne (2009:112) argues that sexual violence toward animals comprises a wide range of actions and that current definitions are too narrow, concerned only with "penetration of the vagina, anus or cloaca of an animal by a human penis." He proposes "animal sexual assault" as a more appropriate term; it recognizes the similarities between sexual victimization of women, children and infants, and animals. When not specifically referring to legislation (in which case I use the common term "bestiality"), I use Beirne's term in acknowledgment of the full range of sexual abuses perpetrated against animals and to situate them as victims rather than objects.

Whereas criminal justice statistics on bestiality are available globally, there is little evidence that this behavior is common practice, though many countries have identified it as a serious offense worthy of serious punishment. Of the limited data available on the prevalence and nature of animal sexual assault, most stem from academic and practitioner studies (see Ascione 2010 for a comprehensive overview of recent studies), which are often limited by sample size and population. Animal sexual assault is considered to have a high "dark figure of crime" (offenses often go unreported and unrecorded), as with child sexual abuse; victims are "voiceless" and helpless. English and colleagues (2003) maintain that the secrecy surrounding (child) sexual assault offenses ensures that most perpetrators never come to the attention of authorities. While in some cultures animal sexual assault is simply regarded as a victimless crime, for all animal victims it is a voiceless one, largely undetected and underreported.

Animal sexual assault is a complex issue in terms of definitions, explanations, and responses. From an international perspective, the complexity increases because of our varied and often paradoxical relationship with animals. How can bestiality remain legal in many countries (Ascione 2010) while simultaneously being deemed illegal (and even an illness) in others? Further, how can the latter then justify *legitimately* torturing and killing animals and also interfering with their genitalia (e.g., for food, clothing, and medicine)? Taken more generally, these inconsistencies in the human-animal relationship make animal sexual assault a unique sexual offense. As a consequence, there is a complicated legislative response, characterized not only by the problems of consent and evidentiary proof but also by tension between civil liberties and animal protection. Similarities can be drawn between animal sexual assault and interpersonal sexual offenses. This chapter, for example, explores recent developments in legislation regulating animal sexual assault. Parallels are evident here between the social and legal context of animal sexual assault and marital rape—both are heavily influenced by religion and, while criminalized in some countries, are widely tolerated and ignored in others (see Woodley 2007 on the complexities of criminalizing and responding to marital rape).

This chapter also explores definitional arguments and debates surrounding the criminalization of animal sexual assault and the approaches to legislating for this and related offenses (largely from a European perspective). While the scope of this book is transnational problems and global perspectives, academic and public debate worldwide has largely ignored bestiality. Because it is legal or believed to be nonexistent in many countries, there is a paucity of global research and statistics on animal sexual assault. Elements of cross-border concern do exist, particularly the Internet as a vehicle for offending and the transnational use of animal brothels, but limited information inhibits a useful global comparison. The rationale for providing a European, and to a lesser degree U.S., comparison is simple:

this is the locus of most academic literature and accessible legislation. This chapter begins with a discussion on definitions and legislative approaches, providing an important overview of the social and legal complexities of this offense. A comparison of relevant legislation follows, which establishes the developments and limitations of legal responses to bestiality. The international scope of the chapter necessitates a broad overview rather than in in-depth discussion, with a focus on legislation—just one aspect of this complex offense—as it provides an essential platform for understanding and responding to animal sexual assault.

BACKGROUND

Animal sexual assault is commonly referred to as "sodomy," "bestiality," "zoophilia," and other more general terms, such as "animal abuse." These terms require further clarification and are examined herein. Animal sexual assault tends to fall into two key categories of crime: animal abuse and sexual abuse.

Definitions of animal abuse vary considerably depending on the ideological perspective of the definer (e.g., animal welfare versus animal rights) and the legitimacy of the abuse (e.g., illegal versus socially condoned abuse). Ascione's (1993:228) definition of animal abuse, which takes a broader approach than most legal definitions, is widely used in academic literature. He states that animal abuse is "socially unacceptable behavior that intentionally causes unnecessary pain, suffering or distress and/or death of an animal." A similar focus on unnecessary suffering is evident in animal welfare legislation worldwide. The United Kingdom, in 1911, was one of the first countries to enact general animal welfare legislation. Much of current animal abuse legislation is contained in the Animal Welfare Act (AWA) 2006 (UK). Under s.4.1 it is an offense to cause "unnecessary suffering" to an animal (defined under s.1.1 as "any vertebrate other than man"). This means abuse is defined not only by "intentional" acts but also by acts (or inaction) the person "ought reasonably to have known" would have caused unnecessary suffering (AWA 2006). Although the AWA 2006 does not specifically identify sexual abuse as an offense, animal sexual assault can be prosecuted under this legislation once unnecessary suffering is proven.

The offense of "intercourse with an animal" is defined in the Sexual Offenses Act 2003 (UK) s.69 as penetration that is "vaginal or anal, either way." This legal definition does not include oral sex or other nonpenetrative offenses. Table 14.1 provides a comparison of the legal terminology used to define this offense in seven countries. The absence of a clear definition in many countries, and the exclusive focus on penetrative sex in the others, is notable (see further discussion below). The Humane Society of the United States (2001) recognizes that animal sexual assault can involve a wide range of behaviors, including "vaginal, anal or oral penetration; fondling; oral-genital contact; penetration using an object and killing or injuring an animal for sexual gratification." By targeting only penetrative acts, legal definitions fail to recognize the full extent of animal victimization. Additionally, by focusing on "unnecessary suffering," legal definitions do not recognize that animal sexual assault may or may not include physical violence (other than the sexual act itself) or force, so may not result in physical injury.

Academics have proposed typologies that categorize the behavior according to the level of violence/harm inflicted. Singer (2001) distinguishes between (1) cruel sexual abuse—requiring physical harm to intensify the sexual experience—and (2) sexual acts not necessarily causing physical injury. Beirne (2009) suggests four categories, factoring in harm to the animal and the motivation of the offender: (1) sexual fixation (e.g., exclusive desire for animals), (2) commodification (e.g., animal brothels), (3) adult sexual experimentation (e.g., animals for sexual gratification—the most common category), and (4) aggravated cruelty (e.g., sadistic sexual acts). These typologies are useful for defining and responding to animal sexual assault as they consider the complexities of the human-animal sexual and emotional relationships, often absent in legislation. Despite their usefulness, though, the distinction between "cruel" and "nonviolent" sexual acts made in Singer's (2001) typology has been utilized by probestiality/ zoophilia campaigners calling for the legalization of "nonharmful" human-animal sexual relations.

Although the terms "zoophilia" and "bestiality" are often used interchangeably, there are many definitions that distinguish between these behaviors (see Miletski 2005 for a detailed discussion). Zoophilia is considered a paraphilia (a deviant but essentially victimless behavior) in the

TABLE 14.1 Comparison of Bestiality Legislation

COUNTRY	OFFENSE (DEFINITION)	LEGISLATION (DEFINITION OF OFFENDER)	MAXIMUM PENALTY (IMPRISONMENT/ OTHER)
Australia	Bestiality	Includes: (a) buggery committed by a man on an animal of either sex (b) buggery committed by an animal on a man or woman (c) penetration of the vagina of an animal by the penis of a man (d) penetration of the vagina of a woman by the penis of an animal *Crime Acts 1958* s59 person who commits the act.	5 years
Barbados	Bestiality	Includes: "sexual intercourse *per anum* or *per vaginam* by a male or female person with an animal" *Sexual Offenses Act* 2002 s10.1 person who commits the act s10.2 person who by the use of force or drugs, causes another to commit act.	s10.1: 10 years s10.2 life
Canada	Bestiality	(not defined) *Criminal Code. R.S.C. 1985 c C-46* s160.1 person who commits act s160.2 person who compels another to act s160.3 person who commits act in presence of child	s160.1: 10 years s160.2: 10 years s160.3: 2 (less a day) to 10 years

EU (legislated against in some countries—e.g., UK, Germany, France, Sweden)
Varied (e.g., bestiality, intercourse with animal)

| Example: UK | Intercourse with an animal | Act includes:
(a) intentionally performs an act of penetration with penis
(b) what is penetrated is the vagina or anus of a living animal
(c) knows that, or is reckless as to whether, that is what is penetrated
Also,
(a) A intentionally causes, or allows, A's vagina or anus to be penetrated
(b) penetration is by the penis of a living animal
(c) A knows that, or is reckless as to whether, that is what A is being penetrated by Varied
Example:
Sexual Offenses Act 2003
s69 person who commits act | Varied (e.g., 2 years |

TABLE 14.1 *(continued)*

COUNTRY	OFFENSE (DEFINITION)	LEGISLATION (DEFINITION OF OFFENDER)	MAXIMUM PENALTY (IMPRISONMENT/ OTHER)
Kenya	Indecent act (not defined)	*Sexual Offenses Act* 2006 s6(d) person who compels, induces, or causes another to act	5 years
South Africa	Bestiality	Includes acts: (a) that cause penetration to any extent what-soever by the genital organs of— (i) A into or beyond the mouth, genital organs, or anus of an animal; or (ii) an animal into or beyond the mouth, genital organs, or anus of A (b) of masturbation of an animal, unless such act is committed for scientific reasons or breeding purposes, or of masturbation with an animal *Criminal Law (Sexual Offenses and Related Matters) Amendment Act* 2007 (no 32) s13 person who commits act	Determined by the judge
United States		(legislated against in 32 states) Varied (e.g., buggery, bestiality, sexual assault) Example: California—"sexual assault" (not defined) "for the purpose of arousing or gratifying the sexual desire of the person" Varied (see Michigan State University College of Law 2014) Example: *California Penal Code* s286.5 person committing the act Varied	Misdemeanor (less than 1 year)

Note: Countries chosen for the availability and accessibility of their legislation.

Diagnostic and Statistical Manual of Mental Disorders (DSM III) and is defined as the "preferred or exclusive method of achieving sexual excitement" (American Psychiatric Association 2000:270). Zoophilia involves sexual attraction to animals, which may or may not include sexual acts. Bestiality, the term most commonly used in legal definitions (see table 14.1), usually refers to human-animal penetrative sex. Academic use of this term generally refers to any sexual act between humans and animals.

ANIMAL SEXUAL ASSAULT AS A CRIMINAL OFFENSE

Ideally society (and thus this chapter) would be past the need to ask the question: why should we consider bestiality as a criminal offense? Unfortunately there remains considerable debate between those proposing bestiality as a "civil liberty" and those arguing that animals be afforded protection against human sexual coercion. Both perspectives are important to consider as these beliefs may account for the variation and difficulties inherent in animal protection legislation.

While this chapter does not attempt to evaluate the effectiveness of specific legislation, it is important to clarify that (1) in some countries where animal protection legislation is provided, bestiality is openly engaged in and permitted (e.g., Denmark, Belgium, and Italy), and (2) in countries where strong legislative (e.g., constitutional) protection exists for animals, there remains significant problems implementing this legislation (e.g., Switzerland). Legislation alone is an ineffective response to animal sexual assault; social support, strong enforcement, and a multiagency approach is an effective response.

ARGUMENTS FOR AND AGAINST CRIMINALIZATION

Animal abuse research in criminology (and related fields) outside of Europe and the United States is almost completely absent, perhaps because for many, animal abuse is a victimless crime, not needing discussion or understanding (Pierpoint & Maher 2012). Beirne (1999) argues that animals, as sentient beings, deserve our attention. They are subjects of criminal law, their rights open to violation, and their abuse is an important indicator and/or predictor of interpersonal abuse. From this perspective, animal sexual assault should be of paramount interest to scholars, practitioners, and the public alike. More recently, in an encouraging development, research in this area is growing, and attempts to address this offense, by veterinary medicine and law, have gained momentum (Beetz 2010).

Coincidentally, the probestiality voice in Europe and America has also grown over the last decade. In Germany, a recent probestiality group campaign against a bestiality ban represented up to ten thousand zoophiles (ZETA 2013). Campaigners (often identifying as zoophiles) present bestiality as a legitimate lifestyle choice (Dekkers 2000) and feel discriminated against and forced to fight a battle for civil liberties similar to one previously fought by homosexuals (Miletski 2005; ZETA 2013). Zoophiles feel justified having a relationship with an animal "partner," viewing the relationship as genuine, mutually consenting, and loving. However, Adams (1995) draws a comparison between these claims and those arguments put forth by child sexual abusers. Singer (2001) lent "intellectual" weight to the probestiality voice in his controversial essay "Heavy Petting" by justifying that animals may mutually enjoy human sexual relations if abuse is absent.

Beirne (2001) counters powerfully, criticizing Singer's position and challenging the probestiality voice. He argues that bestiality is harmful for the same reasons as interpersonal sexual assault, because it involves coercion, produces pain and suffering, and violates the rights of another being. Beirne asserts that coercion characterizes almost all humans-animal interactions; therefore even if an animal "appears" to comply, it cannot freely consent to sex. Increasingly Beirne's position can be seen in new legislation, where animals are characterized as victims. According to the Sex Offenses Review Group (2000), UK animal sexual offenses legislation was developed using the same logic that governs other sexual offenses: "free agreement to sexual activity"—legislators deemed animal consent impossible. Historically, the criminalization of bestiality has been built on a sense that it is a crime against nature and thus against people's morality/sensibility. Accounts over many years from around Europe testify to the court's harsh treatment of animal victims of sexual assault (Beetz 2010). This "new" perception of animals as victims who need to give consent demonstrates a more animal-centered legislative approach.

That it is deemed that animals cannot consent to bestiality is not the end of the debate. Where is "free agreement to sexual activity" in the procedures and practices regularly carried out on animals involving penetration (e.g., artificial insemination) and stimulation (e.g., induced ejaculation) of the genital area (albeit without pain or sexual motivation) (Beetz 2010)? Probestiality campaigners (ZETA 2013) also ask why it is ethical and legal to kill animals for financial gain and for human convenience, while bestiality is outlawed. A key consideration here is that animals, in most cultures, are "owned"; they are without independent status, and their needs are almost always superseded by humans' (Goetschel 2013). How can some acts be acceptable while others (e.g., sexual behavior) are deemed problematic? Bolliger and Goetschel (2005:40) rationalize that although animals are used against their will to meet a multitude of human needs, "most of these actions are socially justified," which is not the case with zoophilia. Hypocrisy seems evident here, but a useful discussion about animal rights would require a chapter of its own and is not dealt with here. It is sufficed to say that the complexities of the human-animal relationship create a significant gray area in which animal sexual assault is argued as acceptable.

Beetz (2010) stresses an animal's "right to dignity," seeing it as a way to sidestep probestiality equality arguments and justify a need for criminalizing bestiality. The Swiss Constitution of 1992 recognizes this: it protected the "dignity of animals," including "protection from excessive exploitation, humiliation, interference with an animal's appearance, as well as sexual integrity" (Federal Constitution of the Swiss Confederation of 18th April 1999 SR101 s.80).

EVALUATION OF LEGISLATIVE APPROACHES

Bestiality legislation has changed considerably over the past century, influenced by changing attitudes toward homosexuality and the separation of law and morality (Miletski 2005). Bestiality and homosexuality were regarded as similar immoral acts and criminalized as "sodomy" or "buggery" (Rydström 2003). Miletski (2005) suggests that bestiality legislation has been greatly influenced by religious and cultural disgust, particularly in Germanic and Anglo-American countries. Legislation was exclusively anthropocentric, particularly concerned with the impact on human morality. In the UK, as was common across Europe and the United States, the removal of legislation criminalizing homosexuality typically coincided with the removal of bestiality as a specific offense.

Some countries do not criminalize bestiality under any legislation, while for others, bestiality can be regulated under animal welfare legislation (according to the World Society for the Protection of Animals 2005, 65 of 192 countries have national animal protection legislation) or sexual offenses legislation. Duffield, Hassiotis, and Vizard (1998), for example, state that although bestiality is not specifically named as a criminal offense, it remains a chargeable offense in most states, prosecuted under animal cruelty statutes. Legislation not primarily concerned with animal protection or sexual offenses can also be used to prosecute bestiality—for example, damage to property, trespass, or indecent conduct. Most European countries and U.S. states have (1) generic animal welfare legislation, which may be used to criminalize harmful sexual acts, and/or (2) sexual offenses legislation that specifically criminalizes bestiality. In addition to legislation that focuses on physical sexual acts (bestiality), recent moves have sought to legislate against related behaviors such as (1) preventing the production, distribution, and ownership of pornography depicting bestiality, and (2) forcing another person to engage in bestiality.

EUROPEAN APPROACH TO LEGISLATION
PROHIBITING BESTIALITY

Using generic animal protection legislation to respond to bestiality is commonplace. Legislation in many European countries (e.g., Denmark, Finland, Hungary, and Slovakia) does not describe animal sexual assault as a specific offense requiring punishment. Slovakian penal law argues that as bestiality can be cruel, certain human-animal sexual behavior is subject to *"cruelty towards animals"* legislation (Hvozdik et al. 2006). Problematically, their state veterinary authorities identify what *they* consider acts of cruelty. This is a subjective process and, as previously discussed, not all sexual animal assault results in obvious visible suffering. There are additional concerns over the extent to which veterinarians are trained to identify sexual assault. Arkow (2004) highlights the limited training veterinarians receive in identifying animal abuse. Swiss legislation also fails to specify bestiality as an offense. However, as previously discussed, they have enshrined the protection of animals into their constitution—thereby affording animals a very strong protection—and passed the Animal Protection Act of December 16, 2005. Given that this act protects animal's welfare *and* dignity, it might reasonably be expected that any animal sexual assault is prosecutable. Not according to Bolliger and Goetschel (2005): although the Swiss penal code clearly protects animals if they have obviously been harmed by a sexual act, other sexual behaviors and actions to facilitate these behaviors (e.g., training or offering an animal for sex) remain permissible. The Ethics Committee for Animal Experimentation of the Swiss Academies of Arts and Sciences (2010:1) criticized the act's terminology as being inconsistent; having "protection of dignity," "taking account of dignity," "violation," and "failure to respect" can create problems when identifying offenses and pros-ecuting offenders.

Animal welfare policy is currently under review in the European Union, prompting policy change in member states. Article 13 of the Lisbon Treaty (Treaty on the Functioning of the European Union) states that "all animals are sentient beings" and expects all member states to "pay full regard to the requirements of animal welfare" when formulating and enforcing related policy. There is no specific EU legislation on "pets," however, this article applies to all captive livestock and animals. The EU animal welfare action plan for 2012–2015 includes development of a general animal welfare law, which would offer a transnational approach to the protection of all animals (Committee on Agriculture and Rural Development 2010). And although there is no specific focus on animal sexual assault, developments in animal welfare and related policy must incorporate changes that recognize ani-mals as sentient beings; arguably this should include recognition of their right to live without sexual coercion. Both the EU plan and legislation could provide greater protection for animals, but leaving room for broad interpretation and enforcement by individual member states may mean this becomes a missed opportunity. In 2002 new additions to the German Constitution (Basic Law for the Federal Republic [GG] [Germany], s.20a) expanded existing provision to "protect the natural foundations of life and animals by legislation" (Vapnek and Chapman 2010:28); however, this did not result in the criminalization of animal sexual assault. It was not until 2012 that bestiality became illegal in Germany (Cottrell 2013). Bolliger and Goetschel (2005:42), citing lessons from the Swiss experience, argue that adding bestiality "as an offense to the catalogue of forbidden actions in ani-mal welfare legislations" is the only way forward. Additionally, they suggest that "physical injuries of animals as a consequence of zoophilic interactions should remain punishable as an offense of animal abuse."

As in Germany, legislation in the UK, France, the Netherlands, and (very recently) Sweden specifically prohibits bestiality. In 2012 the EU received a petition (registered number 812/2012) from animal welfare groups requesting international legislation that specifically criminalized bestial-ity. Around this time there was a public outcry at the apparent growth of "animal brothels" in Germany, following a similar scenario in Denmark. Also in 2012 Germany received considerable media attention when its new legislation criminalized "using an animal for personal sexual activities or making them available to third parties for sexual activities" (Cottrell 2013). The maximum penalty under this legislation is a €34,000 fine. In Sweden, following changes to legislation in 2013, it is now an offense to engage in any sexual act with an animal (Stop Animal Abuse 2013). The maximum penalty is two years' incarceration. Both the German and Swedish approaches create a blanket ban on animal sexual assault (specific definitions were not available in English), thereby eliminating issues of consent and potentially addressing loopholes identified previously in other legislation (e.g., Switzerland). The move toward blanket bans may be evidence of a less anthropocentric and more animal-centered approach that views the animal as a victim. Rather than attempting to, subjectively, measure the level of "suffering," all sexual acts are criminalized. The whole spectrum of sexual victimization that animals can experience is recognized. Despite this progress, the maximum penalties for these offenses would suggest that animal sexual victimization is not considered a serious offense.

COMPARISON OF EUROPEAN AND NON-EUROPEAN LEGISLATION

There is considerable variation in the maximum penalties available in sentencing animal sex offenders (see table 14.1 for bestiality legislation comparisons). U.S. penalties vary state to state, from one year to life imprisonment depending on classification (misdemeanor or felony). In neighboring Canada, an offense is punishable by up to ten years' incarceration, while Australia and African countries legislate more leniently. EU countries have even lower penalties in place. For example, the reintroduction of bestiality legislation in the UK in 2003 reduced the maximum sentence from life to two years' incarceration. It is worth noting that the severity of punishment available may not accurately indicate how seriously the offense is viewed; a maximum sentence may never be used. The UK, for example, recently concluded a sexual offense sentencing consultation to develop sentencing guidelines, which justified omitting "intercourse with an animal" on the basis of it being a "very low volume offense[s] with low maximum sentences available"; in 2011 one offense was sentenced (Sentencing Council 2012:6).

Definitions of animal sexual assault also vary, in terms of both the terminology used and, where a definition is provided, the type of behaviors identified therein. While South African legislation refers to "bestiality," it defines a broader range of behaviors than most other countries using this term. Cultural norms and values often appear to influence these definitions—for example, moral disgust is apparent in the South African rationale, while the need to balance civil liberties and animal welfare is evident in EU countries. The problems with narrowly defined terms (e.g., when bestiality is defined as penetrative sex) have already been discussed. Equally, undefined terms present problems; uncertainty can result, and legal loopholes may appear and may color the process of identifying and subsequently convicting offenders. How legislation distinguishes between the offender and the offense is another important consideration. For example, legislation in Barbados and Canada criminalizes not just those who commit bestiality but also those who compel others to do so. Kenyan legislation recognizes offenders who "compel," "induce," or "cause" another to engage in bestiality. A UK Home Office (2000:31) review proposed that "one aspect of sexual behavior which is potentially very serious, and clearly criminal, is that of compelling others to carry out sexual acts against their will . . . and recommended a new offense to fill this gap." Nonetheless, this offense is not currently recognized in legislation in the UK or most other European countries.

In the same way the Internet has revolutionized the distribution and consumption of mainstream pornography, it has also enabled the development of a transnational "community" who create and share images of animal sexual assault (e.g., zoophilic pornography) (see Pierpoint and Maher 2012). To meet this "revolution," new legislation criminalizes the production, distribution, and possession of zoophilic pornography. According to Miletski (2005), few European countries strictly prohibit this material; it is publicly available in Italy, Spain, the Netherlands, and Denmark, for example. Switzerland prohibits all such material, while in Germany only distribution is criminalized (Bolliger and Goetschel 2005). The UK Criminal Justice and Immigration Act 2008 (UK) s.63.1 makes possession, alone, an offense despite the UK Sentencing Council (2014) placing zoophilic pornography in the most serious category of the Oliver and COPINE scales. Under s.63, the number of charged offenses (including zoophilic pornography) grew from 2 in 2008 to 1,312 in 2013, suggesting this is effective legislation (UKOCD 2013). However, Nair and Griffin (2013) suggest that a possession-only approach is fundamentally flawed. One rationale for criminalizing possession alone may lie within the challenges of regulating the Internet. Prosecuting producers and distributors is a complex problem because of conflicting legislation; "offenders" may originate from countries permitting this behavior. For this reason, Segura-Serrano (2006) argues for international rather than national legislation. Here, a transnational approach to EU animal welfare legislation may demonstrate its worth.

CLOSING NOTES

Unlike with sexual assault of people, there is still pressure to justify the need for legislation that criminalizes animal sexual assault. And depending on the justification, animals are conferred varying levels of protection. It is apparent, when comparing the development of legislation globally, that most countries adopt an anthropocentric perspective; some countries are now incorporating the need to balance human and animal interests, often invoking a "duty of care" approach; and no countries have adopted an animal rights perspective. Sollund (2012:109) argues that providing a "duty of care" is not good enough, as this leads to "uncertainty and variation." Within the EU alone, the wide variation in legislation (including terminology, definitions of what constitutes criminal behavior, and the penalties available) is evident and is creating possibilities for "offenders" to act. One need not embrace a "rights" perspective to identify that animal sexual assault legislation is inadequate in many ways. There are moves in the right direction; some countries are broadening their definition of animal sexual assault, focusing on the animal as a victim, and are proposing an international approach to legislating for this and related offenses. While this might be considered a good starting point, there is still much to be done to ensure that animals receive the protection they have a right to; we need to further develop our understanding of the prevalence, nature, and explanations for animal sexual assault and how countries can effectively respond to it.

DISCUSSION QUESTIONS

1. Why should animal sexual assault be considered a criminal offense?
2. What are the limitations of taking an anthropocentric approach toward legislating for animal sexual assault?
3. Are animal sexual assault and related offenses more effectively legislated nationally or internationally?

REFERENCES

Adams, J. 1995. Bestiality: The unmentioned abuse. *The Animals' Agenda* 15 (6): 29–31.

American Psychiatric Association. 2000. *Diagnostic and Statistics Manual of Mental Disorders.* 3rd ed. Washington, D.C.: American Psychiatric Association.

Arkow, P. 2004. The veterinarian's roles in preventing family violence: The experience of the human medical profession. *Protecting Children* 19 (1): 4–12.

Ascione, F. 1993. Children who are cruel to animals: A review of research and implications for developmental psychopathology. *Anthroozoos* 6:226–47.

——, ed. 2010. *The International Handbook of Animal Abuse and Cruelty: Theory, Research, and Application.* West Lafayette, Ind.: Purdue University Press.

Beetz, A. M. 2010. Bestiality and zoophilia: A discussion of sexual contact with animals. In *The International Handbook of Animal Abuse and Cruelty: Theory, Research, and Application*, ed. F. Ascione, 201–20. West Lafayette, Ind.: Purdue University Press.

Beirne, P. 1999. For a non-speciest criminology: Animal abuse as an object of study. *Criminology* 37 (1): 117–47.

——. 2001. Peter Singer's "Heavy Petting" and the politics of animal sexual assault. *Critical Criminology* 10 (1): 43–55.

——. 2009. *Confronting Animal Abuse: Law, Criminology and Human-Animal Relationships.* Plymouth: Rowman and Littlefield.

Bolliger, G., and A. F. Goetschel. 2005. Sexual relations with animals (zoophilia): An unrecognized problem in animal welfare legislation. In *Antrhozoo's Special Issue: Bestiality and Zoophilia: Sexual Relations with Animals*, ed. A. M. Beetz and A. L Podberscek, 23–45. West Lafayette, Ind.: Purdue University Press.

Committee on Agriculture and Rural Development. 2010. *Report on Evaluation and Assessment of the Animal Welfare Action Plan 2006–2010* (2009/2202(INI)). Brussels: European Parliament.

Cottrell, C. 2013. German legislators vote to outlaw bestiality. *New York Times.* http://www.nytimes.com/2013/02/02/world/europe/german-legislators -vote-to-outlaw-bestiality.html?_r=0 (February 1).

Dekkers, M. 2000. *Dearest Pet: On Bestiality.* New York: Verson.

Duffield, G., A. Hassiotis, and E. Vizard. 1998. Zoophilia in young sexual abusers. *Journal of Forensic Psychiatry* 9:294–304.

English, K., L. Jones, D. Patrick, and D. Pasini-Hill. 2003. Sexual offender contain- ment. *Annals of the New York Academy of Sciences* 989 (1): 411–27.

Ethics Committee for Animal Experimentation of the Swiss Academies of Arts and Sciences. 2010. The Dignity of Animals and the Evaluation of Interests in the Swiss Animal Protection Act. http://www.akademien-schweiz.ch/en/index /Portrait/Kommissionen-AG/Ethikkommission-fuer-Tierversuche.html.

Goetschel, A. F. 2013. The animal voice: ensuring interests through law. Paper pre- sented at the 2013 Voiceless Animal Law Lecture Series Keynote Presentation, Zurich.

Home Office. 2000. *Setting the Boundaries: Reforming the Law on Sexual Offenses.* http://webarchive.nationalarchives.gov.uk/+/http:/www.homeoffice.gov.uk /documents/vol1main.pdf?view=Binary.

Humane Society of the United States. 2001. *Fact Sheet.* http://www.humane society.org/current/facts.html.

Hvozdik, A., A. Bugarsky, J. Kottferova, M. Vargova, O. Ondrasovicova, M. A. Ondrasovic, and N. Sasakova. 2006. Ethological, psychological and legal aspects of animal sexual abuse. *Veterinary Journal* 172 (2): 374–76. doi:10.1016 /j.tvjl.2005.05.008.

Michigan State University College of Law. 2014. *Table of State Animal Sexual Assault Laws.* http://www.animallaw.info/articles/State%20Tables/tbus animalassault.htm.

Miletski, H. 2005. A history of bestiality. In *Antrhozoo's Special Issue: Bestiality and Zoophilia: Sexual Relations with Animals,* ed. A. M. Beetz and A. L. Podberscek. West Lafayette, Ind.: Purdue University Press.

Nair, A., and J. Griffin. 2013. The regulation of online extreme pornography: Purposive teleology (in)action. *International Journal of Law and Information Technology* 21 (4): 329. doi:10.1093/ijlit/eat007.

Pierpoint, H., and J. Maher. 2012. Animal abuse and sex offending. In *Sex Offenders: Punish, Help, Change or Control*, ed. J. Bradford, F. Crowe, and J. Deering. Oxon: Routledge.

Rydström, J. 2003. *Sinners and Citizens: Bestiality and Homosexuality in Sweden, 1880–1950*. Chicago: University of Chicago Press.

Segura-Serrano, A. 2006. Internet regulation and the role of international law. *Max Planck Yearbook of United Nations Law* 10:191–272.

Sentencing Council. 2012. *Sexual offenses Guideline Consultation*. London: Sentencing Council.

Sex Offenses Review Group. 2000. *Setting the Boundaries: Reforming the Law on Sex Offenses*. Vol. 1. London: Home Office.

Singer, P. 2001. Heavy petting. *Nerve*, 2013.

Sollund, R. 2012. Speciesism as doxic practice versus valuing difference and plurality. In *Eco-Global Crimes*, ed. R. Ellefsen, R. Sollund, and G. Larsen, 91–114. Surrey, England: Ashgate.

Stop Animal Abuse. 2013. *Sweden Bans Bestiality*. http://preciousjules1985 .wordpress.com/2013/06/14/sweden-bans-bestiality/.

UKCOD. 2013. *Prosecutions for Possession of Extreme Pornographic Images*. https://www.whatdotheyknow.com.

Vapnek, J., and M. Chapman. 2010. Legislative and regulatory options for animal welfare. In *FAO Legislative Study*, ed. Development Law Service. Vol. 104. Rome: Food and Agricultural organization of the United Nations.

Woodley, M. L. 2007. Marital rape: A unique blend of domestic violence and nonmarital rape issues. *Hastings Women's Law Journal* 18:269–81.

World Society for the Protection of Animals. 2005. *Animal Protection Legislation*. http://www.animalmosaic.org/Images/An%20overview%20of%20animal%20 protection%20legislation_English_tcm46–28491.pdf.

ZETA. 2013. *The Case Against General Criminalisation*. http://www.zeta-verein .de/en/wissenswertes/warum-keine-pauschale-kriminalisierung-von-zoo sexualitat.html.

EDITORS

ALISSA R. ACKERMAN is an assistant professor of criminal justice in the Social Work Program at the University of Washington, Tacoma. Alissa's research focuses broadly on vulnerable populations. She has published scholarly articles on sex offender policy and management and the impact of such practices on offenders, their families, the reintegration process, and communities. Her research on the management of sexual offenders has appeared in several criminal justice journals, including *Criminal Justice & Behavior*, *Journal of Criminal Justice*, and *Justice Quarterly*. She is currently the principal investigator of a national-level study that aims to provide accurate counts and other data regarding the U.S. sex offender population. Additionally, her work with vulnerable groups has led to her research on the lives of the undocumented and the criminalization of immigration. This work has resulted in several peer-reviewed publications on the topic, including articles in the *Journal of Sociology and Social Welfare* and *International Social Work* and an edited book, *The Criminalization of Immigration: Contexts and Consequences* (2014).

RICH FURMAN is a professor of social work at the University of Washington, Tacoma. He is also affiliated with the Ethnic, Gender and Labor Studies Program and the Criminal Justice Program. He received the University of Washington Tacoma distinguished research award in 2011. In 2012 he received the Council for Social Work Education's Partner's in International Education award for his cutting-edge work on transnational social work. He has published over 120 scholarly articles and book chapters. Three of his fifteen books are *The Criminalization of Immigration* (2014), *Transnational Social Work Practice* (2010), and *Social Work Practice with Latinos: Key Issues and Emerging Themes* (2010). His research is concerned with the consequences of globalization on vulnerable populations, and social work's response to globalization. He has conducted research, practiced, volunteered, taught, and consulted in Germany, Colombia, Peru, Costa Rica, Nicaragua, the Philippines, Thailand, and Cambodia.

AUTHORS

JAY S. ALBANESE is a professor and criminologist in the Wilder School of Government & Public Affairs at Virginia Commonwealth University. He has written and edited fifteen books and seventy articles and book chapters and has made keynote and invited presentations in fifteen countries. He has served as chief of the International Center at the National Institute of Justice, the research arm of the U.S. Department of Justice and as executive director of the International Association for the Study of Organized Crime and is a past president and fellow of the Academy of Criminal Justice Sciences. He is currently a member of the executive board of the American Society of Criminology.

RITA AUGUSTYN is a Ph.D. student in the School of Criminology and Criminal Justice at the University of Nebraska at Omaha. Her research interests include older inmate behavior and prison policies, elder abuse and victimization, and sex offender behavior and policies.

CATHERINE BURNS is a lecturer in Asian studies at Griffith University in Brisbane, Australia. She has conducted research on judicial responses to rape in both Japan and Cambodia and is the author of *Sexual Violence and the Law in Japan* (2005). Her teaching and research interests include constructions of crime, gender and sexuality in Asia, intercultural communication, and most recently international development and nongovernmental organizations.

JEFFREY W. COHEN is an assistant professor of criminal justice in the Social Work Program at the University of Washington, Tacoma. He has been teaching criminal justice and related courses at the university level for the past six years. His scholarship focuses on the intersections of gender, masculinities, and crime, as well as research methodology. His current research includes a forthcoming book analyzing media representations of school bullying and their implications for the criminalization of bullying behaviors.

KATHLEEN DALY is a professor of criminology and criminal justice at Griffith University in Brisbane. She writes on restorative justice, indigenous justice, and innovative justice responses to partner, family, and sexual violence. Her book, *Redressing Institutional Abuse of Children*, is forthcoming (Palgrave). She is a fellow of the Academy of the Social Sciences in Australia and past president of the Australian and New Zealand Society of Criminology (2005–09).

PHOENIX J. FREEMAN is a freelance researcher and writer living in Canberra, Australia. His research broadly focuses on criminology, the welfare of vulnerable populations, and health-care provision. His research interests include situational prevention strategies against sexual violence, risk factors for sexual recidivism, addressing manipulation strategies of trans sex offenders, and designing services to be approachable and appropriate for vulnerable populations. He has been professionally involved with service provision to lesbian, gay, bisexual, and transgender (LGBT) populations for nearly a decade and has had ongoing personal and professional interactions with trans people from at least five Western countries. His work with LGBT populations has been additionally informed through his life experience as a gay transman. He is an active participant in the American Society of Criminology's Division on Women and Crime.

CYNTHIA FLORENTINO is a Ronald E. McNair Scholar at the University of Central Florida. She is the chair of the UCF President's Leadership Council. Her research concerns the role of international nongovernmental organizations in global governance and human rights.

MICHELE LEIBY is an assistant professor of political science at the College of Wooster in Ohio, where she teaches courses on human rights, comparative politics, and social science research methods. Her research focuses on wartime sexual violence in Latin America. Her current book project examines the use of sexual violence by state armed forces during the civil wars in El Salvador and Peru. Additional research projects build directly off of earlier findings and include a GIS analysis of the subnational variation in the frequency of sexual violence in Peru and an in-depth, qualitative study of the effects of gender and sexuality norms in Peru on the prevalence of male-on-male sexual violence as well as the prospects for survivors to seek justice and reparation. Her work has been published in *International Studies Quarterly*, *Politics and Society*, as well as in an edited volume on investigating and proving international sex by the Forum for International Criminal and Humanitarian Law.

HELEN LIEBLING is a lecturer-practitioner in clinical psychology and an associate
member of the African Studies Centre at Coventry University (UK). She has
been carrying out applied research with survivors of conflict and postconflict
sexual violence and torture in Africa since 1998. She has numerous journal publications and is author or coauthor of two books, *Ugandan Women War Survivors* (Liebling-Kalifani, 2009) and *Justice and Health Provision for Survivors
of Sexual Violence* (Liebling & Baker, 2010). She has carried out consultancies,
training, and interventions to enhance support for conflict survivors and service providers in conjunction with Isis-WICCE, Kampala.

ERIC MADFIS is an assistant professor of criminal justice in the Social Work
Program at the University of Washington, Tacoma. His research interests are
in juvenile delinquency and juvenile justice, theoretical criminology, homicide and interpersonal violence, school crime and security, youth subculture
and counterculture, masculinities and crime, and hate crime and supremacist
groups. His most recent scholarship explores perceptions of and reactions to
threats of rampage shootings in American public schools.

JENNIFER MAHER is a senior lecturer in the Centre for Criminology at the University of South Wales (UK). Her main research interests are animal abuse, green
criminology, youth gangs/groups, and violence. She is currently conducting
research on the illegal wildlife trade for a project, funded by the European Commission, on the impact of environmental crime in Europe. Her earlier research
includes projects that have looked at animal abuse among youth groups and
gangs. She is currently co-editing *The International Handbook on Animal Abuse
Studies*, has co-edited a special journal issue of *Crime, Law and Social Change*
on animal abuse, and has published internationally in peer-reviewed journals.
She presents at key national and international conferences and has been by
invited by academics and practitioners to guest lecture on animal abuse.

ANNE-MARIE MCALINDEN is a reader in the School of Law at Queen's University
Belfast (Ireland). Her first book, *The Shaming of Sexual Offenders: Risk, Retribution and Reintegration* (2007), was awarded the British Society of Criminology Book Prize for 2008. Her second sole-authored monograph, *"Grooming"
and the Sexual Abuse of Children: Institutional, Internet, and Familial Dimensions* was published as part of Oxford University Press's prestigious Clarendon
Series in Criminology (2012). The primary research for this book was funded by
a small research grant awarded by the British Academy. She is currently working
on a three-year ESRC-funded project (with Shadd Maruna and Mark Farmer)
on sex offender desistance.

CATHY NGUYEN is a social worker in Tacoma, Washington.

ELICKA S. PETERSON-SPARKS is an associate professor of criminology and criminal justice at Appalachian State University in North Carolina. Her research specializations are intimate partner homicide and the impact of religion on criminality.

LISA L. SAMPLE is Reynolds Professor at the University of Nebraska at Omaha. Her research interests include criminal and juvenile justice policy. More specifically, she conducts research in juvenile and criminal justice sentencing disparities, drug control policies, prison reentry programs, and sex offender behavior and policies. She has published in *Criminology and Public Policy*, *Criminal Justice Policy Review*, *Crime & Delinquency*, and *Justice Quarterly*, among other journals.

MICHELLE SANCHEZ is an M.A. candidate in the Interdisciplinary Arts and Sciences Program at the University of Washington, Tacoma.

CHARLES ANTHONY SMITH is an associate professor at the University of California-Irvine. His books include *The Rise and Fall of War Crimes Trials: From Charles I to Bush II* (2012), *Globalizing Human Rights* (2014), and *Understanding the Political World 12th ed.* (2014, with James Danziger). He has published articles in *Law & Society Review*, *Political Research Quarterly*, *Justice System Journal*, *International Political Science Review*, *Judicature*, *Journal of Human Rights*, *Election Law Journal*, *Studies in Law, Politics & Society*, *Human Rights Review*, and *Journal of International Relations & Development*, among other journals, and numerous chapters in edited volumes. He has also served as guest editor for special issues of the *Journal of Human Rights* and *Human Rights Review*.

KAREN J. TERRY is a professor in the Department Criminal Justice at John Jay College of Criminal Justice in New York. Her research focuses primarily on sexual offending and victimization, and she was recently the principal investigator for two national studies on sexual abuse of minors by Catholic priests.

MARY HUIQUAN ZHOU is an assistant professor in the Department of Social Work at the Chinese University of Hong Kong. During her years studying in Boston, she was involved in the anti–human trafficking work of the Boston Police Department, and the Children's Advocacy Center of Suffolk County. Her research focus now is primarily grassroots organization and voluntary action in China. In recognition of her work, in 2010 she received the Emerging Scholar Award from the Association for Research on Nonprofit Organizations and Voluntary Action.